Inventing Tradition

Michael J. Hightower

Inventing Tradition

Cowboy Sports in a Postmodern Age

VDM Verlag Dr. Müller

Imprint

Bibliographic information by the German National Library: The German National Library lists this publication at the German National Bibliography; detailed bibliographic information is available on the Internet at http://dnb.d-nb.de.

Any brand names and product names mentioned in this book are subject to trademark, brand or patent protection and are trademarks or registered trademarks of their respective holders. The use of brand names, product names, common names, trade names, product descriptions etc. even without a particular marking in this works is in no way to be construed to mean that such names may be regarded as unrestricted in respect of trademark and brand protection legislation and could thus be used by anyone.

Cover image: by Jason M. Warren

Publisher:
VDM Verlag Dr. Müller Aktiengesellschaft & Co. KG
Dudweiler Landstr. 125 a, 66123 Saarbrücken, Germany
Phone +49 681 9100-698, Fax +49 681 9100-988, Email: info@vdm-verlag.de

Copyright © 2008 VDM Verlag Dr. Müller Aktiengesellschaft & Co. KG and licensors
All rights reserved. Saarbrücken 2008

Produced in USA and UK by:
Lightning Source Inc., La Vergne, Tennessee, USA
Lightning Source UK Ltd., Milton Keynes, UK

ISBN: 978-3-8364-3699-1

Contents

Contents i
Acknowledgments and Dedications iii
Chapter One — Old Dominion Cowboys 1
    A Primer on Cowboy Sports 1
    Cowboy Ethnography 3
    Inventing Tradition 6
    On the Trail of Old Dominion Cowboys 9
    What's So Special about Cowboy Sports? 12
    Author's Note 15
Chapter Two — The Frontier in American Character Development 16
    A New Kind of Man 16
    The Frontier Revisited: Old Myths, New Realities 27
    From Woodlands to Prairie: The Rise of the Cowboy 38
Chapter Three — The Cowboy in History, Literature, and Showbiz 40
    The Animate Trinity 40
    Honest-to-Goodness Cowboys 46
    Sundown 55
    The West of the Imagination 57
    Between Two Worlds 62
Chapter Four — Nostalgia, Collective Memory, and the Yearning for Cowboy Ways 66
    Inventing Tradition: America at a Crossroads, 1880-1920 66
    The Cultural Trinity 70
        Theodore Roosevelt (1858-1919) 70
        Frederic Remington (1861-1909) 72
        Owen Wister (1860-1938) 74
    From Proletarian to Pop Star: The Resilience of the Cowboy Myth 76
    Old Worn Out Saddles and Old Worn Out Memories: Cowboys in Collective Memory ... 83
    Beyond the Imagination 90
Chapter Five — From Custom to Ritual: Identity Formation and Cultural Expression through Rodeo and Cowboy Sports 92
    The Sociology of Sport 92
    Culture in Action 99

- Rodeo: Cultural Expression through Symbols and Rituals ... 102
- Cowboy Sports: Amateurs in the Arena ... 108
- Toward a Sociology of Cowboy Sports ... 111

Chapter Six — Showtime ... 114
- Run Up ... 114
- Gettin' Western ... 122
- Chow Time ... 130
- Cowboy Up! ... 132
- Quittin' Time ... 137

Chapter Seven — A Sociology of Cowboy Sports ... 140
- Culture, Cowboy Sports, and the Seamless Web ... 140
- Themes ... 143
    - Cowboying ... 143
    - A little less talk and a lot more action ... 144
    - The cowboy says it salty ... 145
    - The hoss bidness ... 147
    - Cowboy up! ... 149
    - Easy come, easy go ... 150
    - Cowboy democracy ... 150
    - It's mighty white out there ... 151
    - Cowboys and cowgirls ... 152
    - What kind of outfit is this anyway? ... 154
    - The animate trinity ... 156
    - The wild and the tame ... 158
    - A community of mavericks ... 159
    - Ritual: the ties that bind ... 162
    - The West of the imagination ... 163

Chapter Eight — Postmodern Cowboys ... 165
- Inventing Tradition and the Elusive Postmodern ... 165
- Identity Formation and Cultural Expression through Cowboy Sports ... 169
- Livin' on the Edge ... 170
- The Lure of Cowboy Ways ... 171
- Cowboy Sports and Postmodernity ... 172

Postscript ... 176
Index ... 177
References ... 181

Acknowledgments and Dedications

I dedicate this work to Old Dominion cowboys for welcoming me into their midst, and cowboys in Oklahoma, New Mexico, and Texas, mostly gone but not even close to forgotten, who taught a young man what they knew, and then some.

Contrary to popular opinion, cowboys depend on team work to get the job done. So do scholars. They should, anyway. Thanks go to Jeff Olick, Krishan Kumar, Sarah Corse, and Paul Halliday at the University of Virginia for giving me the rein I needed to complete the doctoral dissertation that became this book. I'm obliged to Chris Einolf at the University of Richmond for his thoughtful critiques, usually softened by the libations that went with them, and Mark Meier at the University of Virginia for the scrupulous care he took in proofreading and indexing. At the end of the day, of course, mistakes and shortcomings are all mine.

I'd be remiss, not to mention in a heap of trouble, if I neglected to thank my research assistants, Haskell and Colfax, for their willingness to stand still while I scribbled ethnographic notes and their enthusiasm as we continue to hone our cowboying skills.

I especially want to express my gratitude to Judy Walston Hightower for her support and computer savvy. Turns out she's no stranger to cowboy ways herself. I figured that out the first time we saddled up together. I hope my academically minded readers will tolerate a few lines of cowboy doggerel as my way of saying thanks:

> May your horse never stumble,
> your spurs never rust;
> Your belly never grumble,
> and your heart never bust.
>
> May you stay in the saddle,
> your nerve never fail;
> Keep your eyes on the cattle,
> and your mind on the trail.

Michael J. Hightower, PhD
Charlottesville, VA
January 2008

Chapter One — Old Dominion Cowboys

> "When you're sitting on your horse..."
> His voice trailed off as he crouched,
> dropped his hands to his knees, and
> mimicked a cowboy ready to spring
> into action. "When that cow cuts," he
> continued, his voice muted almost to a
> whisper, "and your horse goes with him—
> now that's a thrill. You'll get hooked.
> There's nothing like it!"
>
> Old Dominion cowboy
> Etlan, VA

A Primer on Cowboy Sports

In the spring of 2004, I made my first foray into athletic activities that I have dubbed *cowboy sports*: team penning, team and ranch sorting, and cutting horse competition. Team penning is a timed competition that requires participants on horseback to self-select themselves into teams of three and, within the confines of an arena, separate three cattle from a herd of thirty and pen them in a small corral. Numbers ranging from zero to nine are affixed to their flanks such that there are three cattle numbered zero, three numbered one, three numbered two, and so on for the entire herd. Each ride begins when a team has entered the arena and the nose of one of the three horses crosses a foul line. At that moment, two riders designated to calm and group the cattle, known in penning vernacular as *settling the herd*, exit the arena at a rapid clip. A flagman stationed at the foul line drops a flag, and a judge announces over a public address system which three cattle, all bearing the same number, the team is supposed to pen. Non-designated cattle that cross the foul line are known as *trash cows* and are grounds for disqualification.

Typically, contestants are permitted to participate in a maximum of five teams in each division, and divisions are based on riders' ratings on a scale of one to six indicating their levels of expertise. The same three people are prohibited from participating in more than one team in each division. Two riders can team up for multiple rides as long as they enlist different people as third riders. This prevents the formation of power blocks and encourages riders and their mounts to develop sufficient skills so that they can be effective penners no matter who else is on their team. Contestants pay an entry fee

INVENTING TRADITION

each time they ride into the arena. The top ten teams in the first round of competition in each division are eligible to ride in the final round, or *call backs*. At the end of the day, the most successful penners share the jackpot. Success—that is, *finishing in the money*—is measured by the number of cattle penned and the amount of time it takes to pen them.

Many penners participate in the closely related sports of team and ranch sorting, both of which require self-selected teams to separate cattle from a herd and drive them into a holding pen. Each ride begins when a horse's nose crosses an invisible barrier. At the far end of the arena, two herd settlers do their best to control ten numbered cattle and perhaps a few unnumbered and particularly ornery ones thrown in to spice up the competition. As soon as the barrier is breached, the judge calls out a number between zero and nine, the clock starts, and the herd settlers beat a hasty retreat. Riders then locate and cut out the designated cow and, in  numerical sequence, separate the rest of the cattle from the herd and drive them one at a time into the holding pen. Cattle that enter the holding pen out of sequence are designated as *trash cows* and signal the end of the ride. As with penning, riders are prevented from teaming up with the same people for multiple rides. Contestants pay an entry fee for each sort, and the top ten teams in each division are invited to the *call backs*. Teams that sort the most cattle in the least amount of time split the jackpot.

Arguably, no activity offers more opportunities for horse and rider to demonstrate their prowess than the third sport under consideration: cutting horse competition. Unlike penning and sorting, cutting involves a lone rider, and to the untrained eye, the action is deceptively simple. The ride begins when the horse's nose crosses an invisible barrier approximately half way between the entrance and the far side of an arena, where a herd of cattle stirs quietly. At that moment, a digital clock starts to click off precious seconds. With painstaking movements that belie the breath-taking action to come, the competitor then rides into the herd, separates—or, in cowboy vernacular, *cuts*—a single cow from its mates and prevents it from satisfying its instinct to return to the herd. Under certain conditions, riders can permit the cow to return to the herd and separate additional cattle before a buzzer signals the end of the ride. A rider's only assistance comes from two *herders* stationed at the far end of the arena and two *turn-back men* who remain close to the arena entrance. Their job is to maintain control over the unselected cattle and make sure that separated cattle remain more or less in the center of the arena. Distractions are thus minimized, and horse and rider are free to concentrate with laser-like intensity on the task at hand. Anxious moments pass between the end of one ride and the beginning of the next as a judge tallies the score and relays it to the announcer. Scoring is based on the judge's assessment of the horse's skill in keeping cows apart from the herd and the rider's ability to maintain control with a minimum of interference.

And herein lies the magic behind what some Western horsemen describe as the Cadillac of the horse business. To watch, let alone experience, a cutting horse in action is to enter a world of symbiosis between man and animal that surely dates back to the dawn of civilization. Blurring the lines between the sacred and profane, I long ago settled on the *animate trinity* as appropriate shorthand to describe the union of human, horse, and cow—all mammals, to be sure, but unique and utterly distinct by any reasonable measure. Yet in this ritualized blending of sport and choreography, the differences fade. Seasoned horses mirror the cow's every move. Through a combination of breeding and training that none of us will ever completely understand, they flex their haunches, drop nearly to their knees, and pivot with astonishing speed. The best horses, often valued in the tens and even hundreds of thousands of dollars, have an uncanny ability to remain head-to-head with cattle and anticipate the sharp stops and reverses they make in a desperate bid to rejoin the herd. And what of the rider? What is his or her contribution to the ritual? To the untrained eye, the answer seems to be: not much. Rules require that riders leave their reins alone, maintain a grip on the saddle horn, and rely on their legs to communicate with their mounts. Yet the reality is far more complex, and even the most experienced riders would be hard-pressed to explain the mental and physical connections that play out in the arena.

Cowboy Ethnography

As a native Oklahoman and one-time working cowboy on ranches in the American Southwest, I was surprised and delighted to discover cowboy sports in my adopted state of Virginia or, as the state is known in these parts, the Old Dominion.[1] These sports and their highly professionalized cousin, rodeo, can be traced to the cattle frontier of the late nineteenth century, when men's livelihoods and often their lives depended on their ability to handle livestock. Arguably, cowboy skills have been of less value on the East Coast, where mountains, forests, and consistent rainfall have necessitated entirely different sets of skills to maintain agricultural enterprises. Moreover, Virginia's equestrian tradition is a direct descendent of European horsemanship and lives on today in steeplechase, dressage, and foxhunting—a far cry from the rough-and-tumble sports forged on America's prairies. Even as I strap on my spurs and saddle my horse, I reflect on the oddity of finding horsemen and women who prefer riding Hell-bent-for-leather after cattle to English imports that have shaped Virginia's equestrian tradition. In my expanding lexicon, I refer to my rowdy weekend comrades (myself included) as *Old Dominion cowboys*[2], bound by an ethos that can be expressed most succinctly as *cowboy ways*.

---

[1] As a young man, I cowboyed (a perfectly good verb in cow country, even though Microsoft Word doesn't recognize it) at Farafield Farms in Haskell County, Oklahoma; the Double U Bar Ranch in Colfax County, New Mexico; and *Quien Sabe* Ranch in Gonzales County, Texas.

[2] The moniker *Old Dominion cowboys* represents economy of words rather than gender bias. Indeed, the fact that men and women compete head-to-head and cooperate as teammates is one of the most intriguing aspects of cowboy sports.

INVENTING TRADITION

Such was my delight in finding kindred cowboy spirits that I competed for several months before it occurred to me that I had stumbled across sports that were ripe for an ethnographic study. By the late summer of 2004, I never left the barn where my wife and I stable our horses and maintain a small herd of cattle without a pen and note pad. After seeing a few too many writing implements trampled in the dirt, I decided that a pouch strapped to my flank girth was handier, and certainly more economical, than a shirt pocket. I eventually went high-tech and, when time permitted, slipped off to my horse trailer, closed the door against prying eyes and annoying horseflies, and dictated significant goings-on into a tape recorder.

As I reflected on what had become a propitious union of equine and academic interests, I realized that my methodology was departing from mainstream participant observation that once defined ethnography (Denzin 1997). In most cases of participant observation, the researcher shares in an activity as a prerequisite to observation and analysis. My approach, however, cast me in the role of an *observant participant*, and my units of analysis were none other than the athletic contests in which my horses and I were competing. My research assistants included Haskell, a sorrel gelding, and Colfax, a spirited bay mare with a beautiful blaze running down her face. They deserve credit for standing patiently as I hobnobbed with contestants and scribbled ethnographic notes from my perch in the saddle.

As Lofland and Lofland (1995) recommended in their guide to qualitative research, I was thus starting where I was, morphing personal history and interests into scholarship, and guaranteed both physical and psychological access to Old Dominion cowboy culture by virtue of my standing as a contestant. Riemer (1977) cited three advantages to what he dubbed "opportunistic research": (1) ease of entry into the research setting; (2) rapport between the investigator and the persons being studied; and (3) an increased likelihood of accurate interpretations. Disadvantages include excessive emotional involvement with subjects of the study, the impossibility (given the apparent dearth of cowboy – sociologists) of someone replicating my research, and a legion of methodological pitfalls that simply come with the territory. Weighing the pros and cons, I entered the arena as a cowboy first and researcher second, firmly embedded in my units of analysis, and clearly in a unique position to use ethnography as a window into cowboy sports.

Sitting horseback outside the arena and awaiting my turn to pen, sort, or cut cattle, I thus found myself at the edge of an ethnographic continuum dating back to the early days of the Chicago School, when Park, Dewey, Burgess and their ilk eschewed detached observation for imaginative participation in the lives of others (Adler and Adler 1987; Fine 1995; Matthews 1977). Their immersion in the cauldron of lived experience took a back seat to quantitative methodologies in the 1940s and 1950s, only to make a comeback with a second generation of Chicago School sociologists committed to biographically opportunistic research (Fine 1995). From Goffman's (1973, 2002) dramaturgical perspective of human behavior to Becker's (1963) studies of deviance, sociologists mined the real world for insights to be found in the ways we interact through symbols and meaning systems. Riding the tide of existential literature that probed for meaning in the wake of World War II, ethnographers delved ever deeper into emotions roiling beneath the surface of everyday experience. In contrast to quantitative sociologists in thrall to Parsons and structures and statistics, existentialists posited people as active, empowered subjects in their cultural milieus. As ghettoes went up in flames and students seized control of their campuses, it was perhaps inevitable that sociologists would attempt to place man at the center of philosophy—to imagine him as agent and creator of both meaning and action, a victim of his own peculiar ways, threatened with imprisonment by a society of his own making (Manning 1973). "The emphasis was on understanding the individual as a convergence of social, affective, and cognitive potentials when encountering the concrete situations of everyday life" (Kotarba and Johnson 2002: vii).

Thus have sociologists opened themselves to an ever wider range of possibilities for studying, understanding, and writing about people in a postmodern world that communication researcher McQuail (2000: 114) dubbed as "volatile, illogical, kaleidoscopic, and hedonistic." Convinced that art and sociology draw from much the same wellsprings of human experience, Nisbet (1976) railed against social scientists who write as though the logic of discovery can be summoned by obeying the logic of demonstration. "Only intellectual drouth and barrenness," concluded Nisbet, "can result from that misconception" (p. 5). In their collection of essays on trends, innovations, and problems in ethnography, Clifford and Marcus (1986) showed that virtually no medium is off limits to the sociologist with an imaginative bent, including autobiography, film, the essay, the short story, the poem, and the performance. For Denzin (1997), ethnography has passed through five distinct phases to arrive, in the twilight of the twentieth century, at "a sixth moment" that is pregnant with possibilities. He traced an epistemological aesthetic that has moved from realism to modernism and on to postmodernism, leaving ethnographers to embrace the kaleidoscope of interactional experience while remaining anchored in self-reflexivity. "The ethnographer who wishes to understand another has to build up an understanding based on a deep involvement in the subject's worlds of experience. This means the subject is transformed into a person who is no longer the object of an external voyeuristic gaze" (p. 35). Clark (2002) criticized sociologists' reluctance to confront the false dichotomy between reason and emotion that has constricted our understanding of social behavior. Only by confronting the brute being that lurks within every human breast can we transcend the Cartesian bias toward cognition ("I think, therefore I am") and sociology's reliance on quantitative methodologies to unravel "the complex, highly improvisational, often near chaotic nature of *social life*" (p. 157; Clark's *ital*).

Still, there must be some method to teasing the meaning out of social phenomena. Adler and Adler (1987) contributed to the systemization of ethnographic methodology by distinguishing between three categories of membership along a continuum of participant – observation research: (1) peripheral membership that requires minimal commitment to the social world under scrutiny; (2) active membership, a role that compels the researcher to take on core activities of group members; and (3) complete membership in which the researcher, for all intents and purposes, "goes native" (p. 67). Prime examples of the ultimate immersion in a social setting include Michalowski and Dubisch's (2001) chronicle of a cross-country motorcycle trip from California to the Vietnam Memorial in Washington, DC, undertaken to commemorate casualties of the Vietnam War, and Fontana's (2002) "Short Stories from the Salt," an account of the sociologist-turned-sportsman's participation in high speed racing on the Bonneville salt flats straddling the Nevada – Utah border. Citing Goffman's (1974) assertion that the ethnographer's task is to fill in the gaps of reality to make it appear seamless, Fontana eschewed sociological jargon to provide a riveting glimpse into a subculture that raises speed to an art form and celebrates the emotional roller-coaster that keeps participants coming back to the salt flats. "It is still sociology," wrote Fontana (2002: 202). "I am still trying to capture a temporary still of a moving everyday process so that I can share that understanding with others, if only for a fleeting moment." Castigating the cold, analytical, rational style so common in academic writing, Fontana waxed classical in his plea for a humanistic sociology: "We all need to become like Hermes, the messenger who translated the language of the Greek gods for the everyday Greek folks" (p. 202).

In my case, I've long since gone native, so there's not much I could do about my level of membership in Old Dominion cowboy culture. The trick was to sublimate my cowboying proclivities long enough to figure out what was going on. "We acquire more sensitivity, knowledge, and skill each time we delve into another membership world," concluded Adler and Adler (1987: 87). "We must draw on, expand, and continue to dig deeper into our multiple memberships to enlighten the social science community about the worlds in which we live."

Such is the logic behind analytic autoethnography, an increasingly popular methodology that calls on researchers to immerse themselves fully in their social worlds and become visible, active, and reflexively engaged in textual interpretation. In his survey of realist ethnography,

Anderson (2006) identified five key features of analytic autoethnography: (1) the researcher's status as a complete member researcher (CMR); (2) analytic reflexivity; (3) narrative visibility of the researcher's self; (4) dialogue with informants beyond the self; and (5) commitment to theoretical analysis. Unlike more detached participant observers, analytic autoethnographers have a stake in the beliefs, values, and actions of the people they are studying, so much so that interrogations of themselves and others "may transform the researcher's own beliefs, actions, and sense of self" (p. 383). In terms of the current investigation, analytic autoethnography provided a framework for self-reflexivity that facilitated my mission to mine cowboy sports for all their symbolic richness. I can't say that I have been transformed, but I have certainly become more aware of my position in the spectrum of qualitative research methodologies.

Drawing on complementary sources of data, I thus explore four interrelated questions: (1) In what sense do cowboy sports serve as a vehicle for identity formation and cultural expression?; (2) To what extent do cowboy sports mimic other extreme sports and subcultural activities, and to what extent are they unique?; (3) What macro historical and social forces contribute to the resilience and popularity of cowboy sports?; and (4) What can cowboy sports teach us about postmodern American culture?

Inventing Tradition

Americans experienced the waning of the nineteenth century in a state of collective angst. For all its promise, industrialization was offset by a numbing predictability that flows inexorably from capitalist production. Moreover, socioeconomic dislocations associated with mass production threatened the much-touted American Dream. Anxieties heightened after 1890, when data from the eleventh census confirmed a dawning realization that the frontier had disappeared. Across the land, from corporate boardrooms and the halls of academe to sites of political power, cultural leaders concerned with the preservation of American values contemplated a future with no virgin land to explore, no savages to subdue, and no communities to hew out of the wilderness. Such apprehensions dated back to dawn of the Republic, when America beckoned as an Edenic paradise in a world sullied by civilization. Immigrants from southern and eastern Europe, arriving on American shores with their strange ways and babble of languages, were particularly vexing. "The influx of the 'new immigration', besides threatening protestant hegemony, seemed to coincide with the growth of urban squalor, political corruption, and industrial discontent; anxious observers had no trouble establishing a causal link" (Wrobel 1993: 18).

Thanks to advances in communication and transportation, there was no shortage of activities to alleviate the stresses of modernity. Between 1880 and 1910, organized sports muscled their way into popular culture. Athletes found structured opportunities to test their mettle, and sedentary thrill seekers were delighted to find an endless array of sporting venues to express pent-up emotions.[3] Less robust consumers of culture could choose from a smorgasbord that included dime novels, theatrical productions, and of course Wild West shows, those artful blends of athleticism and showmanship that delivered Western adventure to anyone who could afford a ticket and elevated one character in particular, the cowboy, to iconic status (Kasson 2000; Warren 2005).

As the frontier faded into memory, cultural entrepreneurs became ever more creative in mining the nation's foundation stories to satisfy an insatiable appetite for vicarious adventure. The result, of course, was the Western, the bedrock of American entertainment, and certainly among America's most influential contributions to global culture. But where did the stories behind the narrative come from? Whose stories were they, and how closely did they mirror the national experience? Nobody would be more surprised to see cowboys elevated to mythic status than the lowly cowpoke himself, dust-covered and weary from months on the trail and not at all certain that he would live long enough to squander his meager wages at the next prairie outpost. How are we to explain the cowboy's metamorphosis from laborer on horseback to swashbuckling hero, and why did the kind of hardscrabble work that led many cowboys to early graves evolve into multi-million dollar leisure activities and provide fodder for a global entertainment industry?

As I argue in the following pages, the rise and resilience of the cowboy myth are best understood in the context of dizzying social and economic changes preceding World War I. Across America, old traditions were falling by the wayside. Agriculture was ceding ground, literally and figuratively, to industry; immigrants with strange customs and unfathomable languages were flocking to American cities; conflicts between labor and capital were erupting into violence; and technology, for all its benefits, was reordering lives and relationships. The time was ripe for new traditions to lend cohesion to an increasingly fragmented citizenry and, not incidentally, facilitate social control. In a process most clearly articulated by Hobsbawm and Ranger (1983) in their seminal collection of essays on invented traditions, the four decades

---

[3] Sports also instilled in young men a passion for teamwork that served the interests of industrial production as well as military preparedness. See Mrozek 1983.

leading up to World War I witnessed a reappraisal of America's frontier heritage in the context of perceived social needs. The traditions that appeared during this watershed era were neither arbitrary nor revolutionary; rather, through formalization and ritualization, they laid claim to legitimacy by reference to the past.

New traditions are to be expected during times of rapid change. Sometimes, traditional expressions of culture such as folk songs, physical contests, and marksmanship can be appropriated for new purposes. Symbols and commemorations can also be created out of whole cloth to reflect new social or political realities. In Europe, the state has taken the leading role in promoting new traditions. Witness the modernization of rural France following the Franco-Prussian War, when the Third Republic relied on a combination of railroad building, education, and military service to unify what had heretofore been a bewildering patchwork of languages, customs, and traditions (Weber 1976). Masquerading as representatives of the far left, the centrists who controlled the imagery and symbolism of the regime relied on monuments and public ceremonies to glorify the achievements of 1789, thus leaving no doubt of their commitment to *liberté, égalité, et fraternité*. Commemorations that obscured the blood and thunder of the Revolution tended "to transform the heritage of the Revolution into a combined expression of state pomp and power and the citizens' pleasure" (Hobsbawm 1983: 217).

America's invented traditions have been a much less focused enterprise, particularly with regard to the historic and symbolic role of the West in shaping the national consciousness. Recognizing the nostalgia that accompanied the closing of the frontier, American entrepreneurs, writers, and artists lent their talents to satisfying a market in desperate pursuit of meaning. None were more prominent in promulgating the final chapter of the frontier myth that played out on the cattle frontier between 1865 and the late 1880s to a receptive nation than Theodore Roosevelt in history and politics, Frederic Remington in art and illustration, and Owen Wister in literature. More than anyone, these scions of the Eastern establishment both reflected and reproduced the dialectic in American culture between runaway industrialization and nostalgia for a simpler, more primitive past (White 1968). Yet the success of the vision they promoted represents not so much a process of manipulation as it reveals the eagerness with which consumers accepted mythic portrayals of the frontier story. As Hobsbawm (1983: 307) recognized, "the most successful examples of manipulation are those which exploit practices which clearly meet a felt—not necessarily a clearly understood—need among particular bodies of people."

Even as America's fabled moneymen were moving beyond their nineteenth-century characterization as captains of industry to become "captains of consciousness" (Ewen 1976: 19) in the nascent age of consumerism, those with the power to shape culture were tapping into the frontier narrative as a surefire means of promoting independence, freedom, and rugged individualism as time-honored ideals. Susceptible as they are to mass marketing, it is hardly surprising that sports emerged as the quintessence of all that was good about America—perfect vessels to slake the nation's thirst for authenticity. Nor is it surprising to find that sports rooted in the final chapter of America's conquest of the continent became popular vehicles of nationalistic expression, not to mention outlets for people with more

money than peace of mind. What's more, consumers had a choice: they could either take their entertainment sitting down, or they could experience it up close and personal from the backside of a horse.

Buffeted by a century of bewildering change, the cowboy has yet to relinquish his stake in the popular imagination, embracing the trappings of modernity even as he keeps his boot heels planted in the prairie soil that spawned him. Such is the cloth from which we Old Dominion cowboys weave the fabric of our lives. No matter what we do in our personal and professional lives, we are *cowboys*. When we win, we ride away from the arena in the warm glow of admiration and with ever-so-slightly fattened wallets. When we lose, we load our horses and go home with a vow to do better next time, maybe with another horse, and definitely with a new strategy for working cattle. We are steeped in the context of the Old West. To understand cowboy sports as avenues of identity formation and cultural expression in postmodernity, we must accept the context. Only then can we mine them for their deposits of cultural and symbolic meaning in a nation galloping at breakneck speed away from its frontier heritage.

On the Trail of Old Dominion Cowboys

I begin this inquiry with an overview of the frontier story. Since the dawn of the Republic, writers have made much of the clash between civilization and savagery. Awareness of the frontier's significance in molding the American character crystallized in the work of Frederick Jackson Turner (1977), a young historian from the University of Wisconsin who revolutionized American historiography with his 1893 essay, "The Significance of the Frontier in American History." "Up to our own day," wrote Turner,

> "American history has been in a large degree the history of the colonization of the Great West. The existence of an area of free land, its continuous recession, and the advance of American settlement westward explain American development" (p. 3).

America's creation story was never encapsulated in a single dramatic work or symbolized by a lone archetype. Rather, it emerged over centuries, recorded sometimes in the journals of westward travelers, and other times in tall tales passed around campfires and remote outposts, where lives were shaped by the vicissitudes of frontier life and nobody was overly concerned with the nuances separating fact from fiction. The narrative began when the first bewildered settlers to the New World greeted their surroundings. Behind them, across an endless seascape, was the only civilization they knew. Before them lay uncharted territory whose immensity was beyond all reckoning. But one thing was certain: survival, and perhaps even a privileged place in God's kingdom, depended on bringing settled ways to their new home. Armed with a few rudimentary tools and a conviction that God was on their side, New World settlers built their communities and molded their traditions to the contours of their new home. Across generations, whether blazing trails through the eastern woodlands or homesteading a patch of wind-blown prairie, America's pioneers not only conquered a wilderness; they fostered the development of a typology whose resilience helps make the case for American exceptionalism.

After establishing the centrality of the frontier in American character development and describing its privileged position as a source of imagery and metaphor in our own time, I proceed

INVENTING TRADITION

in the third chapter to outline the socioeconomic factors that coalesced after the Civil War to produce the cowboy, arguably the most prominent figure in the nation's pantheon of mythic heroes. I then describe how this proletarian laborer on horseback was elevated to heroic status in the late nineteenth and early twentieth centuries through mass entertainment: specifically, dime novels, theater, and Wild West shows. With this in the way of background, I turn in the fourth chapter to the tumultuous period between the closing of the frontier and World War I, when Theodore Roosevelt, Frederick Remington, and Owen Wister stood in the vanguard of cultural entrepreneurs from the East who promulgated their own interpretations of cowboy ways to a nation in thrall to Western images. The traditions they invented drew deeply from the wellsprings of history, and they found a voice in a burgeoning entertainment industry that propelled the cowboy—or, more accurately, the cowboy type that was never personified in a single individual—to the realm of mythology (Smith 1950). Even today, Western images and metaphors have seeped into the popular consciousness to such an extent that the cowboy has been lifted from the prairies that nurtured him to a state that isn't found on any map: America's "fifty-first state of mind" (West 1995: 131).

If mass media have served as a port of entry for Western themes to infiltrate culture, then collective memory is their natural storehouse. Toward the end of my fourth chapter, I suggest that nostalgia and collective memory studies have much to say about the yearning for cowboy ways. Halbwachs (1992), a pioneer in conceptualizing the ways that we construct our identities through memory, is particularly germane to the current study. He distinguished between history, which aims to establish objective truth, and memory, which relies on personal recollections shaped by external stimuli and interpersonal communication. Collective memory is thus not a given, but rather a socially constructed notion. It is, of course, people rather than groups and institutions who remember, but their individual memories are heavily influenced by the social contexts in which they are located. Given the tenuous links between historical cowboys and fictional characters raised to heroic status through the magic of mass entertainment, it seems reasonable to examine the resilience of the Western myth through the lens of socially-constructed memory.

After placing the cowboy in his historical and sociological contexts and exploring his privileged position in our collective memory, I review the literature on sport sociology as a prerequisite to investigating rodeo and cowboy sports within the rubric of cultural sociology. Scholars interested in sport as a reflection and reproduction of Western themes have tended to focus on rodeo (Boatright 1964; Errington 1990; Lawrence 1982; Slatta 1994; Stoeltje 1989, 1993; Westermeier 1987). Since its inception in the late nineteenth century, rodeo has evolved from spontaneous demonstrations of cowboy skills into a professionalized and, at the highest levels of competition, lucrative collection of athletic contests that typically includes saddle bronc riding, bareback bronc riding, steer wrestling, calf roping, team steer roping, barrel racing, and bull riding. As a rule, nationalistic pageantry and showmanship laced with earthy humor add to the entertainment value of these ritualized performances and, at the same time, distract audiences from the prospect of injury and even death that contestants face every time they ride into the arena. For the purposes of this inquiry, rodeo is pertinent insofar as it reveals themes and patterns of action that are mimicked in cowboy sports. Within the literal confines of an arena and the structural parameters of highly regulated competition, penning, sorting, and cutting cattle exhibit a brand of athleticism and a dimension of culture whose contours can best be revealed through an interplay of history, social theory, and ethnography.

In my sixth chapter, I make the transition from scholarship to horsemanship. Rather than attempt to recount every competition, clinic, or practice session that my horses and I have attended, I have condensed dozens of experiences into a single narrative. In this composite sketch, stripped of identifiers (with the exception of my feisty mare, Colfax, her sidekick, Haskell, and my old grey mare, Caroline) and set in a fictional location, I weave in fifteen themes that emerged from my fieldnotes. Thus is chronology sacrificed to expediency. My technique might be problematic for the historian, but it enabled this cowboy-turned-sociologist to provide a context for the delineation of themes and elaboration of theory.

With cultural sociology as my rubric and sports as my window, I close this dissertation with two chapters exploring the themes that link the cowboy era and the invented traditions that it spawned, our collective memory of the frontier, and my units of analysis. Chapter Seven, "A Sociology of Cowboy Sports," is a straightforward thematic analysis. This paves the way for my eighth and final chapter, "Postmodern Cowboys," in which I return to my research questions and situate cowboy sports in postmodernity. Ironically, what seems to hold this shifting mosaic together is contradictions that Americans have never quite resolved. The wild versus the tame, independence versus community—these and other tensions in American culture provide a matrix for contextualizing cowboy sports.

Ethnographic evidence gathered in the course of this project suggested two social theorists whose insights are key to unraveling the meaning that Old Dominion cowboys invest in their sports: Georg Simmel, whose interest in the tightening grip of modernity led him to theorize about efforts to create distance from mind-numbing routines; and Erving Goffman, whose dramaturgical perspective has much to teach us about the tensions between self and society that confound our search for contentment. Together, these theorists build a compelling argument that escapism comes in many guises, and that humans can be remarkably creative when it comes to cultural expression and identity formation beneath the homogenizing pall of modernity.

As Cohen and Taylor (1976: 27) wrote in their seminal book about resistance to everyday life, "The regularized nature of our life begins to loom within consciousness as a cause for dissatisfaction, as a reason why we feel that something must be done about it." In his polemic against America's obsessive individualism, Slater (1970) made a compelling argument that consumerism has become a substitute for direct, visceral experiences and has driven a wedge between people that makes community problematic and collective life utterly unsatisfying. Our only recourse is to cast about for an identity to bring some semblance of congruence to our hollow lives. "Americans have created a society in which they are automatically nobodies," wrote Slater, "since nobody has any stable place or enduring connection. The village idiot of earlier times was less a 'nobody' in this sense than the mobile junior executive or academic. An American has to 'make a place for himself' because he does not have one" (p. 110). In a similar vein, Berger et al (1974) blamed the West's obsession with progress, and specifically its manifestation in technology, for divorcing modern man from pre-industrial modes of consciousness and coupling his identity with the implacable logic of the machine. Suffering from a deepening condition of homelessness, we have become appendages of our creations, anonymous and interchangeable, forced into a straightjacket of conformity to forces we can neither understand nor control. Riesman's (1953) lonely crowd, Putnam's (1995) evidence of declining social capital, Bellah et al's (1996) cult of individualism, and McPherson et al's (2006) study of social isolation in America complete the picture of a culture in crisis, struggling for a means to reignite communal values. As I hope to show in the following pages, such unflattering pictures of a listless culture in thrall to shopping malls and whiz-bang technology find their antithesis in the historical and emotional mimesis that keeps Old Dominion cowboys coming back to the arena.

What's So Special about Cowboy Sports?

Cowboy sports are by no means the only activities that draw on historical experience. Civil War reenactments, Renaissance fairs, antique car shows, and Shakespearean festivals are only a tiny sampling of the options available to people who yearn for a taste of history. Cowboy action shooting, an activity that allows participants to act out their fantasies by donning Western garb, adopting fanciful names, and shooting blanks from vintage weapons is the most recent addition to our repertoire of activities that satisfy the need for historically-based authenticity.[4] Similarities notwithstanding, Old Dominion cowboys constitute a subculture that occupies a special place in the realm of sport and leisure. A cursory glance at the main features of penning, sorting, and cutting cattle suffices to place them in a league of their own. First and foremost, these sports are not simply reenactments torn from the pages of history. Rather, they are timed competitions that bring financial rewards as well as a psychic thrill that lies at the center of this investigation. Simply put, they are uniquely suited to scholarly inquiry under the overall rubric of cultural studies and the specific category of sport sociology.

Distinguishing characteristics of penning, sorting, and cutting cattle can be briefly outlined. First, each of these sports requires skill on the part of riders and their mounts. Accomplished riders finish in the money; those less fortunate leave the arena empty-handed. Second, as is the case in any equestrian sport, contestants assume the risk of physical injury.[5] Third, simply attending a competition presents a wide range of logistical headaches. Contestants

---

[4] For more information on the latest craze in historical reenactments, see Jesse Dukes' report on National Public Radio's *Weekend Edition* (November 20, 2005), "Reliving 'Gunsmoke' with Cowboy Action Shooting," at http://www.npr.org/templates/story/story.php?storyId=5020633. Coincidentally, I listened to this report as I was traveling to a competition in the Shenandoah Valley near Waynesboro, Virginia.

[5] Since I began participating in cowboy sports, a woman who was known in Old Dominion cowboy circles as a particularly fierce competitor died in a fall from her horse. Another woman was thrown from her horse and broke her arm during a team penning clinic near Spotsylvania, Virginia. On a personal note, I have never regained full use of my right index finger because Haskell, my sorrel gelding, decided to pitch a fit when I was gathering cattle in preparation for a practice session. As near as I can recall, I jammed my finger as I was pressing my hand against the saddle horn in preparation for what was supposed to be a controlled, albeit unexpected, dismount.

begin the day early as they hitch up trailers and haul their horses, tack, and equipment to arenas that are often many miles from home, only to repeat the process after hours of sitting on the backside of a horse between rides, often under a blistering sun, and always, it seems, downwind from the dust.

A fourth issue is expense. Like the proverbial black hole, horsemanship in all its guises requires a seemingly endless stream of investment that only begins with the acquisition of a horse. Once committed, penners, sorters and cutters have little choice but to spend their money on vehicles, trailers, equipment, board, feed, veterinary and hoof care, and in some cases, continuing education for both horse and rider under the tutelage of some renowned trainer. As the author can attest, few reach the point where their winnings can even begin to defray their entry fees, let alone other expenses. Rather than complain about their empty wallets, participants exhibit, at least in public, a nonchalance toward money that would be familiar to some cowboy fresh off the trail, eager to empty his pockets during a night on the town and oblivious to the consequences.

Finally, penning, sorting and cutting require cooperation on several levels. As the terminology indicates, these are team sports. Penners and sorters who fail to communicate with their teammates, and cutters who fail to heed the advice of their herders and turn-back men, are doomed not only to failure on any given run, but also to negative sanctions from other participants and the very real prospect of being unable to find riders at subsequent competitions. At the same time, Old Dominion cowboys belong to a union that I refer to as the *animate trinity* of human, horse, and cow. In spite of digital clocks, state-of-the-art horse trailers, websites, and all the other trappings of modernity that have rationalized the arena, ours is a ritual that has been replicated, one way or another, in pastoral societies across time and culture. Insofar as these sports elicit emotional reactions from a time out of mind, I have designated contestants as *mimetic cowboys*—that is, sportsmen and women who derive pleasure and even construct their identities not only by imitating the ways of their pastoral forebears, but also by experiencing emotional tensions created during the adrenaline rush of penning, sorting, and cutting cows that would just as soon not be bothered. Arguably, tensions generated in the arena create the kind of emotional jolt that humans need to maintain their sanity. Elias and Dunning (1986: 89) provide a hint of what is to come in their essay, "The Quest for Excitement in Leisure":

> "In a simple or complex form, on a low or a high level, leisure activities provide, for a short while, the upsurge of strong pleasurable feelings which is often lacking in the ordinary routines of daily life. Their function is not simply, as is often believed, a liberation of tensions but the restoration of that measure of tension which is an essential ingredient of mental health."

To prevent Old Dominion cowboys from fading behind a veil of theory that obscures more than it reveals, I have attempted to let them speak and act for themselves—to form their penning and sorting teams, spur their horses, hobnob with friends as they anticipate moments of glory in the arena, and curse the cattle for their contrary ways. As an observant participant, I had plenty of latitude to let this robust subculture disclose meaning on its own terms. My findings certainly have something to say about macro social forces that nurture cowboy sports. They also open a window on American culture at the threshold of a century that is taking us ever farther, both temporally and metaphorically, from the Old West. How the closing chapter of America's frontier history is remembered and commemorated in sport, together with the cowboy's

INVENTING TRADITION

significance as a source of identity formation and cultural expression, are surely of more than passing interest to a nation traveling at light speed away from its roots and toward an uncertain future.

Whether practicing in my own arena, participating in a clinic under the tutelage of some seasoned cowhand, or battling for my share of the jackpot, I have found ample opportunity to embrace Old Dominion cowboys as a subculture that has thus far escaped the attention of sociologists and historians alike. The challenge has been to combine the documentary evidence of the historian with theoretical perspectives derived from sociology, maintain a balance between the objectivity of a sociologist and the subjectivity of an observant participant, and frame my findings in the context of cultural sociology, all the while keeping my horses healthy and maintaining my standing as an Old Dominion cowboy. From the outset, it's been quite a ride.

With the possible exception of religion, no other institution commands the mystique, nostalgia, and romantic allure that are found in sport. For Weiss (1969), sports are ceremonies whose formality and solemnity invoke a sense of the sacred, and athletes carry a spark of the divine. "An athlete once was, and still can be, treated as a sacred being who embodies something of the divine in him," wrote Weiss in his philosophical inquiry into the world of sport. "He is credited with the dignity of embodying a supreme value. While functioning as a single, organic being, self-contained and well geared toward the future, he is seen, through the help of a ceremony, to be adjectival to a more remote reality" (p. 153). Reflecting on sports as an institution, Edwards (1973) emphasized that sport is characterized by non-utilitarian loyalties and commitments, ritualized behavior, expressive symbolism, and ideological creeds that justify athletics as the embodiment of the good life. "In sum, sport is essentially a secular, quasi-religious institution" (p. 90). Building on Durkheim's (1995) analysis of religion as a socially constructed vehicle for socialization and Goffman's (1959) dramaturgical perspective of face-to-face interaction, Birrell (1981) examined sport as both a vehicle for communication and role clarification and as a social ceremony akin to religious observances.

Thus does scholarship confirm what most of us feel in our hearts and know in the depths of our souls: sport occupies a special and even sacred space whose allure spans cultures and generations.

The sports examined in these pages have a special appeal whose origins lie in that great swath of open country between the Oklahoma – Arkansas line and the Rockies, where cattle trails once crisscrossed the land and young men with more guts than sense rode into history and unwittingly provided fodder for an enduring myth. Their story, and its resonance in our own time, lives on in a subculture of cowboys and cowgirls in Central Virginia whose ranks are swelling and whose horses are chomping at the bit for a chance to display their prowess in the arena. We are certainly Old Dominion cowboys, but even more, we are mimetic cowboys, curiously at odds with, yet symptomatic of, our postmodern age.

Author's Note

Any reservations I might have had about morphing my equine and academic interests were put to rest in October 2004, when my girlfriend (and, since March 2006, my wife) and I attended the Blue Ridge Team Penning Association's banquet to commemorate the end of the season. A couple in their fifties that I had become fond of was seated across the table. The woman had been teaching school for the better part of three decades, and her husband was holding down a white-collar job that, as I learned in the course of our conversation, had long since lost its charm. As we chatted over roast beef and potatoes and sipped iced tea, I popped my standard question: "So, how'd you get into team penning?"

My question was addressed to the man. But before he could answer, his wife—fated, unfortunately, to break her arm the following spring when her gorgeous new horse bucked her into the dirt—chimed in, "Well, it was either this or a red sports car."

I didn't buy it. There's more than that to being an Old Dominion cowboy.

Chapter Two — The Frontier in American Character Development

> "He who would wish to see America in its proper light, and to
> have a true idea of its feeble beginnings and barbarous rudiments,
> must visit our extended line of frontiers, where the last settlers dwell,
> and where he may see the first labours of settlement, the mode of clearing
> the earth, in all their different appearances. Where men are wholly left
> dependent on their native tempers and on the spur of uncertain industry,
> which often fails when not sanctified by the efficacy of a few moral rules."
>
> *J. Hector St. John de Crèvecoeur*
> *Letters from an American Farmer (1782)*

A New Kind of Man

For Europeans in the eighteenth century, America beckoned as a land of opportunity. Those with the temerity to seek their fortune on the far side of the Atlantic sent back tales of pristine forests, endless supplies of game, and vistas unsullied by civilization. To harness those resources for productive purposes, people whose survival depended on adaptation to a strange and often hostile environment found that Old World traditions weren't necessarily up to the task. Their characters shaped and moral compasses honed by the vicissitudes of probing into the wilderness, America's frontiersmen came to symbolize the regeneration to be found in a state of nature. As villages and tiny outposts coalesced into communities, pioneers and their progeny thus produced a character type representing a blend of Old and New World cultures. Forged in the crucible of the frontier, this new man, this American, had the rare distinction of enjoying mythological status even as he was going about the practical business of settling a continent.

Among the most prescient accounts of America in its formative years comes from the pen of J. Hector St. John de Crèvecoeur, a Frenchman dubbed by D.H. Lawrence as the "emotional...prototype of the American" (Crèvecoeur 1997: vii). Born in Caen to a family of minor French nobility, Crèvecoeur arrived in Canada in 1755 and signed up with a French regiment in the St. Lawrence Valley. Holding the rank of lieutenant when the French and Indian Wars broke out, Crèvecoeur found himself fighting against the British at the Plains of Abraham, a battle that left the French General Montcalm dead and Canada in British hands. Wounded in action, Crèvecoeur eventually resigned his commission and traveled through Pennsylvania and New York before marrying and settling down in Orange County, New York. It was there, from 1769 until the outbreak of the American Revolution, that Crèvecoeur cultivated his Pine Hill estate and wrote *Letters from an American Farmer*, arguably the first work of American literature to influence New World travelers and ignite the passions of anyone interested in the moral, spiritual, and mythological foundations of a nation struggling into being.

As a freeholder far removed from European tenancy, Crèvecoeur represented not only the advantages that accrue to independent farmers, but also the rhetorical and philosophical ideals of the Enlightenment. Like Jefferson, who extolled farmers as nothing less than "the chosen people of God" (p. xviii), Crèvecoeur tapped into a tradition of literary reference dating back to Antiquity. Borrowing from European themes and fables suggesting the possibility of new life in America, Crèvecoeur's letters paint a portrait of an agrarian society in harmony with the natural world. His description of the life he was carving out as a simple farmer in the New World reflected physiocratic theory that was gaining a foothold in Enlightened thought—that is, the belief that the wealth and virtue of nations resides in the cultivation of the land and that, as a consequence, agrarian nations are the most contented. "In this sense," wrote Manning in her introduction to Crèvecoeur's collection of letters,

> "we may see Crèvecoeur as putting together an early mythology of America by translating European motifs to an American context, much as Washington Irving would later do when he naturalized the European folk-tale of Peter Klaus as the story of 'Rip Van Winkle'" (pp. xxv-xxvi).

But there was another, more sinister dimension to life on the frontier. Separated from his fellows by vast expanses of wild country, the frontiersman learned to live by his wits, endure whatever hardships an unforgiving environment had to offer, and respond to lawless brutality in kind. Children reared in such circumstances had nothing to contemplate save the example set by their hardscrabble parents. As connections with the civilized East became ever more tenuous, frontier conditions fostered what Crèvecoeur referred to as "a mongrel breed, half-civilized, half-savage," fully at home neither with his fellows nor among the beasts of the forest. Braving a frontier that receded ever westward, untold thousands left the known for the unfathomable and participated in the formation of an entirely new character that continues to resonate in the national consciousness. In Letter III of his book, Crèvecoeur provided a fitting response to his own inquiry into American exceptionalism that has echoed through generations of Americans in search of an identity commensurate with their unique heritage:

> "The American is a new man, who acts upon new principles; he must therefore entertain new ideas and form new opinions. From involuntary idleness, servile dependence, penury, and useless labour, he has passed to toils of a very different nature, rewarded by ample substance.—This is an American" (pp. 44-45).

Even in Crèvecoeur's time, prescient observers glimpsed the seeds of change in European industrialization and its tentative forays onto American soil. Perhaps the Frenchman, contentedly farming his land and recording his thoughts far from the centers of power, is to be forgiven for failing to see the contradiction between pastoral life and economic progress. His vision was essentially static and anti-historical. Borrowing a page from Virgil's *Eclogues*, Crèvecoeur's ideal was the middle state, "a place apart, secluded from the world—a peaceful, lovely, classless, bountiful pasture" (Marx 1967: 116). Cultivated nature, and not primitivism, offered the best prospects for a contented and fulfilling life.

Crèvecoeur has been criticized for failing to recognize the enduring power of religion in the American polity. Moreover, he seems to have turned a blind eye to potential conflicts in a nation founded on the twin pillars of free enterprise and self-governance. Could *homo oeconomicus* uphold the democratic principles for which the revolutionary generation was prepared to die? Or was the fledgling nation, founded on such high hopes, destined to fall into the hands of despots?

INVENTING TRADITION

Such questions, clearly beyond Crèvecoeur's analytical powers, were very much on the mind of his contemporary, Thomas Jefferson. Deeply imbued with scientific rationalism that he'd picked up in the *salons* of Paris, Jefferson had no illusions about the looming conflict between the pastoral ideal and the economic forces that were transforming Europe. Nor did he romanticize the dreariness and danger that lay in wait beyond the line of settlements. His Virgilian landscape was not a pastoral utopia, but "a real place located somewhere between the *ancient regime* and the western tribes" (p. 122). At its center was the independent, rational, democratic husbandman, uncorrupted by market forces that seemed inevitably to transform reasonable men into bestialized appendages of the machine. Much of Jefferson's career in politics was dedicated to preserving this vision of a land of yeoman farmers whose values could only be preserved in the context of an agrarian republic.

Visions of a Garden of Eden, though tempered by harsh realities, gained currency throughout the nineteenth century not only among cultural and intellectual elites, but also among politicians who, like Jefferson, believed in America's unique and divinely inspired destiny (Nash 1967). None captured the essence of American exceptionalism more empirically than Alexis de Tocqueville, the peripatetic Frenchman whose penetrating insights earned him a place in the historical and sociological canons. Accompanied by the French publicist Gustave Auguste de Beaumont de La Bonninière, Tocqueville traveled across the Atlantic in 1831 to study the American penal system. Their findings were eventually published, but Tocqueville had his mind on matters of far greater import. His most famous work, *Democracy in America*, was published between 1835 and 1840. In two volumes of uncommon prescience, Tocqueville laid bare the influence of social and political institutions on the American character.

Like Crèvecoeur, Tocqueville (1945) perceived Americans as a breed apart whose unique make-up was shaped by a combination of inherited values and the challenges posed by an expanding frontier. Weaned in a culture of rigid class distinctions, Tocqueville was mesmerized by Americans' commitment to equality. "The more I advanced in the study of American society," wrote Tocqueville, "the more I perceived that this equality of condition is the fundamental fact from which all others seem to be derived and the central point at which all my observations constantly terminated" (vol. 1: p. 3). His extensive travels brought him into contact with an enormous variety of people and occupations, and he came away convinced that Americans were writing the latest chapter in a story dating back to the thirteenth century, when the first stirrings of democratic thought penetrated the European mind. Relentless in plumbing the wellsprings of American character, Tocqueville underestimated the visceral fear, even hatred, that the wilderness evoked in people who faced its dangers every day. He arrived in Michigan Territory in July 1831 with an interest in exploring the woods. "But when he informed the frontiersmen of his desire to travel for *pleasure* into the primitive forest, they thought him mad" (Nash 1967: 22).

Tocqueville was deeply impressed with the sense of personal independence that seemed to be embedded not only in political institutions, but also in religious and economic life. "The new American republic of the nineteenth century," he wrote (vol. 1: 40), "was the era of the independent citizen as surely as it was defined by the town and national expansion." In contrast to Crèvecoeur, Tocqueville recognized the possibility that America's brand of individualism could degenerate into isolationism without the mitigating effects of civic involvement. Yet he was also convinced that a nation of farmers, bound together in voluntary associations and committed to a sense of community, was the best antidote to despotism and the most likely guarantee that the free enterprise system would not degenerate into a welter of mutually antagonistic individuals bent on self-aggrandizement at the expense of their neighbors (Bellah et al 1996).

Flush with insights into the new nation's commitment to equality and independence, Tocqueville turned his attention to America's steady march across the continent. Fueled by a restless disposition perceived as threatening to his contemporaries back in Europe, Americans in the mid-nineteenth century headed for the frontier in droves. Motivated by a desire for riches, people who joined the great westward migration reproduced the pattern of decentralized, egalitarian democracy that had already branded the settled East as a new kind of polity. In the process, they unwittingly participated in adding a new dimension to a character type, clearly evident in Crèvecoeur's day, that was already a mainstay of myth as well as a cultural ideal with the power to shape communal life: the frontiersman—independent to the core, practical in outlook, and impatient with distinctions based on anything but ability. Wrote Tocqueville (vol. 1: 294),

> "It would be difficult to describe the avidity with which the American rushes forward to secure this immense booty that fortune offers. In the pursuit he fearlessly braves the arrow of the Indian and the diseases of the forest; he is unimpressed by the silence of the woods; the approach of beasts of prey does not disturb him, for he is goaded onwards by a passion stronger than the love of life. Before him lies a boundless continent, and he urges onward as if time pressed and he was afraid of finding no room for his exertions."

As settlers probed beyond the Alleghenies, novelists on both sides of the Atlantic set their sites on adventurers whose lives represented a precarious balance between civilization and savagery. The earliest treatment in fiction of man in a state of nature to meet with commercial success was Daniel Defoe's *The Life and Strange and Surprising Adventures of Robinson Crusoe* (1986). Originally published in 1719 and widely viewed as the first English novel, Defoe's book captivated readers with tales based on the actual experiences of Alexander Selkirk, who had run away to sea in 1704 and requested to be left on an uninhabited island for five years. Resurrected in fiction, Selkirk entered the common lexicon as Robinson Crusoe, a poor wretch "cast upon a horrible desolate island, void of all hope of recovery...singled out and separated, as it were, from all the world to be miserable" (p. 69). From such bleak beginnings, Crusoe met his extraordinary challenges head on and fashioned a crude civilization from the resources at hand. For generations of readers and, eventually, moviegoers, his name has been synonymous with man's ingenuity in mastering a hostile environment. What's more, Defoe imbued his character with a realization that conquering the frontier is a virtuous undertaking—that man's encounter with nature offers the prospect of moral rejuvenation. After twenty-three years on his island home, Crusoe reflected that

> "it may not be amiss for all people who shall meet with my story to make this just observation from it, viz., how frequently, in the course of our lives, the evil which in itself we seek most to shun, and which, when we are fallen into, is the most dreadful to us, is oftentimes the very means or door of our deliverance, by which alone we can be raised again from the affliction we are fallen into" (p. 178).

INVENTING TRADITION

Defoe's theme of man in a state of nature was taken up later in the century in Jean-Jacques Rousseau's *The New Heloise* (1968). Set in the small villages of Vevey and Clarens, the author's paean to rural life became one of the best selling French novels of all time. In her introduction to an English translation of *The New Heloise*, McDowell asserted that, with the exception of Voltaire's *Contes*, Le Sage's *Gil Blas*, and some of Proust's novels, no other eighteenth-century French novel up to the time of Rousseau's death enjoyed even one-tenth its circulation. Between its original publication in 1761 and 1800, ten editions were published in English, leaving readers in England and America with ample opportunity to enjoy one of the most popular novels of the age. Although renowned as a passionate love story, *The New Heloise* reflected Rousseau's bias toward wild and uncultivated places, where, in the absence of civilizing constraints, people could give free reign to their emotions. In one of his early letters to his beloved, Rousseau's character Saint-Preux described how anxious he was "to wander at my leisure through the savage places which constitute in my eyes the charms of this country" (Part I Letter XVIII: 57). In this and subsequent writings, one of the founding fathers of the French Enlightenment both reflected and cultivated readers' awareness of civilization's corrupting influence and the renewal to be found in natural settings. In his sweeping history of Western legal theory, Kelly (1992) recognized in Rousseau a dissenting spirit that refused to bow to the dictates of rationalism that was rolling like thunder across the cultural landscape of Europe and America. Expressing romantic sentiments that would one day challenge the *zeitgeist* of his age, Rousseau voiced a longing for the wild and primitive as a palliative for an uncompromising faith in reason.

> "He struck a chord on the frontiers of the emotions and the intellect: the preference, which he made fashionable, for what had grown free-range rather than under cultivation, for the spontaneous rather than the artificial, lent a sort of authority to whatever had the quality of the pristine and the unforced and original; but incidentally, too, tended to exempt what could be passionately felt, and passionately expressed, from the scrutiny of reason" (p. 253).

Few fictional characters in nineteenth century literature have been more celebrated than Natty Bumppo, the archetypal frontiersman who appears under various sobriquets in all five of James Fenimore Cooper's *Leatherstocking Tales*. "The character was conceived in terms of the antithesis between nature and civilization, between freedom and law, that has governed most American interpretations of the westward movement" (Smith 1950: 60). Published between 1823 and 1841, Cooper's stories found an audience simultaneously drawn to and repelled by the exigencies of frontier life. In *The Pioneers* (1964), we find this troubling dichotomy personified in the Judge, who represents the values of law and social organization, and of course Natty Bumppo, a child of the frontier destined to stay one step ahead of the steadily advancing line of white settlement. "This is the same conflict between the laws of Man and the laws of Nature," wrote Spiller in his afterword to the 1964 edition of *The Pioneers*, "that Huck Finn debated on his raft and that has occupied American fiction from Captain Ahab to Frank Cowperwood and beyond" (pp. 443-44).

Cooper's frontier romances codified and systematized the representations of the frontier that had evolved haphazardly since the early seventeenth century through such diverse media as personal narratives, sermons, newspaper stories, street ballads, and pulp fiction. Recognizing the opposition between Whites and Indians as the fundamental historical trope of his time, Cooper explored racial tensions as a key to unlock other basic oppositions that were coming to a head in Jacksonian America and would continue to plague the national polity throughout the nineteenth century, including masculine and feminine ways of thinking about the "Indian question" and class envy between landed gentry and yeomen farmers, masters and slaves, and even commanders and their subordinates. His spectrum of racial and cultural compromises, ranging from racially pure Whites and Indians to racial and gender hybrids, provided generations of imitators and dime-novelists with a repertoire of stereotypes that could be adapted to changing fashions and audiences (Slotkin 1992).

In *The Scarlet Letter* (2003), first published in 1850, Hawthorne's depiction of the wilderness surrounding Salem, Massachusetts, conjures up medieval fears of the unknown—a place devoid of law, fit only for wild beasts and terrors of the imagination. "The image is that of a man in an alien environment where the civilization that normally orders and controls his life is absent" (Nash 1967: 2). For Hester Prynne, Hawthorne's hapless heroine, the freedom fostered in the wilds of New England opened the floodgates of sexual temptation and doomed her to a life of shame as an adulteress. As the forces of modernity accelerated toward the end of the nineteenth century, readers searching for lighter fare were treated to Mark Twain's *The Adventures of Huckleberry Finn* (1948). First published in 1885, Twain's rollicking account of adventure on the Mississippi River won over the hearts of millions and secured the author's berth in America's literary canon. Determined to escape his Aunt Sally's *civilizin'* ways, Huck, together with his faithful companion, Jim, gave us a whole new vocabulary to reflect on the perils and promises of life on the edge of civilization.

Perhaps the richest repository of reflection on the frontier's role in shaping the American character can be found in professional historiography. In his survey of historical writing from Bancroft to Boorstin, Noble (1965) found little difference between the world views of modern historians and the Puritans who flocked to the New World in the seventeenth century. Convinced that erecting a simple society in harmony with nature was the only way to preserve man's covenant with his Creator, the Puritans arrived in Massachusetts with a mandate to return to the primitive church—to escape the burden of history and establish God's laws in a pristine wilderness. From Bancroft's paeans to Jackson's Everyman who bounded into the American narrative in the 1830s to Boorstin's artful blend of history and sociology in the 1960s, historians have been the main spokesmen for this cultural tradition. Their perspectives resonate today in a nation whose people, and certainly their leaders, perceive the United States as the last great hope of humanity. "The American people," wrote Noble, "believe that their historical experience has been uniquely timeless and harmonious because they are the descendants of Puritans who, in rejecting the traditions and institutions of the Old World, promised never to establish traditions and institutions in the New World" (p. 4).

Utopian dreams, perhaps most clearly reflected in John Winthrop's vision of erecting a city on a hill as a beacon to true believers, certainly found fertile soil in the New World. Yet it wasn't long before fissures began to appear in the bedrock of Puritan values. Even as they were erecting their churches on American soil, the Puritans found themselves wrestling with a quandary that has plagued moralists and philosophers to our own time: Can man's covenant with God be preserved in a world bent on economic and material progress? Subsequent generations immersed in a rising tide of science and technology fared no better in extricating themselves from the horns of their dilemma. Even the *philosophes* of the Enlightenment were unsure how to reconcile their faith in reason with their equally strong conviction that the human race was better off in a state of nature. If man's salvation lay in a return to primitivism, then didn't science and technology set us on the road to perdition? Could the noble savage of the Enlightened imagination coexist with modernity?

Casting about for a solution, the *philosophes* drew a collective sigh of relief when they found Benjamin Franklin. Here at last was the combination they had been looking for: a rationalist, scientist, and humanitarian, clad in homespun breeches and beaver-skin hat, spouting down-home homilies and captivating his European hosts with his elegant simplicity. Voltaire's perfect philosopher died in 1790, but the vacuum that he left was quickly filled by the titan of the American Enlightenment, Thomas Jefferson, whose dreams of an agrarian democracy sustained hopes that America could fulfill its dual promise as the capital of progress and antithesis to the perils of civilization. As America's agrarian empire stretched ever westward, the Christian and eschatological foundations of Puritan ideology gave way to Jefferson's secular vision. For him as well as countless settlers who pulled up stakes to embrace an uncertain future, the achievement and safety of republican institutions depended on the availability of land capable of sustaining generations of self-supporting freeholders (Slotkin 1992). This vision of the frontier found its philosophic voice in the Romantic Movement. Taking their cue from Rousseau's state of nature thesis, nineteenth-century Romantics and their heirs, the Transcendentalists, believed that intuition represented the reason of the heart and was capable of lifting man from his squalid history and delivering him into communion with nature. Simplicity in the Garden, not reason, was man's best hope for a renewed covenant with God.

Bancroft was an eyewitness to the American juggernaut of the nineteenth century, and his writings are suffused with insights into the paradoxes inherent in a nation committed to progress, yet yearning for a return to primitivism. His mantle was taken up by Beard, Becker, Parrington, and Boorstin, all attuned to America's ambivalence toward its Western lands, and all determined to unravel the meaning behind a nation struggling to escape the snare of history. As guardians of the national covenant, they accepted the moral burden of expressing a ritual drama that was most clearly evident along the fault line between savagery and civilization.

Most prominent among the chroniclers of American exceptionalism was Frederick Jackson Turner. Born in 1861 in Portage, Wisconsin, Turner was an eyewitness to the settlement of the Old Northwest. As a young professor slogging through obscurity at the decidedly backwater University of Wisconsin, Turner accepted Bancroft's version of economic determinism and saw the existence of abundant, free, and virgin land as the key to unlocking the secrets of America's past. He also believed that the central drama of American history was the common man's struggle against European influence, represented in the New World by the colonial and, later, Eastern aristocracy. His interest in this clash led him to the ever-shifting line of frontier settlements, where new societies in the making came in conflict with Eastern privilege and financial power. For Turner, Jefferson was the first prophet of democracy, and Jackson's victory in 1828 was a watershed insofar as it represented the natural potential born of free land and a victory for frontier democracy (Noble 1965).

Keenly aware of the changes that were rumbling through American society after the Civil War, Turner recognized the significance of the land runs in Oklahoma Territory that began with the opening of the Unassigned Lands on April 22, 1889. Packing his interdisciplinary approach to the study of human affairs, Turner, only 32 years old and representing a university that was far from the center of the academic world, traveled to Chicago in the summer of 1893 to present a paper at a meeting of the American Historical Association (Faragher 1994). Across town, people from all parts of the globe were flocking to the World's Columbian Exposition to celebrate the four hundredth anniversary of Columbus' arrival in the New World and marvel at the latest in science and technology. From the ivory tower of academic history to the cacophony and entertainment of a world-class extravaganza, America seemed to have reached a crossroads, poised precariously between its pioneering past and a future that was approaching with breakneck speed.

Attendance was light on July 12 when, toward the end of the evening session, Turner stood to deliver his paper. The professor's youth and lack of notoriety at a conference of intellectual heavyweights were partly to blame for the dearth of attendees, but there was also competition from more alluring entertainment at the nearby exposition. Bearing the unassuming title, "The Significance of the Frontier in American History," Turner's (1977: 3) paper included a prophetic passage from the census of 1890:

> "Up to and including 1880 the country had a frontier of settlement, but at present the unsettled area has been so broken into by isolated bodies of settlement that there can hardly be said to be a frontier line. In the discussion of its extent, its westward movement, etc., it cannot, therefore, any longer have a place in the census reports."

Nobody could have guessed that Turner's paper would one day blow through the halls of academe like a prairie wind storm to become the most familiar model of American history. "The existence of an area of free land," wrote Turner in an oft-quoted passage from his *chef d'oeuvre*, "its continuous recession, and the advance of American settlement westward explain American development" (p. 3). Reduced to its essentials, the frontier thesis begins with the assertion that laws and customs from the Old World had little relevance in the American wilderness, where an abundance of land and dearth of people fostered innovation and experimentation and put a premium on practical skills.[1] Mobility and its corollary, wastefulness, were all but inevitable in a land of seemingly endless resources. The acquisition of material wealth trumped cultural creativity, and class distinctions that shaped European civilization gave way to democratic polities in which status was based on abilities rooted in the exigencies of frontier life. Grimly determined to win at all costs, Americans either took their leisure activities too seriously or avoided them altogether. "And, most important of all, men found that the man-land ratio on the frontier provided so much opportunity for the individual to better himself that external controls were not necessary; individualism and political democracy were enshrined as their ideals" (Billington 1966: 3). Over the course of three centuries, these traits were revitalized over and over again as the frontier receded ever westward. Moreover, the vast majority of people who declined to join in the exodus and remained in the settled East experienced the frontier as a safety valve. The Siren call of the West was, after all, within everyone's earshot, and even people who opted to stay home could fantasize what lay beyond the horizon.

---

[1] Turner certainly acknowledged Old World influence in shaping the American character, but he insisted that it be examined in the context of America's unique development. In essence, he was calling into question the so-called "germ theory" that conferred primary importance on the European origins of New World societies and posited that American institutions evolved in the forests of Europe among Teutonic tribes. See Pierson, in Hofstadter and Lipset 1968: 16-17; and Jacobs 1994: 6.

INVENTING TRADITION

Whatever their field of study, scholars from the dawn of the twentieth century to the end of the 1920s "worshipped at Turner's shrine and glorified the frontier as a molding force that had shaped the course of civilization" (pp. 14-15). The validity of the frontier thesis seemed to be borne out by travelers from overseas who, in the footsteps of Crèvecoeur (1997) and Tocqueville (1945), knew that something was hatching on the far side of the Atlantic that had no precedents in the Old World. In his perusal of hundreds of travel accounts from the eighteenth and nineteenth centuries, Billington (1966) found a consensus that Americans were considered wasteful, democratic, and inquisitive, and that these traits became more pronounced as one journeyed from east to west.

Turner's thesis was by no means original. His genius lay in piecing together a variety of scattered ideas and concepts to form a unified interpretation of one phase of American history, and his contribution to our understanding of the American character was to unite demographic and historical facts into a meaningful pattern and to reveal relationships that had thus far escaped scholarly scrutiny. An alleged lack of originality was of little consequence to Faragher (1994: 1), who was unequivocal in his assessment of the frontier thesis: "Turner's essay is the single most influential piece of writing in the history of American history." Webb (1964: 6), who certainly ranks at the forefront of America's cadre of frontier historians, referred to Turner's paper as "the most influential single piece of historical writing ever done in the United States." Even Pierson (Hofstadter and Lipset 1968: 15-42), whose reexamination of Turner's thesis was the prerequisite to an overhaul of its main tenets, acknowledged that "his brilliant papers have been the bible, and today still constitute the central inspiration, of an extraordinary and widely-held faith" (p. 16). Jacobs (1994), a lifelong student of Turner whose biography of him verges on hagiography, credited the historian from Wisconsin with revolutionizing American historiography. "Whatever may be said about Turner's theory of frontier development, we must acknowledge that he remains one of America's major historians. He is remembered as a gifted theorist in his understanding of and accounting for the varied origins of American civilization" (pp. 11-12).

When Turner died in 1932, the intellectual climate in the United States was changing. As the Great Depression cast its pall across the land and trade between nations bound the globe into ever tighter webs of interdependency, scholars questioned an interpretation that focused on agrarianism rather than industrialism, rugged individualism rather than state planning, and optimistic nationalism rather than political internationalism (Billington 1966). In the ensuing years, Turner has been criticized for his hyperbole, insensitivity to gender and cultural nuances, and even failure to come up with a workable definition of the frontier. Hofstadter and Lipset (1968) gathered a collection of essays by scholars who acknowledged American historiography's debt to Turner even as they deconstructed his thesis. Pierson concluded that the frontier thesis was "too optimistic, too romantic, too provincial, and too nationalistic to be reliable in any survey of world history or study in comparative civilization" (p. 36). The fundamental problem was its internal inconsistency. Turner's rubric calls on us to reconcile nationalism with sectional tendencies, frontier ingenuity with repetition of eastern traditions and institutions, improvement of civilization achieved through the abandonment of civilization, and idealism as the fruit of Western materialism. Boatright dismissed Turner's emphasis on frontier individualism as a myth that has more to do with the social and economic predilections of historians than empirical evidence. "One who examines the folkways of the settlers is impressed by the numerous ways in which the principle of mutuality finds expression in frontier life" (p. 45). Lee was primarily interested in migration, and he criticized Turner for failing to acknowledge Americans' penchant for moving as a building block of the national character. "Most of the effects, desirable and undesirable, that were attributed by Turner to the frontier can, with equal or better logic, be attributed to migration, and in addition, the migratory theory does not collapse or depend upon tradition for its maintenance after the frontier is gone" (p. 66). For Bogue, Turner failed not only to investigate the implications of the West as "a form of society" (p. 73); he also neglected the alchemic processes involved in transforming settlers primarily of European stock into bona fide Westerners. Drawing on research in the social and behavioral sciences, Bogue departed from strict historiography to examine frontier settlements as crucibles of character formation in ways that escaped Turner's poetic sensibilities.

Gates, treading where few frontier historians bothered to go,[2] examined the role of laborers and tenant farmers in shaping Western communities. Finding census figures unreliable and even deceptive, Gates consulted county deed records, local newspaper advertisements, and correspondence of land dealers and landlords to reveal a dimension of frontier culture that has been obscured by the attention given to yeoman farmers and their democratic proclivities. Finding that the frontier was not necessarily the gateway to paradise, landless immigrants carried their resentments with them as they moved westward. With the closing of the frontier, the areas in which they settled often became fertile ground for Populists and labor agitators. Citing evidence from mid-twentieth century sociology regarding the emergence of political democracy in public housing projects, Elkins and McKitrick called Turner to task for not offering a conceptual framework to test his hypothesis that there was an organic connection between American democracy and the frontier. Their model, based on settlement patterns in the Old Northwest, the Southwest frontier of Alabama and Mississippi, and the Puritan frontier of Massachusetts Bay, includes periods of problem-solving and homogeneous populations as variables and an absence of leadership structures as key factors in the formation of democratic polities. Mikesell pinpointed a neglect of comparative research as the principal failing of Turner and his disciples. "Without the perspective afforded by knowledge of developments in foreign areas, it is not possible to interpret the significance of the American frontier" (p. 152). He suggested that Canada, Australia, and South Africa provide the most fruitful comparisons. As was the case in North America, their frontiers emerged in the context of rapid economic and social change, where relationships between aboriginal peoples and immigrants, together with environmental factors, were causal variables in national development. Yet Mikesell failed to see how comparative study could either confirm or deny Turner's most challenging assertion: that the frontier was a major influence on the formation of national institutions. Perhaps it is here, in the bewildering maze of causes and effects, where historians need to recognize their limitations and call in reinforcements from the social sciences. Historians can certainly blaze a trail into the thicket, but in the absence of social theory, they might never find their way out.

For Shannon, it was high time to perform a post-mortem on one of the weakest pillars of the frontier thesis: the labor-safety-valve theory. Gleaning evidence from census reports, Shannon found scant evidence that disgruntled workers from the east traded in their industrial tools for plowshares and migrated west in droves. Farm growth west of the Mississippi between 1860 and 1900 simply was not very impressive, and as Gates showed, much of the population

---

[2] Gates mentioned not only Turner, but also Paxson, Riegel, and Billington as historians who glossed over the role that tenant farmers and laborers played in the settlement of the West. See Gates, in Hofstadter and Lipset 1968: 102.

increase came not from landowners, but rather from tenant farmers and hired hands. Moreover, immigration figures indicate that Europeans were particularly susceptible to the call of the West: witness the Scandinavian settlement of the North Central states. Perhaps most damning was the fact that labor unrest reached a crescendo in the 1870s and 1880s, precisely the period when free land was supposed to seduce easterners from their angst-ridden lives. "Nevertheless," concluded Shannon, "old stereotypes of thought die hard. Quite often they expire only with their devotees" (p. 185).

On the other hand, it may be that critics of the labor-safety-valve theory were asking the wrong questions. Simler suggested that the theory makes sense if we shift our focus from demographics to economics. Whether or not eastern laborers became farmers is beside the point; the fact remains that worker mobility in a region of scarce labor and abundant resources was a significant factor in stimulating economic development in the West. Murphy and Zellner were likewise reluctant to bury this aspect of Turner's theory. Citing sequential growth patterns that "gave a solid foundation to the rags-to-riches saga" (p. 216), they acknowledged the psychological influence of the safety-valve theory that continues to shape our metaphors of westward migration. "American social history," concluded the authors, "indicates quite clearly that the 'belief' in a safety valve had a potent effect upon social action in America" (p. 216).

In her overview of criticism that has been leveled at the frontier thesis, Young (1970) found a consensus among historians claiming that Turner's fixation on agrarianism and isolationism downplayed America's roots in European culture, ignored its membership in an Atlantic and world community, and distorted its importance as a major industrial power. To understand the relationship between national identity and the frontier, Clementi (1981) conducted a comparative study of three archetypes from the Americas: the North American pioneer, the Brazilian *bandeirante*, and the Argentine *gaucho*. Although she acknowledged Turner's contribution to our understanding of the North American case, she felt that criticism was warranted insofar as he eschewed scientific methodology and omitted salient facts from his interpretation. Cronon (1987) suggested that his vocabulary was more that of a poet than a logician and that his "fuzzy language" carries the weight of thoughtful analysis only because his central terms—frontier, democracy, individualism, and national character—were so broad and ill-defined. In his review of contemporary historiography, Faragher (1993) found that Turner's ghost was finally giving way to rival interpretations of the Western experience that call attention to such factors as urbanism, immigration, and the environment. He further chided Turner for failing to recognize the possibility that the American West was, in essence, a plundered province, tyrannized by eastern capital and under the sway of the federal government.

Yet the fact that what some scholars dismiss as "the shibboleth of the frontier" (p. 109) has survived to be castigated in our own day is testimony to its enduring value. For all its shortcomings as an explanatory text, Turner's thesis "expresses some of the deepest myths and longings many Americans still feel about their national experience" (Cronon 1987: 160). Memories that foster collectivities are not necessarily reflected in official history. Even literate societies depend on myth as a wellspring of identity and cultural expression. We continue to rely on the frontier thesis not because it stands up to the rigors of academic history, but because of its simplicity and movement, its sense of sequence, and its ability to lend narrative power to facts supplied by historians. In short, it tells a story about what it means to be an American—a story of people across generations working with the tools at hand to mobilize resources and build communities. "What endures is Turner's commitment to history as contemporary knowledge; his understanding that debates about the past are always simultaneously debates about the present. It marks him as America's first truly modern historian" (Faragher 1994: 4). Jacobs (1994) came to much the same conclusion, asserting that Turner's insight into the foundations of American character, informed by literature and sociology as well as history, provides a jumping off point for theorizing about America's past. The patriotic self-image that Turner and his disciples fostered is certainly in keeping with American values, and his insistence that such traits as individualism, inventiveness, and exuberance for freedom grew out of frontier conditions rang an historical bell that has yet to stop pealing. Even as modernity shapes and reshapes the landscape, the West, both geographically and in the high country of the mind, survives as the memory bank of the frontier experience. "Thus the history of the bygone frontier days becomes a memory, a myth that helps us to comprehend the legacy of the West" (p. 246).

Of course, it didn't take an award-winning historian or a copy of the 1890 census to prove that the frontier was on its way out. One had only to peek out the window to see that big changes were in the wind. Modernity in all its guises was plowing through traditions like a hot knife through butter, sometimes for the better, and sometimes not. Even as caravans of hopeful settlers ventured onto the great prairies and scratched out communities destined to become great cities, America's peculiar penchant for exploration was making itself evident science, technology, and politics. Eradicating diseases, harnessing the power of the atom, putting a man on the moon, and other accomplishments too numerous to mention have all been framed in the familiar context of conquering a frontier. Meanwhile, the end of America's westward trek coincided with and perhaps even spawned opportunities for overseas expansion in the Caribbean and the Philippines. Clearly, the spirit that has captivated observers since the dawn of the Republic continued to flow like an underground river through the national psyche to become a cornerstone of America's collective consciousness.

The Frontier Revisited: Old Myths, New Realities

Turner (1977: 5), never one to let precision get in the way of an inspiring story, gave a whole new dimension to ambiguity when he characterized the frontier as an elastic term that "for our purposes does not need sharp definition." Such fuzziness notwithstanding, Turner and his successors were in general agreement on at least one thing: the frontier consisted of areas of Anglo-American penetration that had yet to enjoy the full benefits of civilization (Forbes 1968). Seen in what is best described as a nationalist context, the westward movement of Anglo-Saxons was one-sided and ethnocentric, and the frontier was a place of inter-group contact between pioneers of primarily European heritage and others who weren't. Historians have done their part to inculcate this vision in the popular consciousness with such phrases as "the cattle frontier." The uninitiated might assume that reference was being made to a border between various breeds of cattle, but Americans steeped in their nation's creation stories know this to mean the phase of Anglo-American history when cattle kingdoms spread out across the West.

Conceiving of the frontier as a point of contact between distinct groups leads us to question its much-touted disappearance in 1890. Geographically and metaphorically, the frontier remains very much alive not only in terms of racial and ethnic divisions, but also in the realm of the imagination, where physical borderlands have given way to vague frontiers of knowledge. Frontiers can also take on social and political meaning. Turner was barely in his grave when members of President Franklin D. Roosevelt's New Deal brain trust suggested that the demise of economic stimuli generated on the old frontier necessitated national pump priming through

INVENTING TRADITION

legislation.[3] The same theme resonated in President Woodrow Wilson's New Freedom program of progressive legislation and President Harry Truman's Fair Deal (Jacobs 1994). President John F. Kennedy chose the "New Frontier" as a slogan to represent the theme and style of his upcoming campaign. Sixty-seven years almost to the day after Turner delivered his paper in Chicago, Kennedy stood at the podium in the Los Angeles Coliseum to accept the Democratic Party's nomination for the Presidency. Using Wild West metaphors that tapped into a reservoir of latent ideological power, Kennedy called on his fellow Americans to accept the challenges posed by international Communism abroad and systemic poverty at home. "I stand tonight facing west on what was once the last frontier," declared this scion of the Eastern establishment.

> "From the lands that stretch 3000 miles behind me, the pioneers of old gave up their safety, their comfort and sometimes their lives to build a new world here in the West...[But] the problems are not all solved and the battles are not all won, and we stand today on the edge of a new frontier—the frontier of the 1960s, a frontier of unknown opportunities and paths, a frontier of unfulfilled hopes and threats...For the harsh facts of the matter are that we stand on this frontier at a turning point in history" (Slotkin 1992: 2).

Kennedy's rhetoric, as familiar to his old comrades at Harvard as it was to his listeners in Los Angeles and the millions in between, evoked a complex set of symbols resonant with heroes and adventures that represented morally justified stages of historical conflict. In the years to come, soldiers fated to defend Southeast Asia from the scourge of Communism made liberal use of frontier imagery to describe, and indeed to justify, the horrors inherent in their own crusade. Vietnam was Indian country, search and destroy missions were games of cowboys and Indians, and the fort was to be protected at all costs. Such talismans were revived with special poignancy during the presidency of Ronald Reagan, the actor-turned-statesman whose gift was to distill complex issues into Western morality plays scripted in Hollywood. Whatever one's politics, there's no denying Reagan's mastery of frontier rhetoric. He spoke the language of the West, of an imaginary world in which there was no society, only individuals, and of self-reliance, suffused with a conviction that America was naturally endowed with the right to rule the world (Michalowski and Dubisch 2001).

Even as Reagan was molding affairs of state to the contours of his own Western values, Associate Supreme Court Justice Sandra Day O'Connor was fulfilling her duties to the Constitution with flourishes, verbal and otherwise, that had been cultivated under Western skies. She often cited her upbringing on the Lazy B, a cattle ranch straddling the Arizona – New Mexico border, as the source of her fierce independence. "The power of the memories of life on the Lazy B is strong," recalled O'Connor and longtime ranch manager Alan Day (2002: 315) in their memoir, *Lazy B: Growing Up on a Cattle Ranch in the American Southwest*.

> "It surges through my mind and my heart often...We know that our characters were shaped by our experiences there as surely as Arturo Gonzales shaped his clay sculptures in art class at Radford School. The value system we learned was

---

[3] Roosevelt, who had been exposed to Turner's work at Harvard, often stressed the concept that an ordered economic society must take the place of unbridled individualism in order to preserve democracy and unbridled individualism. See Jacobs 1994: 111.

simple and unsophisticated and the product of necessity...Verbal skills were less important than the ability to know and understand how things work in the physical world. Personal qualities of honesty, dependability, competence, and good humor were valued most. These qualities were evident in most of the people who lived and worked at the Lazy B through the years."

In the wake of 9/11, President George W. Bush sounded like a lawman preparing to dispense justice from the business end of a Colt 44. The smoke was still smoldering at the World Trade Center and the Pentagon when the president called for Osama bin Laden to be brought in dead or alive, as if sending a posse, six-guns a-blazin', after the world's most wanted man would put an end to terrorist threats. One is reminded of Senator Mark Hannah's assessment of Theodore Roosevelt, badlands rancher and hero of the Rough Riders, as a dangerous man—cocky, impetuous, progressive, and full of anti-business notions. After William McKinley was elected President in 1901 with the hard-riding Roosevelt on the winning ticket, Hannah reminded his fellow Ohioan what would happen if he should die in office: "Look what we've got—that damned cowboy is President of the United States!"

Of course, as President Bush discovered to his chagrin at the annual Group of Eight (G8) Summit of Industrialized Nations in July 2006, cowboy diplomacy has its limits. Unaware that there was a live feed nearby, he offered British Prime Minister Tony Blair his take on the escalating violence along the Israeli – Lebanese border. With Hezbollah missiles raining down on northern Israel, Bush sounded more like a sheriff in an R (or perhaps, these days, PG)-rated Western than the leader of the free world. "What they need to do is get Syria to get Hezbollah to stop doing this shit, and it's over," he said as he snarfed down dinner rolls and rocked back in his chair like some cowpoke sidled up to a hitching post. Picking up on CNN's suggestion that the president was up to his old cowboy ways,[4] the global media declared open season on Bush's less than nuanced approach to international relations.

In less time than it takes for a duck to light on a June bug, publics worldwide were making the connection between President Bush's scatological humor and the cowboy of Western lore: simple, rough-hewn, and unmindful of what civilized folks might think of him. Rather than run for cover, White House press secretary Tony Snow played down the incident. Alerted to his gaffe, Bush asked to see the transcript from the Summit's four minutes of uncensored statesmanship. "So we showed him the transcript," said Snow, "then he rolled his eyes and laughed."[5] Such barnyard banter might not win very many friends abroad, but it suits the folks back home just fine. Bush "used an expletive to express his view," said Roderick Hart, a professor of communications and government at the University of Texas in an interview with *USA Today*. "That's the way plain folks talk and probably will play pretty well in the heartland

---

[4] Shortly after Bush's candid take on Middle East diplomacy on July 17, 2006, a CNN reporter framed his story in the context of President Bush's blunt and earthy bravado that falls under the rubric of cowboy ways. A video featuring the presidential *faux pas* is available at http://www.cnn.com/2006/WORLD/europe/07/18/bush.tape.reaction/index.html.

[5] See Jim Rutenberg, (July 18, 2006), "Bush's Policy Chit-Chat: Undiplomatic Prose," *The New York Times*, VOL. CLV.... No. 53,644: A6.

INVENTING TRADITION

and beyond."[6] The president returned to his favorite rhetorical sandbox during a press conference the day after Republicans took what he described "a thumpin'" in the midterm elections of 2006. At one point, a reporter questioned his ability to establish a working relationship with Congresswoman and soon-to-be Speaker of the House Nancy Pelosi, a woman who has made no secret of her contempt for President Bush and his Administration. In a flourish of Western bravado that captures the essence of American political campaigns, the president said simply, "This isn't my first rodeo."[7]

Of course, cowboy imagery struts its stuff on lesser stages as well. In the wake of the same elections that sent President Bush running for metaphorical cover, there was speculation that George Allen, one-time governor and Republican senator from Virginia with a yen for cowboy ways and a horse to boot, would get over the thumpin' he took from Democratic challenger Jim Webb and run for another office. "I don't think we've seen George Allen hang up his cowboy hat yet," commented Albemarle County Republican Lee E. Goodman, counsel for the Republican Party of Virginia.[8] It doesn't take much imagination to conjure up the headline that will one day blaze above the fold of Virginia newspapers: "George Allen Rides Again."

Meanwhile, *Time Magazine* has been conducting its own exploration of cowboy imagery in American projections of power. To provide historical context for America's contemporary challenges, the magazine publishes an annual "Making of America" issue. Past issues have profiled Meriwether Lewis and William Clark, Ben Franklin, Thomas Jefferson, and Abe Lincoln. The fifth issue in the series featured Theodore Roosevelt—"that damned cowboy," according to an apprehensive Mark Hannah—a larger-than-life figure who dragged his nation into the twentieth century. His commitment to the strenuous life, recorded in his highly acclaimed histories and hammered into policy throughout his career in politics, was hewn largely from the two years he spent as a cowboy in the Dakota Territory.[9] Roosevelt's rough-riding proclivities were brought up to date in the magazine's July 17, 2006 issue. With a giant cowboy hat imprinted with the Presidential seal and stylish Western boots gracing *Time*'s cover, co-authors Mike Allen and Romesh Ratnesar proclaimed that Bush's cowboy diplomacy had reached a dead end. Midway through the Administration's second term, cracks were developing in the "muscular, idealistic and unilateralist vision of American power" that prevailed after nine-eleven. Wild West rhetoric was giving way, however grudgingly, to a strategic make over based on diplomacy and cooperation with allies. "As much as anything," concluded Allen and Ratnesar, "it's confirmation of what Princeton political scientist Gary J. Bass calls 'doctrinal flameout.' Put another way: cowboy diplomacy, R.I.P."[10]

---

[6] See David Jackson, (July 18, 2006), "Live Mike Captures Bush's Tough Talk at G8 Summit," *USA Today*: 5A.

[7] Presidential news conference, (November 8, 2006). *National Public Radio*.

[8] See Bob Gibson, (November 10, 2006), "Allen Stands Aside; Webb Wins: Step Shifts Senate Balance to Democrats," *The [Charlottesville, Virginia] Daily Progress*: A6.

[9] See Kathleen Dalton, (July 3, 2006), "The Self-Made Man," *Time*, Vol. 168, No. 1: 48-50.

[10] See Mike Allen and Romesh Ratnesar, (July 17, 2006), "The End of Cowboy Diplomacy," *Time*, Vol. 168, No. 3: 20-26.

On the other hand, maybe cowboys have just gone overseas. The next week, *Time* columnist Joe Klein tried to sort out the players in Iran's convoluted power plays that confound American policy makers, particularly in the wake of hostilities between Israel and Hezbollah that erupted in the summer of 2006. Using a metaphor that needs no elucidation for readers back home, Klein suggested that "the Iranian government's cowboy faction might be strutting its stuff."[11]

Writing for *The New Republic*, correspondent Robert Kagan clearly recognized the cowboy myth as such a strong signifier that it needs no elaboration. Under the title, "Cowboy Nation," he debunked the myth that America has been a reluctant player on the world stage, satisfied with the status quo until goaded into action by some malevolent or revolutionary force. On the contrary, "The United States has never been a status quo power; it has always been a revolutionary one, consistently expanding its participation and influence in the world in ever-widening arcs."[12] Long before the nation's founding, Americans began their relentless push westward, wresting control of great swaths of land from France, Spain, and Russia, and exterminating Native Americans along the way. International adventures began with the Spanish-American War and continue in our own time in foreign lands too numerous to mention. Driven by enlightened liberalism and its belief in universal rights and self-determination, America has been anything but a reluctant hegemon. In true cowboy fashion, Americans have rarely shrunk from a fight. More often than not, they've drawn first. What is particularly apropos about Kagan's assessment of America's cultural proclivities is that he used the word "cowboy" only once—in his title. No sense wasting ink.

Among the most holistic approaches to frontier history and its influence on postfrontier generations flowed from the pen of Walter Prescott Webb (1964). Webb's boom hypothesis of modern history suggests that the American experience was but a single chapter in a narrative spanning some four centuries, beginning with the voyages of exploration in the late Middle Ages and ending in the 1890s, when free land was no longer there for the taking. Sparsely-settled regions of the globe constituted the Great Frontier, and the wealth that poured into the coffers of nations that exploited them produced a drama whose final act has yet to be written. The principal actors—population, land, and capital—were certainly present prior to the age of discovery, but their ratios were insufficient for a boom. With the discovery of new lands, however, tiny populations encountered resources on a scale heretofore beyond imagining. Economies were transformed, and cultures bound by centuries of tradition were unleashed to discover new avenues of expression. Recognizing that no resources are unlimited, Webb speculated what would become of humanity as swollen populations approach scarcity or exhaustion.

> "Then the scholars will look back on the age when the Golden Door opened, and men marched out to the Great Frontier to create the greatest boom that the world has known; they will make myths and legends about it, and in poetry and literature express their yearning for New Frontiers. They will see the frontier as the great factor in the age called modern, see it clearly as the lost factor which they would so love to find" (p. 28).

---

[11] See Joe Klein, (July 24, 2006), "The Iran Factor," *Time*, Vol. 168, No. 4: 31.

[12] See Robert Kagan, (October 23, 2006), "Cowboy Nation," *The New Republic*, Issue 4,788, Vol. 235: 20-23.

INVENTING TRADITION

Adopting a multi-disciplinary approach that would have met with Turner's whole-hearted approval, Billington (1966) concluded that, even though the frontier experience may not have been the single causal variable in American character formation, it was certainly of major importance. In an environment where traditional controls and values were weakened, pioneers found themselves in a state of mass *anomie*. Their societies were fluid, ever changing, and unstable. Accustomed behaviors failed to bring predictable results, and experimentation seemed to be the most likely avenue to success. Simply put, the frontier had a corrosive effect on individuals and institutions, and the more group culture acted upon and molded their personalities, the more pioneers realized, however subconsciously, that conformity to their unique social environment was easier than resistance.

> "Sufficient to say that the findings of social scientists, particularly in the fields of motivation, personality, culture, and spatial mobility, do suggest logical means whereby three centuries of expansion did alter the behavioral patterns of the frontiersmen, and to a lessening degree of their descendants of the twentieth century" (p. xiii).

Acknowledging the tendency among contemporary historians to reveal new patterns in the mosaic of Western America, Deverell (1994) suggested that the Old West provides ideal texts for the analysis of power. Like Forbes (1968), Deverell (1994) assumed the primacy of the Anglo-Saxon experience—a one-sided, mega narrative embracing all the pieces of the hardy pioneer epic, scattered like toys in America's favorite sandbox.

> "It is a mythic image cultivated by all sorts of entities, from journalists to politicians to corporations, and it is a view fiercely protected by nostalgia and sentiment. It is a West both understood and explained by Ralph Lauren, Frontierland, Levi's, High Noon, rodeos, Ronald Reagan, as well as countless history texts and tests. We all know about this West, the West of little houses and prairies, good and bad guys, Conestogas, and lusty days of yesteryear" (p. 188).

If the West, an awe-inspiring land of prairies, majestic mountains, and tall tales commensurate with their setting, resides in our imagination as a dreamscape reminding us what it means to be American, then what happens to those who fail to embrace the archetypes of the independent farmer, the rugged cowboy, or the self-sacrificing schoolteacher? Scratch deep enough, and what emerges is a contestation for power. "Then the entire experiment—democracy, egalitarianism, the American Dream—is brought into question" (p. 201). The Edenic dream of happy yeomen and contented families fulfilling God's promise breaks down into a nightmare that reveals the limits of America's promise of success and upward mobility. Through the prisms of gender, race, and ethnicity, new visions and interpretations of the frontier experience suggest that the one-size-fits-all approach fails the test of historic accuracy and perhaps even common sense. Arguably, a cultural approach to the frontier experience gives us the tools we need to transcend the one-dimensional myth and uncover underlying tensions and complexities in American history.

Clearly, a concern with the West as an image of American culture and a crucible of cultural identity pervades traditional historiography. After poking the requisite holes in Turner's thesis, Young (1970) suggested that the dialectic between nature and civilization has shaped

Americans' definition of culture since the early seventeenth century, when Puritans made their first forays into virgin lands. "Defining the West as a state of nature and a theater for progress, Americans projected upon the area a central tension in European primitivism, the tension between the static concept of a natural paradise and the restless ideal of progress" (p. 140).

As we have seen, these polarities found reconciliation in the myth of the garden and its celebrated denizens, yeoman farmers, tethered to the Old World by language and custom, yet susceptible to change as warranted by the vicissitudes of frontier life. Building on Turner's insight even as they have castigated its shortcomings, generations of scholars have probed the dialectic to discover character traits unique to Americans, from anti-intellectualism and pragmatism to the extraordinary creativity summoned by the challenges of the natural environment. A primary theme that emerges from these studies is that transactions between men, rather than encounters with nature, have been the focus of analysis. "Further, it is in such social processes as migration and the forming of new communities that mid-twentieth century historians find a common identity between their culture and that of their pioneer ancestors" (p. 148).

For Young, the myth of the garden, framed either as myth or ideology, falls short of explaining the formulation and administration of public land policies. Her pattern of explanation rests on the utopianism that lay at the heart of most nineteenth-century values concerning Western lands. Inspired by a vision of yeoman farmers tilling their land beyond the influence of eastern capital, policy-makers devised programs such as the Homestead Act of 1862 as mechanisms to ensure universal access to resources. Yet from its beginnings, the land system rarely lived up to the Jeffersonian ideal. No sooner did the settler lay claim to his land than some instrument of industrial society mobilized its assets "in unequal combat for the rich resources of the western domain" (p. 158). The dialectic between paradise and progress thus played out in the self-destructiveness of the liberal system. With the fruits of liberty available to independent farmers and monopolies alike, the system sacrificed equality to progress, paradise to institutional power. In short, the utopianism that fueled nineteenth-century land policies bore the seeds of its own destruction, thus providing yet another source of cultural tension for subsequent generations.

If the frontier has indeed been central to American identity, then we would do well to synthesize prevailing attitudes toward, and definitions of, the wilderness. Nash (1967) traced its etymology to early Teutonic and Norse languages that conveyed an idea of being lost and confused. "The image," wrote Nash, "is that of a man in an alien environment where the civilization that normally orders and controls his life is absent" (p. 2). Wilderness, then, is more than a place; it is a state of mind fixed somewhere along a continuum between the wild and the tame, between the savage and the pastoral—or, as Nash put it, between the primeval and the paved. Demons and spirits that haunted the Judeo Christian imagination accompanied settlers to the New World and compelled them to transform the wilderness into a new Eden. In a morality play that spanned generations, pioneers sustained by a commitment to their nation and their God set about conquering their surroundings much as an army would vanquish its enemy.

Subjugation of the wilderness was a primary source of pioneer pride—until, that is, it became apparent that there were limits to God's bounty and that there might be something about untamed lands worth saving. By the eighteenth century, the reconciliation between the allure of the wild and man's need to tame it was represented by the "middle state," a pastoral ideal espoused by Jefferson and his French contemporary, Crèvecoeur, that was poised between the extremes of civilization and savagery. "It is a moral position perfectly represented by the image of a rural order, neither wild nor urban, as the setting of man's best hope" (Marx 1967: 101). Instilled with a more sanguine perspective of wild places, scientists, writers, and artists far removed from the frontier idealized the wilderness as a place not be feared and reviled, but rather to be sought as a sanctuary from civilization. Romantics and Transcendentalists who followed in their footsteps fostered an appreciation for the spiritual truths to be found in the wilds through intuition. Outdoor enthusiasts in our own time seem to have heeded Thoreau's suggestion that wildness and refinement are not fatal extremes; rather, they blend to become equally beneficent influences on the human soul. Nash (1967) asserted that modern disputes over the proper uses of wilderness revolve less around policy than personal attitudes and beliefs. Simply put, the issue between wilderness and civilization generally takes the form of ambivalence in a single mind than a conflict between people.

Turner's contention that westward expansion dominated American development would never have attained universal acceptance unless it had reflected prevailing ideas and attitudes. In his seminal book about the influence of the West on the American consciousness, Smith (1950) identified two visions of American Empire that have occupied the imaginations of statesmen and visionaries: an empire based on command of the sea, and an agrarian republic stretching across the continent. Ever since America's earliest explorers set out in search of a passage to India, the second vision has prevailed. Commonly understood under the rubric of manifest destiny, this view of what America might become was given whole new meaning with Jefferson's bargain-basement deal to purchase Louisiana from Napoleon in 1803. Lewis and Clark's exploration of this vast territory was only the beginning of a quest to explore America's interior and extend the benefits of civilization past the Alleghenies.

Beyond the practical considerations of pushing back the frontier, the importance of the Lewis and Clark expedition lay in the realm of imagination. It foreshadowed a century-long drama whose actors included mountain men and trappers, trail blazers and gunslingers, cowboys and Indian fighters—in short, a pantheon of cultural icons whose legendary exploits blurred the distinction between fact and fiction. In terms of the nation's creation story, nineteenth-century pioneers enacted a myth that embodied the future and "gave tangible substance to what had been merely an idea, and established the image of a highway across the continent so firmly in the minds of Americans that repeated failures could not shake it" (p. 17). Jefferson's vision of an agrarian republic peopled by yeomen farmers remained central to the myth of America as garden of the world long after the last trail had been blazed and the last Indians had been reduced to wards of the state. "From the time of Daniel Boone," wrote Smith, "the popular imagination had constantly formed the facts of the westward movement in accordance with the requirements of myth" (p. 102).

Sanford (1961), another of the myth-critics who have done so much to expose the subconscious origins of human endeavors, has given us what might be the most protean perspective of the Edenic myth. His wide-ranging survey takes us from Old Testament stories and millennial movements that captivated the medieval imagination to the city on a hill image that emboldened Winthrop's parishioners in colonial New England to recreate God's kingdom in America. Even Columbus, imbued with a missionary zeal that transcends time and culture, "wished to open the world to the Gospel in fulfillment of Biblical prophecy of the Second Coming" (p. 39). Young (1970) suggested that the quest for paradise helps to explain the eschatological myths of ancient Mesopotamia, India, Greece, early Christian communities, and pre-Columbian America. For Sanford (1961), the common thread that weaves these spiritually charged chapters of history into a coherent pattern is the search for a lost Eden; that is, a conviction that the paradise rejected so tragically by Adam and Eve can be reactualized at the end of time. Yet the Edenic paradigm is not simply a static reflection of farmers tilling their fields in some idealized vision of agrarian bliss, nor an image of the wilderness, sinister and foreboding. Rather, it is an imaginative complex that places agrarianism and wilderness in a dynamic relationship with other values.

Consciously or not, Americans have always sought the middle path between civilization and savagery. Whether pushing the frontier to the edge of the Alleghenies or setting out on the Oregon Trail, New World settlers have tended to idealize nature and rely on it as a standard for criticizing civilization. Thus, the search for paradise lost "has been the most powerful and comprehensive organizing force in American culture" (p. vi). This spiritual mission quickly became subordinate to that of an earthly paradise and manifested itself on many levels: on the psychic plane as an infantile regression to the womb; on the moral plane as a wish to recapture lost innocence; on the political plane as an assertion of individual freedom; on the religious and aesthetic plane as a wish to transcend temporal existence; on the sexual plane as a desire to develop relationships beyond the gaze of an over rationalized civilization; and on the plane of personal fulfillment as a rebellion against routines and a yearning for new experiences. Ultimately, the quest for paradise lies at the heart of myth, the purpose of which is to help make life meaningful, coherent, and ordered, no matter how miserable the present. Moreover, myth contributes to historical change insofar as people want to behave in conformity with the dramatic world portrayed in myth. "History moves, if it moves at all, in the mass, and mass psychology is peculiarly dependent on myth" (p. 25).

Writing at the height of the Cold War, Sanford concluded his *tour de force* with a suggestion that crises both at home and abroad were fostering not a deepening and maturing of the popular mind, but rather a resurgence of anti-intellectualism (a strain that has never been far beneath the surface of American culture) and an interest in the Western genre of entertainment, all in "a search for security in the earlier symbols and traditions of nationality" (p. 261). The main theme in these trends was a regression to nature and a reliance on cultural heroes endowed with an intuitive sense of right and wrong and a repertoire of skills nurtured on the far side of civilization. Character types represented by the Lone Ranger, Roy Rogers, Hopalong Cassidy, and Davy Crockett, to name the most prominent, have served as guardians of the public conscience—all forged in the crucible of the frontier, and all occupying privileged places in the national mythology. As we will see, similar forces are at work in our own, postmodern world, where popular culture and sports provide outlets for angst-ridden Americans trapped in the money nexus and yearning to connect themselves to a culturally defined vision of paradise.

At the dawning of the twenty-first century, it is tempting to dismiss myths as vestiges of our primitive past—stories that served a purpose for people who had no other way to explain natural phenomena, but that have little relevance in a world awash in technological marvels. For Robertson (1980), myths might indeed be irrational insofar as they appeal to faith rather than reason, but that does not imply that they have lost all meaning. Handed down through generations in ways that escape conscious thought and bedevil the historian's craft, myths provide workable ways to resolve social contradictions, and they provide a means of understanding experience that lies beyond the Western logic embodied in science and reason (Gordon 1981). Contrasts and conflicts that arise among people and ideals "are somehow reconciled, smoothed over, or at least made manageable and tolerable" (Robertson 1980: xv) by myths. The stories that we tell about people and events that have occupied American spaces live on in rituals, sacred places, social groups, and even games and sports. They often revolve around heroes and heroines who, unlike the one-dimensional celebrities served up by modern pop culture, have something important to tell us about our own lives.

What's more, mythological images reveal themselves in odd moments. Former Secretary of State Henry Kissinger was once asked by an Italian interviewer, Oriana Fallaci, why he enjoyed movie-star status. His reply? Americans, droned the peripatetic envoy in his baritone and heavily accented voice, liked the fact that he acted alone.

> "Americans like the cowboy who leads the wagon train by riding ahead alone on his horse, the cowboy who rides all alone into the town...with his horse and nothing else. Maybe even without a pistol...this cowboy doesn't have to be courageous. All he needs is to be alone, to show others that he rides into the town and does everything by himself..." (p. 6).

For Robertson, America has always stood at the cutting edge of history, proclaiming its mantra of progress, power and prosperity to anyone who cared to listen, and often shoving it down their throats. Unable and certainly unwilling to outrun their myths, Americans continue to rely on a familiar repertoire of stories and slogans to maintain social cohesion, particularly in a world that seems about to fall apart at the seams due to forces beyond our control. In Thanksgiving rituals, we relive the Pilgrims' first dark years in the New World and celebrate the bounty that is still within our reach; from George Washington's savage slashing of the iconic cherry tree, we remind ourselves that honesty is always the best policy and that, metaphorically, a child challenging his parent is not unlike a colony standing up to its overlords. Freudians might even suggest that a hatchet serves as a perfectly good substitute for a phallus. The point is that myths simultaneously describe the past and provide imperatives for present and future action. Archetypes that have insinuated themselves into the national mythology include the Puritans, determined to replicate God's kingdom in the wilderness; the frontiersmen, a broad category of pathfinders that includes settlers, backwoodsmen, sodbusters, and cowboys; and pioneers, whose wagon trains snaked across the prairies to herald the coming of civilization. All three prototypes are celebrated in canonical texts, and all three contribute to a narrative of fierce individualism, reconciliation between the frontier and its settlement, and even paganism and Christianity.[13]

Puritans, backwoodsmen, and pioneers contributed to the frontier narrative in unique ways, but their common denominator was an acceptance and even celebration of violence. In his cultural history of America's westward trek, Slotkin (1992) traced the development of mythic and ideological formulations that constitute the myth of the frontier. He posited culture-making as a process that involves three interlocking and closely related concepts: ideology—a system of beliefs, concepts, and values that define a society's way of interpreting its place in the cosmos; myth—stories drawn from the wellsprings of history that dramatize a society's moral consciousness; and genres—expressive forms that articulate ideological concepts directly and explicitly. Over time and through repetition, mythic stories become conventionalized and abstracted. Landmarks in America's grand narrative such as the Alamo and Custer's Last Stand are thus reduced to complex symbols. Though subject to revision according to historical contingencies, they practically ooze symbolic meaning, and they provide us with a prism through

---

[13] In his insightful review of Robertson's book, Gordon stressed the author's insistence that historical methods are inadequate to illuminate meanings behind human actions. See Gordon 1981: 446-50.

which to interpret current phenomena. The language we use to express their meaning is metaphorical and suggestive rather than logical and analytical and reflects our culture's most persistent concerns. And in ways that circumvent official history, the language of metaphor helps us to frame our memories. Drawing on a treasure trove of frontier tales, Americans have learned to look beyond family, ethnicity, and workplace to find symbols of a national culture and shared identity.

Due to his focus on the development of a national myth and ideology, Slotkin approached the dialectic between producers of culture and their audiences from the producer's side, thus minimizing the ways that audiences receive cultural messages. Nevertheless, his approach is effective insofar as it reveals the dynamics of myth-production by mass media that claim to serve as spokesman for America's national culture in its totality. "The Myth of the Frontier," wrote Slotkin, "is our oldest and most characteristic myth, expressed in a body of literature, folklore, ritual, historiography, and polemics produced over a period of three centuries" (p. 10). According to this myth, the conquest of the frontier and displacement of Indians through extraordinary acts of violence enabled pioneers over generations to achieve self-identity, a democratic polity, and an expanding economy. What is unique in American history is not so much the pervasiveness of violence as the symbolism that it carries in the popular imagination and the political uses to which it is employed. Spiritually and psychologically, America's heroes represent the savagery lurking beneath our civilized veneers as well as the regeneration that is possible through struggle against dark forces.

In her study of the frontier's role in shaping national identity, Clementi (1981) suggested that the United States, Brazil and Argentina produced character types of mythological proportions. America, of course, produced the pioneer, "the incarnation of all the highest virtues: work, the spirit of initiative, and fidelity to the values fixed by the religious community" (p. 38). Together with the *bandeirante* of Brazil and the *gauchos* of Argentina, America's hunters, lumberjacks, laborers, Indian fighters, herdsmen, and others too numerous to mention spawned archetypes that continue to exert a powerful pull on the consciousness of their respective nations. Granted, frontier stories cannot claim unlimited validity. The formation of cities and the all-too-common failures of those who fell short of the American Dream lie outside the explanatory power of frontier mythologies. Nevertheless, tales handed down through the generations about our ancestors' conquest of the wild have yet to lose their resonance "as the successful, harmonious, conciliating and inspiring key to great undertakings" (p. 39).

In a brief, yet provocative, overview of pop culture heroes, Leverenz (1991) takes us from the patriarchal simplicity of Natty Bumppo and his ilk to Robert Bly's *Iron John: A Book about Men* (1990), a nationwide bestseller that empowered middle-class men to reclaim their masculinity in a culture that devalues fathering and eschews male friendship. Woven in the fabric of American mythology are familiar characters such as Daniel Boone and Davy Crockett who have embodied shifting definitions of manliness. Under the influence of the marketplace, Americans in the twentieth century have looked to avenging heroes, often half animal and half human, who descend into the evil underclass to rescue a helpless bourgeois civilization. "From Tarzan to Batman," wrote Leverenz,

> "the myth expresses the paradox of a collectively empowered middle class in which men feel personally powerless or unmanly except as they compete in the workplace. Simultaneously, the mass-market myth appeals to a fantasy of

working-class remasculinization through often sadistic violence, diffusely directed against black men, gay men, and women" (p. 759).

In essence, Leverenz posited a myth of late twentieth-century American manhood descended from Crèvecoeur's new man, Tocqueville's backwoodsman, Jackson's Everyman, and even Turner's frontiersman: to be both civilized and savage, wild and tame—in short, to occupy a place where refinement exists in harmony with wilderness. For Leverenz, the changing myth of male masculinity has evolved mainly in relation to the gaze of male peers and male authority and continues to reflect hostility toward women and ambiguity toward sexual identity. Moreover, as long as capitalism structures male identity through role-playing and competition in the workplace, the craving for Real Man myths will continue to exert a powerful pull on people who feel ever more estranged from lived experience. Perhaps future generations will look back on our own with a mixture of awe for the elegance and resilience of our mythologies and revulsion toward the violence that teases us away from the sources of our postmodern angst.

From Woodlands to Prairie: The Rise of the Cowboy

Between Tocqueville's American sojourn and the outbreak of the Civil War, life beyond the pale of civilization was giving birth to a variation on the frontier character type that has stirred the popular imagination ever since. Just as the eastern woodlands fostered real-life characters like Daniel Boone and fictional creations along the lines of Natty Bumppo and Huckleberry Finn, so did the Great Plains provide a setting for the cowboy. We will probably never know just when the term "cowboy" muscled its way into the common vernacular. It might have been on the eve of Lincoln's election to the Presidency in 1860, when the first of the so-called dime novels was published to capitalize on fascination with the Wild West. It was certainly in vogue five years later. By then, some five million of these cheap thrillers had been snatched up by readers eager to participate, however vicariously, in the American odyssey (Robertson 1980).

What is certain is that, by the time Daniel Boone's progeny emerged from the eastern woodlands to confront the great prairies, a new type of frontiersman was in the making. From his broad-brimmed hat to his high-heeled boots, more affectionate toward horses than women and wary of settled life, this new actor on the American stage represented a blend of trail blazer and Southern gentleman, with a sprinkling of the famed Mexican *vaquero* thrown in for good measure. He was a direct descendant of Daniel Boone, who actually settled on the far side of the Mississippi in his golden years, and Kit Carson, the mountain man and pathfinder who, at some point in his storied career, swung himself onto the backside of a horse to become the prototype of the hardscrabble herdsman. The trans-Mississippi West was a new wilderness, and the cowboy, like the frontiersman in the forests, was a harbinger of civilization who learned how to survive in his new environment and led the way for anyone with the temerity to follow. Ironically and perhaps tragically, the cowboy's role in opening the West to civilized ways heralded the end of his way of life and brought America's westward trek to its *dénouement*.

Frantz and Choate (1955) suggested that the cowboy existed on three levels: the historical level, about which most Americans remain woefully ignorant; the fictional level, in which the cowboy has played a prominent role since the days of the dime novel; and the level of folklore, where the cowboy stands as an idealized creation of the American folk mind. To appreciate the cowboy's resilience in American culture, we need to understand something about the socioeconomic factors after the Civil War that determined his place in history. Only then will we be able to explore authentic cowboy ways, largely by consulting memoirs left to us by cowboys with a flair for narrative. With this in the way of background, we will be poised to consider the myriad ways that cowboys were celebrated in fiction, theatrical presentations, and exhibition entertainment, all against the backdrop of a nation struggling to maintain its values in a period of rapid-fire change.

Distilled less from historical experience than the doubts and fears of Americans between 1880 and 1920, images nurtured in the West of the imagination outlived and transcended the reasons for their manufacture (Murdoch 2001). Unlike Arthurian tales or Greek myths gestated over time in the depths of the unconscious, cowboy stories sprang up after the Civil War and were already fading into memory by the late 1880s, and the legends they left behind were propagated by a small group of cultural entrepreneurs with specific agendas. Drawing on the resources of an increasingly market-driven society, cowboy myths not only left a lasting impression on the national psyche; they also found cultural outlets far removed, in time and place, from their native soil.

Chapter Three — The Cowboy in History, Literature, and Showbiz

"Ma," says she, "do cowboys eat grass?"

"No, dear," says the old lady, "they're part human."

Charles M. Russell
Trails Plowed Under (1927)

The Animate Trinity

In the opening decades of the nineteenth century, the Great Plains that would one day support the range cattle industry still belonged to Indians. Comanches and Apaches dominated lands to the Southwest, while bands of Sioux and Cheyenne held sway in the north. The region's designation as the Great American Desert dates back to Coronado's travels in 1541, when the famed explorer reported to his king that nothing but an inhospitable wasteland stretched east of the Rockies. Subsequent explorers over the next three and a half centuries confirmed Coronado's assessment and left the impression of a mysterious landscape where anything was possible (Frantz and Choate 1955; Slatta 1997).

Meanwhile, far to the south, the Nueces Valley of southern Texas was teeming with an estimated four million Longhorn cattle that were the direct descendants of herds brought to the New World by Spanish conquistadores in the early sixteenth century. When Texas was wrested from Mexican control and the Rio Grande accepted as the international boundary, Mexicans retreated south of the border, and American cattlemen simply appropriated cattle roaming between the Rio Grande and Nueces Rivers as public property. Wild, tall, sway-backed and big-eared, and outfitted with a fearsome set of horns, the legs of a race horse, and hides impervious to mesquite thorns, Longhorns were built to withstand just about anything

that their harsh environment could dish out.

Longhorn cattle shared their terrain with another Spanish import: Mustangs. Their ancestry goes back to colonial Virginia and the Carolinas, where breeders mixed English stallions with native mares to produce short, muscular animals that were quick but lacking in endurance over the long haul. These horses were ideal for racing, the sport of gentlemen in the seventeenth and eighteenth centuries. Mares, known in some circles as Chickasaw Indian ponies, were descendants of Spanish stock that were brought to the New World in the holds of

Columbus' ships when they weighed anchor in Cadiz.[1] In all likelihood, their ancestors were Barbs, fast horses from the deserts of North Africa that arrived on Iberian shores during the Muslim invasion of 711. Because of English and Indian attacks on Spanish settlements in Florida, some horses escaped and lived in the wild, where they were available for anyone who could catch and break them (Slatta 1995). Escaped horses from Spanish outposts in the West not only transformed native American cultures; they also constituted the foundation for wild horse herds that provided many a cowboy with a reliable mount and continue to symbolize Western freedom. Endowed with legendary intelligence, strength, agility, stamina, and cow sense, these scrappy little horses were a perfect match for the ornery Longhorns that they would one day prod to Kansas and points north (Frantz and Choate 1955).

Even though horses were imports from the Old World to the New, they captured the spirit of the West, and they continue to symbolize the wildness that lurks beneath the veneer of civilization. One looks in vain for a more potent symbol of the frontier than the legend of the White Mustang. Alternately known as the White Steed of the Prairies, the Pacing WhiteStallion, the Phantom White Horse, and the Ghost Horse of the Plains, this storied creature was rumored to be feral (formerly domesticated) and, as such, even more intractable than horses that have known nothing but freedom. Allegedly roaming from the mesas of Mexico to the Dakota badlands, the White Mustang radiated the untamed spirit of the 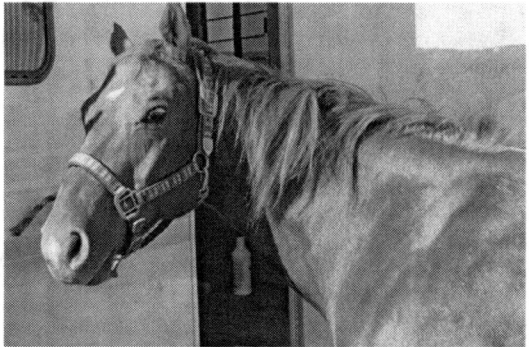 West, and tales of his eventual capture and self-induced starvation to avoid enslavement came to symbolize the conquest of the frontier. The White Mustang's death was a perfect expression of frontier duality: the impulse among frontiersmen to conquer and subdue the very wildness that they treasured. "The White Steed," wrote Lawrence (1985: 64), "as an object of beauty, a thing apart, unsuited to a pragmatic world, must inevitably be sacrificed, and thereby attains universal significance." The White Steed's cousins that found themselves on the south end of north-bound cattle after the Civil War were officially designated as Quarter Horses in 1940, long after their work in building the range cattle industry was done (Slatta 1995).

Even though Mustangs and their equine kin have long since been pressed into the service of civilization, they retain a spark of wildness that can never be entirely tamed. Like yin and yang, the wild and the tame are woven into the relationship between humans and horses. We are at once attracted and repelled by their explosive energy, and on some level we crave it as an antidote to the numbing predictability that came with the closing of the frontier and the onset of modernity. Based on hair-raising experiences both in and out of the arena, I can state with some authority that modern-day cowboys ignore this ancient duality at their peril.

Rounding out the trinity was, of course, the cowboy. Like the *gauchos* of Argentina and the *llaneros* of Columbia, the western American cowboy was strongly shaped by his Hispanic legacy. Differences between cowboy types notwithstanding, all three remain important

---

[1] Conflicts with Mexico in the nineteenth century, combined with Anglo racism, fostered a tendency to minimize Spanish contributions to America's equine tradition. See Slatta 1995: 24.

throughout the Americas "as symbols of rugged individualism, unbending principle, and frontier spirit and courage" (Slatta 1997: 95). Moreover, they exhibit similarities that help to explain the influence that they continue to exert on their respective national identities. Perhaps the most obvious attribute shared by these kissing cousins is their insistence on staying in the saddle. From the Argentine pampas to the plains of West Texas, any herdsman worth his salt considered footwork beneath his dignity. Of course, as is so often the case with cowboy ways, there are practical reasons behind entrenched customs. For one thing, cattle are known to stampede at the bizarre sight of a pedestrian.[2] Yet the cowboy's reluctance to dismount also has a direct bearing, however subconscious, on the preservation of culture. As a working cowboy in Oklahoma, New Mexico, and Texas, and in the course of my competitive ventures in Central Virginia, I have both participated in and marveled at a range of activities that are possible, and even comfortable, on the backside of a horse.[3] And I have known cowboys whose proficiency in the saddle stands in complete contrast to their clumsiness on foot. The bowlegged cowpuncher is more than a myth; he is very much alive and well, bent to the contours of his trade and in dire need of chiropractic treatment.

Like the Quarter Horse, the American cowboy's antecedents go back to colonial days, when so-called cattle hunters gathered cattle in the public lands of Virginia and the Carolinas and herded them into cowpens stationed throughout the Piedmont and Atlantic Coast (Frantz and Choate 1955). Hispanic influence came by way of the Mexican *vaquero*,[4] a figure dismissed as untrustworthy and unnecessarily hard on stock by Alamo-obsessed Texans (Fishwick 1952). When

---

[2] In his memoir of plying the cattle trails in the 1870s and 1880s, Teddy Blue Abbott was highly critical of cowboys who didn't have sense enough to remain in the saddle. "You couldn't get off your horse unless you rode over the hill, because if [the cattle] saw a man afoot that would settle it. You might be watering below a cut bank, and some fool would ride up there and show his head over the bank—and away they'd go." See Abbott 1939: 216.

[3] Over the years, I've hobnobbed with friends, picnicked, sunbathed, composed ethnographic notes, and even withdrawn funds from an ATM without ever climbing off my horse.

[4] Owen Wister, author of *The Virginian* (2002), was one of the most prominent chroniclers of the American West to note that Mexicans were the original cowboys. Indeed, "cowboy" is a translation from the Spanish *vaquero*. Invoking the racism that has infused the cowboy myth since its inception, Wister claimed that American cowboys were an improvement over the despised aliens from south of the border. See Munden 1958: 114. See also Boatwright 1951: 160-63. According to Adams, the massacre at the Alamo stirred up such intense hatred for Mexicans that cowboys dropped many of the customs that came by way of the *vaquero*, including methods of roping cattle and saddle design. See Adams 1971: 22.

Eastern cowmen moved west, they took their lore and terminology with them, but modifications necessitated by culture and geography were not long in coming. The eastern cowhunt became the western roundup, and cowpens were henceforth known as corrals, a term they borrowed from their Mexican neighbors (Frantz and Choate 1955). American cowboy culture's debt to Mexico is reflected in equipment and language that remain critical to ranch work as well as equestrian competition. Tack includes a *bozal*, or bosal, the nose band of a hackamore; *chaparreras*, or chaps (pronounced "shaps"), leather leggings that provide protection from skin-piercing vegetation and, as the author can attest, traction in the saddle; and *la reata*, or lariat, an indispensable tool for snaring cattle in need of branding and doctoring (Slatta 1997).

Together, Longhorns, Mustangs, and cowboys, set in an epic environment and informed by stock lore of colonial origins, constituted the key players in a unique industry. They coalesced when cattlemen arrived in Texas determined to supply western beef to burgeoning markets back East. Like Coronado and subsequent travelers across the vastness of America's heartland, eastern cattlemen and farmers had always looked askance at the barren plains stretching from western Missouri to the Rockies. Accustomed to steady rainfall and cultivated pasturage, they had little use for the buffalo grass and mesquite that seemed to render the entire region unfit for agriculture (Boorstin 1974). All that changed toward the end of the Civil War. Legend has it that an ox train traveling through Wyoming was caught in a blizzard and had to be abandoned. When the driver returned the following spring to see what had happened to his livestock, he expected to find nothing but skeletons. Instead, his oxen were very much alive—fat, happy, and clearly well-nourished by native vegetation.[5]

The story, like so many that come to us from Western lore, is probably apocryphal. Yet it serves to illustrate a dawning realization that the arid West, long shunned by travelers heading for more promising lands beyond the Rockies, was home to fairy-tale grasses that required little rain and enabled cattle to survive even the harshest of Western winters. Dazzled by the prospect of buying a mangy Longhorn steer for three or four dollars in Texas and selling it in Kansas City or St. Louis for thirty or forty dollars, cattlemen set about devising a way to round up cattle and get them to market (Frantz and Choate 1955).

A few intrepid souls attempted to drive cattle to the West Coast along the California Trail, but an arid climate, an unforgiving terrain, and the threat of Indian raids rendered the route unprofitable. Cattle drives through the Indian Territory to Missouri often ended in disaster when thieves made off with livestock and farmers, wary of Texas fever and determined to protect their crops from being trampled, wreaked havoc in any way they could. It was left to an enterprising young Illinoisan by the name of Joseph G. McCoy to point the way to riches. Already in the cattle business and anxious to get his hands on Texas Longhorns, McCoy cut a deal with the Hannibal & St. Joseph Railroad, which ran from Kansas City to Chicago, to supply beef to Chicago (Boorstin 1974). His next task was to select the most convenient little town along the Kansas Pacific where he could build the facilities needed to handle large numbers of cattle. He chose a nondescript railroad depot at Abilene, Kansas, four hundred miles north of the Red River and a thousand miles from the Nueces Valley, as the destination for northbound cattle drives.

---

[5] In his memoir of driving the Circle Dot herd from south Texas to Montana in 1882, Andy Adams claimed that northern climates were beneficial for horses as well. "It does seem incredible," wrote Adams, "but it is a fact nevertheless, that a horse, having reached the years of maturity in a southern climate, will grow half a hand taller and carry two hundred pounds more flesh, when he has undergone the rigors of several northern winters." See Adams 1903: 322.

INVENTING TRADITION

Within sixty days of purchasing the entire town site and 480 additional acres for the grand sum of $2,400, Abilene was transformed into a well-equipped cattle capital, complete with a shipping yard, barns, offices, and state-of-the-art scales. McCoy then sent agents deep into the Indian Territory to enlist drovers to bring their herds to the burgeoning cowtown.

And come they did. During the first season in 1867, some twenty-five thousand cattle passed through Abilene. On September 5 of that year, twenty carloads of cattle were shipped off to Chicago. Seemingly overnight, Abilene became the commercial capital of Texas. The era of the great cattle drives had begun (1974; Frantz and Choate 1955).

Even the most visionary cattlemen must have been daunted by the hazards of driving livestock across a rugged landscape populated by predators and hostile Indians with a taste for beef. It was a big problem that called for creative solutions. And it was a challenge tailor-made for young men whose skill in handling livestock was matched by a zest for adventure. Many likely candidates were battle-hardened veterans of the Civil War who were eager to begin life anew in the West. Others included ex-slaves, army scouts, Mexicans, drifters who felt constrained in increasingly populated regions east of the Mississippi—in short, just about anyone with the grit to trade his former life for endless days in the saddle and tense nights under the stars, prepared to mount up at a moment's notice in the event of an Indian raid or a stampede. Most outfits consisted of a foreman and from three to a dozen cowboys, a cook, and a *remuda* man to tend the extra horses that were needed on their epic journeys (Savage 1976).

Frantz and Choate (1955) estimated that no more than 40,000 men drove cattle from Texas to the northern railheads and ranges after the Civil War. In their seminal work on Negro cowboys, Durham and Jones (1965) claimed that 5,000 of those men were black, "slaves on horseback," and they did "no more and no less than cowboys of other races and nationalities" (p. 3). Porter (1971) estimated the cowboy population during the heroic age of the cattle industry between 1866 and 1895 to be in the vicinity of 35,000. By perusing extant lists of trail-herd outfits that identified their members by race, he calculated that slightly more than sixty-three percent were white, twenty-five percent were Negroes, and somewhat less than twelve percent were Mexicans (p. 495). What's more, blacks rarely shrank from the toughest jobs their outfits had to offer. "These Negro cowboys," wrote Porter, "whether on ranch or trail, were generally regarded as good workers, who got along well with others and who took pride in their work. A white Texan, a former cowboy and rancher, went so far as to write that 'there was no better cowman on earth than the Negro'" (p. 497). Although they occasionally ran into prejudice, there is no question that black cowboys made a significant contribution to the range cattle industry and the mythology that it spawned. Their competence was unquestioned, their commitment to their outfits was exemplary, and their exploits, from breaking broncos to bringing in their herds, were extraordinary.

Whatever the cowboys' provenance, the trails they followed from Texas to Abilene and similar cowtowns that were sprouting across the prairie—from the Chisholm Trail and, slightly further west, the Western Trail that cut straight through the Indian Territory and ended in Kansas to the Goodnight-Loving Trail that skirted west through the highlands of New Mexico and Colorado before winding its way to Cheyenne— became fodder for legend. And the cattle they coaxed and prodded along the way, wilder than deer and as hardy as the landscape that sustained them, entered the national consciousness as symbols of the Western experience. "The Texas Longhorn," wrote Boorstin (1974: 7), "put the cowboy on horseback, kept him in the saddle, and fixed the rhythm of his life. The wildness of the Wild West, then, was in large part the wildness of the Texas Longhorn."

Because the cattle business required few people to maintain successful operations, cow country was thinly peopled, and the society that it bred was overwhelmingly masculine, primitive, and rough. With few exceptions, cowboys were young men bound by a code of ethics that put a premium on hard work and loyalty to their employers. Tales of drunken revelries and saloon fights notwithstanding, the average cowboy was a sane and sober individual who lived a lonely but not unhappy life. He undoubtedly cursed bad weather and the misfortunes that came with the territory, but when the sun shone and the prairie sparkled with wild flowers, he must have counted himself very fortunate indeed. According to Edward Everett Dale, an historian from Oklahoma and an accomplished cowpuncher in his own right, "He liked his work, was proud of his job, and like every man on horseback, whether he be called knight, *chevalier*, *Ritter*, *caballero*, or cowhand felt himself distinctly superior to the man who walked" (1937: 6).

Thus did the cowboy and his mount contribute to one of humanity's most enduring narratives. Literally and symbolically, the man on horseback has always radiated the kind of power that transcends earthly existence. Moreover, the ancient union of man and horse represents a synthesis of civilized and bestial qualities. "Horses extend their human riders into the world without enclosing them, something machines seldom do," concluded Lawrence (1985: 195) in her study of human-horse relationships. "Through this process people become a part of the equine animal's forward thrust, reconfirming the human status as part of nature." As Schwartz (1988) asserted in his analysis of equestrian imagery in European and American political thought, the horse and rider represent the fluid boundaries between nature and culture, animals and humans, men and women, and even society and the state.

Any experienced cowhand knows how Texas Longhorns were trailed to northern pastures and railheads, but how are we supposed to trail the cowboys? Unlike elites, commoners leave little evidence of their passing. The cattle frontier lay far beyond urban centers, where newspapers and other means of record keeping have always devoted disproportionate attention to city matters. Given their nomadic ways, herdsmen have generally been wary of officialdom and kept their distance. This was particularly true in Latin America, where *gauchos* and *llaneros* were valued for their equestrian skills and eagerly sought by military recruiters (Slatta 1997). Because they eschewed mutual aid societies and unions, cowboys left no lists of dues-paying members or minutes of organizational meetings. Other documents that become fodder for historians such as wills, inventories, bank accounts, safety deposit boxes, and probate records are of little use when it comes to reconstructing the life of the cowboy. In most cases, the cowboy's final will and testament was reflected in the closing stanzas of an old song that was no doubt sung over many a campfire, "When the Work's All Done This Fall":

> Fred you take my saddle;
> George, you take my bed,
> Bill you take my pistol
> after I am dead.
>
> Then please think of me kindly
> when you look upon them all,
> For I'll not see my mother
> when the work's all done this fall.

INVENTING TRADITION

> Poor Charlie was buried at sunrise,
> no tombstone at his head,
> Nothing but a little board,
> and this is what it said:
>
> "Charlie died at daybreak,
> he died from a fall,
> And he'll not see his mother
> when the work's all done this fall.[6]

Fortunately, literacy was not altogether uncommon on the trail.[7] Cowboys able and willing to record their experiences have left us a treasure trove of first-hand descriptions of what it was like to participate in the great northern cattle drives. Although much has been written by and about cowboys, I have chosen three celebrated memoirs to establish a baseline for authenticity. Granted, authenticity is treacherous ground, particularly in a study of socially constructed identity and cultural expression rooted in historic discourse. Nevertheless, the historical and emotional mimicry built into cowboy sports leaves us no choice but to return to the source. We need to identify the wellsprings of the cowboy's allure so that we can make sense of the mythology it spawned and the sports that commemorate cowboy ways. Only then can we unravel cowboy sports as avenues of identity formation and cultural expression and situate them in their social and historical contexts.

Here, then, are excerpts from the recollections of three honest-to-goodness cowboys, provided as background for later chapters where I explore the interstices between frontier history, the traditions (invented and otherwise) that it fostered, and the mimesis behind cowboy sports. Near as I can tell, this is about as real as it gets.

Honest-to-Goodness Cowboys

Twenty years after his cowboy adventure, Andy Adams wrote *The Log of a Cowboy: A Narrative of the Old Trail Days* (1903). Adams was a boy in Georgia when Sherman's army marched through his county, slashing and burning its way to the sea. Anxious to begin life anew in the West, his father, a veteran of the Confederate army, relocated the family to Texas. When he was old enough, Adams hired on with an outfit that set out on April 1, 1882, with some 3,100 Longhorn cattle from Brownsville, Texas, bound for the Blackfoot Agency in Montana. Because

---

[6] For the full text of this and other cowboy songs written for the harmonica, see the *Giant Harmonica Fakebook*, a downloadable e-book, available online from Harmonica Country at http://www.harmonicacountry.com/index.html.

[7] Frontier ambivalence toward tradition was reflected in the fact that many cowboys were avid readers and often went out of their way to find something to feast their eyes on. In a region where literature was hard to come by, cowboys made do with whatever they could find, including labels on cans and scraps of old newspapers. See Billington 1966: 77. For an amusing account of cowboy ingenuity in the literary desert of the Old West, see Walker 1960: 307-18.

of their brands featuring a dot in the middle of a circle, Adams referred to his bovine charges as the Circle Dot herd. Under the guidance of his foreman, Jim Flood, Adams took up his position and prepared for the adventure of a lifetime. Two point men rode in the lead to direct the herd, and outriders known as *swing men* kept the cattle in check. "With six men on each side," wrote the cowboy-turned-chronicler, "and the herd strung out for three quarters of a mile, it could only be compared to some mythical serpent or Chinese dragon, as it moved forward on its sinuous, snail-like course" (p. 28).

Adams clearly respected his foreman. Early on, he found that "there was plenty of horse-sense in Flood's advice" (p. 29). Flood's first admonition to rookies was never to let the herd know it was under restraint. Turning to the equine member of the animate trinity, Flood asserted that "a man afoot is useless" to underscore the importance of caring for horses. "Accidents will happen to horses," said Flood, "but don't let it be your fault; keep your saddle blankets dry and clean, for no better word can be spoken of a man than that he is careful of his horses" (p. 29). More advice was no doubt offered during social hour at the end of a hard day's ride, but mainly, the men gathered around the campfire for conversation ranging from the practical to the outrageous. As Adams recalled, "The stories told may run from the sublime to the ridiculous, from a true incident to a base fabrication, or from a touching bit of pathos to the most vulgar vulgarity" (p. 31).

Adams waxed poetic when he described Flood's choice of a horse to ride on a visit to an old friend who had been spotted driving another herd nearby. The passage warrants quoting in its entirety, for it speaks to the special bond between man and horse that has lost none of its timbre since the cattle trails closed forever. Adams' recollection also reflects an awareness of what had been lost by the time his log was published in 1903—a nomadic way of life that was obsolete practically before it began, and a culture unable to withstand the pressures of modernity. In a morality play signaling the age-old tension between the wild and the tame, cowboys owed their survival to frontier skills even as they paved the way for civilization. They were thus agents of their own demise, caught in the nexus of a wilderness that shaped their identities and a civilization representing man's penchant for progress.

> "We all knew what horse he would ride, and when he dropped his rope on 'Alazanito,' he had not only picked his own mount of twelve, but the top horse of the entire *remuda*,— a chestnut sorrel, fifteen hands and an inch in height, that drew his first breath on the prairies of Texas. No man who sat him once could ever forget him. Now, when the trail is a lost occupation, and reverie and reminiscence carry the mind back to that day, there are friends and faces that may be forgotten, but there are horses that never will be. There were emergencies in which the horse was everything, his rider merely the accessory. But together, man and horse, they were the force that made it possible to move the millions of cattle which passed up and over the various trails of the West" (p. 124).

Cowboys didn't reserve their sense of awe just for horses. In yet another instance where reverence for nature bumped up against the advancing tide of civilization, Adams seems to have nearly fallen out of his saddle when the Circle Dot herd crossed the Red River into the Indian lands (the current state of Oklahoma) at Doan's Crossing and he took time to survey his surroundings. "The Country was as primitive as in the first day of its creation," he recalled.

"As we wormed our way up this narrow divide, there was revealed to us a panorama of green-swarded plain and timber-fringed watercourse, with not a visible evidence that it had ever been invaded by civilized man, save cattlemen with their herds. Antelope came up in bands and gratified their curiosity as to who these invaders might be, while old solitary buffalo bulls turned tail at our approach and lumbered away to points of safety. Very few herds had ever passed over this route, but buffalo trails leading downstream, deep worn by generations of travel, were to be seen by hundreds on every hand. We were not there for a change of scenery or for our health, so we may have overlooked some of the beauties of the landscape. But we had a keen eye for the things of our craft" (pp. 122-23).

Much later, as the Circle Dot herd snaked along the Rosebud River somewhere near the Montana line, Adams once again lapsed into a reverie inspired by the wonders around him. "The month was August, and, with the exception of cool nights, no complaint could be made, for that rarefied atmosphere was a tonic to man and beast, and there was pleasure in the primitive freshness of the country which rolled away on every hand" (p. 329).

When they weren't marveling at the wonders of nature and tending to their herds, cowboys lapsed into storytelling. Their proclivity to exaggerate was legendary and gave rise to a rich folklore suffused with humor and hyperbole. Fearing that the cattle were going blind from thirst during a particularly hellish stretch, one man resorted to standard cowboy communication to get his point across. "It was no vague statement of the man who said if he owned hell and Texas, he'd rent Texas and live in hell, for if this isn't Billy hell, I'd like to know what you call it" (p. 64).

Frontier humor was nothing less than an antidote to tragedy and frustrated hopes. If cowboys were laughing philosophers, it was because they needed relief from hardships. Faced with the prospect of Indian raids, predators, and storms, and suffering from a loneliness that affects herdsmen to this day, cowboys adopted a joking attitude toward death and a tendency to exaggerate that reflected the immensity of their landscape. "Spread-eagle oratory on whatever plane," observed folklorist and historian Mody Boatright (1942: 55), "cannot be accounted for except as a psychological corollary of geographical expansion. Neither can the humor of the frontier." Hence the cowman who claimed not that he owned a million acres, but rather, that he simply used Arizona for a calf pasture; that it was a three-day ride from the front gate to the house; and that his range reached so far that the sun set between headquarters and the west line camp (1949).

Similarly, ludicrous imagery and non-sequiturs conveyed more than mere recitation ever could. Invoking the code of the West, a man surrounded by hostile Indians claimed he wasn't scared; "he just didn't know where to get" (p. 72). The story was told of a man who woke up with a rattlesnake on his chest. Nonplused, he reached for his six-shooter and blasted it. His listener recalled a similar incident out on the Pecos in '83. He woke up in much the same fix, but his weapon was out of reach. What did he do? "Well, seeing there wasn't anything he could do, he just shut his eyes and went back to sleep" (p. 77). Turning to the cowboy's favorite object of ridicule, there could be no clearer sign of a tenderfoot than someone who described a tall horse as, say, "sixteen hands," the standard nomenclature for equine measurement. A cowboy would simply say that he needed to pack a lunch on the way up.[8] Adams (1971), a lifelong collector of Western lore (a scholar, not to be confused with Andy Adams the memoirist), attributed the cowboy's salty turn of phrase to his individual liberty, lawlessness, and an acceptance of his own standards of conduct and communication. In the absence of education and the vocabulary that comes with it, he became a painter of word pictures, or mental images laced with exaggeration and absurdities that expressed the essence of his life in ways that transcended conventional language. "His general impatience of rule and restraint, his democratic enmity to all authority, his extravagant and often grotesque humor, his extraordinary capacity for metaphor—these are indicative of the spirit of the West, and from such qualities its language is nourished" (p. 4).

When it came to conversations about the vicissitudes of nature, most everyone had something valuable to contribute. Not so with matters of the heart. Whenever card game banter turned to romance, cowboys revealed a hard-nosed practicality that ensured their survival on the frontier. Accustomed to an overwhelmingly male milieu and preoccupied with the challenges of driving thousands of cattle to market over an unforgiving terrain, these men had little use for the subtle nuances of love, sex, and marriage. "Yarn followed yarn;" recalled Adams (1903: 82), "for nearly every one of us, either from observation or from practical experience, had a slight acquaintance with the great mastering passion. But the poetical had not been developed in us to an appreciative degree, so we discussed the topic under consideration much as we would have done horses or cattle."

Recognizing the eternal mysteries lurking in the feminine persona, cowboys attributed female qualities to the most unlikely obstacles, particularly forces of nature. What emerged among these trail-hardened herdsmen was ambivalence toward women. Theirs was an attitude poised delicately between condescension toward the gentler sex and fear, tinged, perhaps, by a conviction that women were simply beyond all understanding. Foreman Jim Flood was annoyed when he lost three days to pulling horses and cattle from the quicksand of the South Canadian River. "Well, in all my experience in trail work," said Flood as he gazed back at the dozen animals struggling in the quicksand, "I never saw as deceptive a bottom in any river. We used to fear the Cimarron and Platte, but the old South Canadian is the girl that can lay it over them both" (p. 163). Not long after a stopover in Dodge City, a cowboy made a similarly disparaging reference to women to express his frustration when the cattle balked at crossing Slaughter's Bridge:

> "Jacklin swore that he would bed that herd at the entrance, and hold them there until they starved to death or crossed, before he would let an animal turn back. But cooler heads were present, and the Rebel mentioned a certain old adage, to the effect that when a bird or a girl, he didn't know which, could sing and wouldn't, she or it ought to be made to sing" (p. 227).

---

[8] I learned something about cowboy humor when I was cowboying at the Double U Bar Ranch near Cimarron, New Mexico, in the summer of 1974. I was lagging behind a group of cowboys when my horse started to buck. I managed to stay on until I caught up with my comrades. They could scarcely contain their glee with this impromptu entertainment. Sporting a grin that pretty much told me what was coming, one of them nodded toward my horse and said, "Seems like that horse of yours got a pretty rough lope." Nothing more needed to be said to remind a young and relatively inexperienced cowboy (but by no means a tenderfoot!) of his place in the pecking order.

INVENTING TRADITION

Without question, cowboys took their work seriously. Yet their communicative patterns reveal an awareness of their own shortcomings that was never far beneath a veneer of masculine self-confidence. The result was a self-deprecating humor that bequeathed to posterity a rich repository of metaphors reminding us of our frailties and, not incidentally, our tenuous relationship with the Almighty. A cowboy from another outfit, Nat Straw, described how fortunate he felt to have kept his herd together through a dry spell, ride good horses, and have plenty of good grub to eat at the end of the day. "I always did claim that it was better to be born lucky than handsome" (p. 85), said the cowpuncher. Another cowboy marveling at his good fortune expressed uncommon optimism as he contemplated a future as propitious as his present. "I can't help it," he gushed, "but some day I'll marry a banker's daughter, or fall heir to a ranch as big as old McCulloch County" (p. 86). Light-hearted mockery of religion was another staple of cowboy communication. As one man commented over breakfast, "I think that when the Almighty made this country on the north side of the Brazos, the Creator must have grown careless or else made it out of odds and ends" (p. 109). Such buoyancy and humor signaled the cowboy's optimism, faith in democracy, and shared pride in man's mastery over the continent that ultimately heralded the demise of his nomadic culture (Boatright 1942).

Perhaps the most distinctive feature of cowboy communication was the use of metaphor. Just as self-deprecating humor and tall tales expressed a world view born of vast horizons and dangerous work, so did metaphors, sprinkled as liberally in cowboy banter as fleas on a dog's back, reveal a culture that was inseparable from the forces of nature that defined it. During the Circle Dot herd's stopover in Dodge City, Adams listened as Colonel Shanghai Pierce, "possibly the most widely known cowman between the Rio Grande and the British possessions" (1903: 201), regaled his listeners with his story of selling a thousand beef steers to some Yankee army contractors.

> "Well, my foreman and I were counting the cattle as they came between us. But the steers were wild, long-legged coasters, and came through between us like scared wolves. I had lost the count several times, but guessed at them and started over, the cattle still coming like a whirlwind..." (p. 202).

Always amused by tales of trickery, particularly when Yankees and greenhorns were on the receiving end, the cowboys roared when Pierce finally got to his punch line. In frustration, the contractors allowed Pierce and his foreman to estimate a thousand head. When the herd settled down the next day, the contractors realized that they were 118 head short and tried to compel Pierce to make it right. "They wanted to come back on me," concluded the legendary cowman, probably with a wink or a broad grin, "but, shucks—I wasn't responsible if their Jim Crow outfit lost the cattle" (p. 203). Later, as they pushed their herd across the Nebraska line, Circle Dot cowboys bracing themselves for a taste of city life "set out for Ogalalla, happy as city urchins in an orchard" (p. 264). One can imagine a subsequent scene in a crowded music hall as musicians mustered up for a fiddling contest. One man delighted his audience with a rendition of "The Arkansaw Traveler." Then, the "little, old, weazened mendicant took his cue, and cut into 'The Irish Washerwoman' with a great flourish, and in the refrain chanted an unintelligible gibberish like the yelping of a coyote, which the audience so cheered that he repeated it several times" (p. 267).

Adams' log crackles with adventure: cattle stranded in quicksand, perilous river crossings, stampedes, camaraderie around the campfire under a star-studded sky, and even gunplay during what must have been a memorable night in Dodge City. What goes largely unwritten is the mind-numbing monotony of prodding cattle across a treeless landscape. His account was published some twenty years after his cowboy days, so it seems only natural that Adams would highlight the excitement and downplay the drudgery that he and his fellow proletarians on horseback experienced in their trek across the great prairies. On at least one occasion, however, he allowed himself to relive the days that seemed to stretch to eternity between hair-raising adventures. Reverting to metaphor to get his point across, Adams recalled a stretch in July after his outfit had taken on supplies in Ogalalla and was "snailing along" the North Platte River en route to the Blackfoot country. "Our long hours in the saddle, coupled with the monotony of our work, made these supply points of such interest to us that they were like oases in desert lands to devotees on pilgrimage to some consecrated shrine" (p. 275). Still, few cowboys were willing to trade their work for something less grueling, much less return to "the old States" back east. One man who had gone home to Tennessee for a visit cautioned his companions against the lure of more settled employment elsewhere. Lands east of the Mississippi were too crowded, too pretentious, and too competitive. Everybody was "rapidly getting locoed," he claimed, clearly relieved to be back in the saddle with only horses, cattle, and rough-hewn men for company. Perhaps most damning was the ubiquity of standard-bred horses that would be completely useless on a cattle drive. "No," he explained to his mates in a paean to the equine athletes that made their lives possible, "they would never fit here—it takes a range-raised horse to run cattle; one that can rustle and live on grass" (p. 236).

And what of the danger that lurked around every bend? Cowboys were clearly aware of just how fleeting life could be, but they factored that into their lives as an occupational hazard and let providence decide their fate. The story passed along the trail that one of Shanghai Pierce's men had met his Maker in a tragic accident; his horse had acted up and fallen backward, causing the rider's gun to discharge. After several men had visited the fallen cowboy's shallow grave, Rod Wheat, a cowboy with the Circle Dot herd, more or less summed up the prevailing attitude toward death: "As for myself, I'm not going to fret. You can't avoid it when it comes, and every now and then you miss it by a hair" (p. 276). As Adams himself recalled, "There was nothing different about this grave from the hundreds of others which made landmarks on the Old Western Trail, except it was the latest" (p. 276).

Five months on the trail fostered camaraderie between cowboys that few of us can ever hope to replicate. Yet Adams reserved his final tribute not for his fellow drovers, but for their four-legged partners that made the entire adventure possible. After the Circle Dot herd was delivered to agents of the Blackfoot Agency, the cowboys enjoyed a brief shopping spree and a round of drinks before boarding a train for the return trip to Texas. One way or another, all of them had endured the pain of separation and loss. "But at no time in my life, before or since," wrote Adams, wistful even at a remove of nearly twenty years, "have I felt so keenly the parting between man and horse as I did that September evening in Montana. For on the trail an affection springs up between a man and his mount which is almost human" (p. 382). Recalling the tribulations that man and horse had overcome together, Adams expressed a sentiment that was surely in the heart of many a cowpuncher:

> "And on this drive, covering nearly three thousand miles, all the ties which can exist between man and beast had not only become cemented, but our *remuda* as a whole had won the affection of both men and employer for carrying without serious mishap a valuable herd all the way from the Rio Grande to the Blackfoot

Agency. Their bones may be bleaching in some coulee by now, but the men who knew them then can never forget them or the part they played in that long drive" (p. 382).

Adams' recollections find corroboration in E. C. "Teddy Blue" Abbott's *We Pointed Them North: Reminiscences of a Cow Puncher* (1939). Abbott, one of Montana's most celebrated cowboys, was in his seventies when he collaborated with Helena Huntington Smith to write his memoirs. Born in 1860 in the County of Norfolk, England, Abbott moved with his family to Nebraska and spent more than a decade, from 1871 to 1886, on the south end of north bound cattle. Clearly a precocious sort, Abbott acknowledged that other cowboy chroniclers had by and large gotten their facts straight. Yet he admonished them for not telling their stories right. "Other old-timers have told all about stampedes and swimming rivers and what a terrible time we had, but they never put in any of the fun, and fun was at least half of it" (pp. 7-8). And for the most part, it was Texas cowboys, scattered like quail from the Rio Grande to Alberta, who were having all the fun. Tough, fearless, and prone to violence, these men were forces to be reckoned with. "They used to brag that they could go any place a cow could and stand anything a horse could. It was their life" (p. 11). But even these hard-riding men knew their limits. "In fact there was only two things the old-time cowpuncher was afraid of, a decent woman and being set afoot" (p. 13). Beaten and abused by his father and surrounded by cowboys, all the young Abbott could think of was getting old enough to leave home and join the ranks of his heroes. "And all the time I was living with Texas cowpunchers, the most independent class of people on earth, and breathing that spirit" (p. 19).

When Abbott was finally old enough to fulfill his dream, he found all the independence that he'd been longing for. In 1884, he spent eight carefree days in Miles City, Montana, recovering from an injury that didn't seem to curtail his spirit. "Those were the days when I didn't have a care in the world," recalled Abbott wistfully. "I had plenty of good horses to ride, and the girls said I was the best-looking cowboy on the Powder River. And they cleaned me down to my spurs" (p. 101). Those same girls (known as *sporting women* in range vernacular) were only too happy to divest their customers of their money, but they were held in respect just the same. Abbott remembered a man who "half killed" another for beating a girl. "It was none of his business," wrote Abbott. "It was just the idea of mistreating a woman" (p. 121). Such was chivalry in cow country as cowboys rode to the rescue of ladies in distress, even as they shrank in fear from female attentions.

> "We didn't consider we were fit to associate with them on account of the company we kept. We didn't know how to talk to 'em anyhow. That was what I meant by saying that the cowpunchers was afraid of a decent woman. We was so damned scared for fear we would do or say something wrong—mention a leg or something like that that would send them up in the air" (pp. 206-07).

Like Adams, Abbott took time to relish his surroundings. On April 10, 1883, he set out from Texas with an outfit bound for Montana. "After you crossed Red River and got out on the open plains it was sure a pretty sight to see them strung out for almost a mile, the sun flashing on their horns" (p. 71). Even so, the discomfort and drudgery was more than some men could stand, particularly those designated to *ride drag* directly behind the herd. "I have seen them come off herd with the dust half an inch deep on their hats and thick as fur in their eyebrows and mustaches, and if they shook their head or you tapped their cheek it would fall off them in showers" (p. 72).

As was the custom on the cattle frontier, Abbott let hyperbole seep into his descriptions. Annoyed by the ignorance of the manager and part owner of one of the herds that he prodded north, Abbott claimed that "what he didn't know about a trail herd would make a book so big you couldn't load it on a flatcar without a block and tackle" (p. 83). Even when annoyance turned to enmity, nobody was exempt from the unspoken law of hospitality. "The law of hospitality on the range was very strict," recalled Abbott. "You had to feed and shelter your worst enemy if he came to your house in a storm, and if you refused him shelter you had better leave that country" (p. 139).

Hardships notwithstanding, Abbott reveled in the independence that had long since abandoned his contemporaries back East. In the spring of 1886, he met Charles Russell, the famed painter who dedicated his life to preserving the vanishing West on canvas and who appreciated, perhaps more than most, the quality of independence. One day, Abbott encountered an Assiniboine Sioux who mesmerized him with tales of Indian ways before the coming of the white man. Shortly thereafter he ran into Russell and described the experience. "I said: 'God, I wish I'd been born a Sioux Indian a hundred years ago,' and I told him the story." Russell, who had once dismissed cowboys as nothing but "white Indians" (pp. 22-23), replied: "Ted, there's a pair of us. They've been living in heaven for a thousand years and we took it away from 'em for forty dollars a month" (p. 159).

Abbott's memoir is shot through with references to the qualities that distinguished cowboys from men afoot: pride, a determination to earn the respect of their peers, loyalty to their outfits, and generosity. And like Adams, he was keenly aware of the slender thread that kept him and his fellow cowboys tethered to the earth. He knew a man who was killed in a stampede near the Blue River in 1876. His own brush with death came in the fall of 1888, when his horse threw him in a stampede and raging cattle came within inches of crushing him, leaving him slightly injured but miraculously in one piece. But it was all in a day's work for men satisfied to let fate take its course.

> "Well, it was all in the game, and all cowpunchers knew it when they were riding like that; they all knew that might be their fate with the next jump the horse took. But they didn't quit and didn't hesitate to risk their lives for their outfits" (p. 219).

A review of cowboy memoirs would be incomplete without mention of Charlie Siringo's *A Texas Cowboy, or Fifteen Years on the Hurricane Deck of a Spanish Pony* (1950). On the title page of the first edition, published in 1885, a thirty-year-old Siringo described himself as "an old stove-up 'cow puncher,' who has spent nearly twenty years on the great western cattle ranges" (p. xli). In his introduction to the 1950 edition, J. Frank Dobie, a renowned historian of the West, cited the extraordinary number of printings of Siringo's classic as a clear indication of its popularity, particularly among Eastern readers hungry for tales of Western adventure. "Whatever the total number of copies printed, *A Texas Cowboy* has been, by far, Siringo's most-read book, also the most-read non-fiction book on cowboy life" (p. xiv). Slatta (1994) came to much the same conclusion, citing *A Texas Cowboy*, along with the aforementioned accounts by Andy Adams and Abbott, as an authentic memoir in a sea of tall tales that have more to do with authors' need for posthumous recognition than accuracy or even credibility. Unlike Adams and Abbott, Siringo didn't try to place his experiences in a larger context. Philosophy was not his strong suit. "Charlie Siringo had almost nothing to say on life; he reported actions...His cowboys and gunmen were not of Hollywood and folklore. He was an honest reporter" (Siringo 1950: xxxv).

Nevertheless, Siringo's down-to-earth reporting does give us glimpses into authentic cowboy culture. Like his peers, Siringo was always a stone's throw from destitution, and he was clearly impressed with anyone able to capitalize on opportunities afforded by the range cattle business. Recalling the story of two brothers who parlayed their ranching interests "for the snug little sum of one hundred and ten thousand dollars" (p. 46), Siringo took a rare moment to reflect on life's possibilities, aided by the kind of hyperbole that helped chroniclers of the West make their point.

> "That shows what could be done in those days, with no capital, but lots of cheek and a branding iron. The two Pierce's had come out there from Yankeedom a few years before poorer than skimmed milk" (p. 46).[9]

For the most part, Siringo stuck to the facts. From the backside of his Spanish pony, he careened from one hardship to the next. Somewhere along the "Cimeron,"[10] his meager campfire turned into a raging inferno that nearly scorched his horse and destroyed what few possessions he carried. He was often alone between trail drives, usually hungry, and almost always suffering from heat, cold, or some other discomfort dished out by Mother Nature. He nearly died of smallpox, seemingly accepting of the fact that nobody was willing to take him in. The horror of an Indian raid is preserved in his matter-of-fact description of a mass killing near Dodge City, Kansas.

> "On riding through the streets that morning, crowds of women, some of them crying, seeing we were just in from the South, flocked around us inquiring for their absent ones, fathers, brothers, lovers and sons, some of whom had already been killed, no doubt; there having been hundreds of men killed in the past few days" (p. 107).

Hardships notwithstanding, Siringo seemed to be amused by Eastern attitudes toward cowboy life. During a round-up in the Texas Panhandle, he visited a Christian colony and attended a church service, where the reverend was preaching "about the wild and woolly Cow Boy of the west; how the eastern people had him pictured off as a kind of animal with horns, etc." (p. 112). Like Adams and Abbott, much of Siringo's affection and admiration were reserved for his horse, "one of the most intellectual animals that exists" (p. 113). His recollection of having to abandon his horse, Whisky-peet, is reminiscent of Adams' sorrow when he and his comrades left their mounts behind in Montana and boarded the train for Texas. "Leaving Whisky-peet behind was almost as severe on me as having sixteen jawteeth pulled," wrote Siringo, using the cowboy's telltale hyperbole to drive his lesson home. Such was life on the range, preserved for future generations by a chronicler who wanted posterity to know the truth

---

[9] Adams (1903) has already introduced one of the brothers, Shanghai Pierce, as one of the West's most revered cattlemen.

[10] This is a reference to the Cimarron River in Oklahoma.

about cowboy life and culture. According to Dobie, "No record of cowboy life has supplanted his rollicky, reckless, realistic chronicle" (p. x).

Couched in cowboy vernacular, Siringo's paean to Whisky-peet brings us face-to-face with the duality between the wild and the tame that was just as real to honest-to-goodness cowboys as it is to competitors in contemporary cowboy sports. Even as horses are viewed as machines perfectly suited to the rhythms of the animate trinity, they are held in a reverence that transcends utilitarian and athletic needs. Across time and culture, the horse has transformed and uplifted those who have purported to be its masters. Steeped in symbolism and endowed with an energy that touches on the spiritual, this remarkable animal has never been far from the center of human value systems. Given our heightened awareness of ecological issues, the horse compels us to rethink our relationship with nature and to question our presumption in dominating other forms of life. Literally and symbolically, the subjugation of the Wild Steed of the Prairies came at a high a price insofar as it sacrificed the wildness we crave for the benefits of civilization. It also forced us to become ever more inventive in our efforts to mimic the historical and emotional intensity of a lost heritage—that is, to find a balance between the wild and the tame. "Horses, like the wind and the sea, belong to the realm of nature," wrote Lawrence (1985: 195) in her study of the unique and often contradictory bond between humans and horses.

> "[Y]et they also belong to the domain of man. Embodying simultaneously the spirit of both spheres, horses are unique in the complexity and duality—and often the contradictory elements—of the values they express. In their mobility and wildness, their perpetuated capacity to revert to the feral state, horses always represent freedom. Their power and strength are a reminder of the capacity for rebellion against restraint which may once again surface even after so long a history of obedience."

Sundown

By the early 1880s, enthusiasm for ranching on the western plains was approaching mania. Investors in Great Britain and even Continental Europe were vying for an opportunity to get rich on American beef. A curious brand of American feudalism was taking shape that bore a striking resemblance to society in medieval Europe (Dale 1937). Ranchmen were appropriating grazing lands from Texas to the Dakotas that encompassed more territory than many a European kingdom, and the cowboys who brought their herds up from South Texas and tended them in their new surroundings were as ubiquitous as the knights and men-at-arms of Old World barons. Save for a few nineteenth-century conveniences and decidedly different scenery, feudal lords might have felt right at home in the American West. White (1965: 193) reminded us that "the horny-handed plowmen and craftsmen who populated our continent" were descendants of the medieval proletariat, by far the largest segment of medieval Europe's population, whose influence on subsequent generations has been obscured by more celebrated achievements preserved on the printed page. Revolvers, barbed wire, and windmills are among the icons of the Wild West that were elaborations of cowboys' medieval legacy. How many of us would recognize in the cowboy's jingling spurs the faint echo of a thirteenth-century stockman on his way to tend his cattle? And who in our own time would suspect that a posse's choice of a tall tree and a short rope as an appropriate means of dispatching some unfortunate cattle rustler had its antecedents among pagan Scandinavians, for whom hanging was the preferred method of making sacrifices to the god Odin? "To comprehend ourselves as Americans," concluded White, "we must recover, and relate ourselves to, our deeper past, the Middle Ages" (p. 202).

Yet events were conspiring to bring the era of the great cattle drives to an abrupt and tragic end. Prescient observers saw it coming as ever-expanding herds over grazed the land and cattle prices edged downward. The heavy cost of fencing and exorbitant dues charged by proliferating cattlemen's associations added to stockmen's woes. But it was Mother Nature that dealt the blow from which the range cattle industry never recovered. A killing cold that descended on the Plains during the winter of 1885-86 was followed by a dry summer that left scant forage. Then, blizzards the likes of which nobody had ever seen wiped out entire herds. For weeks on end, the range was blanketed in snow. Blinding winds piled cattle up against fences and sent them careening to their deaths in ravines and canyons. When winter finally turned to spring, retreating snows revealed a range littered with the carcasses of cattle that had finally found the limits of their endurance. "Spring came at last," recalled Teddy Blue Abbott (1939: 202) after surviving the most brutal winter of his cowboying career. "The coulees in some places were piled deep with cattle where they had sought shelter and died, and the ones that were left were nothing but skin and bone and so weak they could scarcely stand." For years thereafter, it was not unusual for farmers migrating to the Great Plains to come across lifeless stalks of willows that desperate cattle had gnawed on in a futile attempt to stave off starvation (Boorstin: 1974).

Those same farmers were the advance guard of a changing economy. Like the rivalries between Athens and Sparta, Rome and Carthage, England and Spain, and America's antebellum South and its industrializing neighbor to the north, the clash between farming and ranching in the nation's heartland produced a new order that was unlike either of the first two and, at the same time, contained elements of both. Dale (1937) used the metaphor of parenthood to describe the fusion of East and West that began in the closing decades of the nineteenth century. The father of the new society was the roaring cow country, primal and pastoral, contemptuous of settled ways. Its mother was the agricultural society that hesitated at the eastern edge of the great prairies before making its first tentative incursions in the decades following Appomattox. Into a region of Longhorn cattle and hard-riding men came wagons loaded with the accouterments of an alien civilization: plows and hoes, pitchforks and cook stoves, feather beds and barnyard animals. Most of all, they brought wives and children, whose homes, schools and churches were soon competing with saloons and lonely cow camps.

Values, too, were in a state of flux. Cowpunchers disdained the penny-pinching habits of their new neighbors, while homesteaders feared and frankly disliked the swashbuckling man on horseback and his spendthrift ways. Yet economic necessity, a rapidly expanding population[11] and, not incidentally, the lure of romance that led many a cowhand to trade his horse for a plow and take up with some farmer's daughter, left farmers and cowboys with little choice but to get along, first through toleration, then a reluctant endurance, and finally an embrace that sounded

---

[11] Between 1870 and 1890, population growth in the prairies states was roughly as follows: the Dakotas, 14,000 to 719,000; Nebraska, 122,000 to 1,058,000; Kansas, 364,000 to 1,427,000; and Texas, 818,000 to 2,235,000. The population of Oklahoma Territory, estimated at 61,000 in 1890, rose to 400,000 by 1900. See Dale 1937: 11.

the death knell of a culture whose meteoric rise and fall belies its importance in the formation of the American character and resilience in many forms of cultural expression.

By the dawn of the twentieth century, great swaths of cow country were succumbing to the plow. Nevertheless, cattle ranching, restricted in geographic scope and subject to ever more rules and regulations, continued to demand the kind of expertise that only experienced cowboys had to offer. Like all industries, cattle ranching has been transformed by technology and the effects of a global economy. Nevertheless, cowboys managed to stake their claim to posterity. Today, whether they're branding cattle, mending fences, or keeping track of their herds with spreadsheets and satellite tracking systems, cowboys continue to tug on our collective consciousness as symbols of a frontier heritage.

The West of the Imagination

Edward Zane Carroll Judson, a contributor to *New York Weekly* with a penchant for seafaring stories, spent much of the summer of 1869 touring the West, prowling for tales that would satisfy readers back East. Writing under the pseudonym Ned Buntline, Judson also wrote fiction for Beadle and Adams, a New York publisher that had harnessed the power of steam to print cheap novels at the rate of 8,000 per hour. The firm's first series rolled off a rotary steam press in 1860, just fifteen years after the newfangled technology had been patented in New York. Over the next few years, dime novels, typically 35,000 words in length and printed on inexpensive paper in press runs of 60,000, became a staple of popular culture and provided most readers with their only glimpse of the Wild West (Murdoch 2001).

Yet it was a glimpse that rarely squared with reality. Tall tales that hatched along the frontier line featuring the likes of Mike Fink, Paul Bunyan, and Davy Crockett had long since become the most popular and enduring means of representing the West. In the nineteenth century, the locus of the tall tale migrated west of the Mississippi, where remoteness from civilization and a bizarre landscape spawned stories that were credible to entertainment-starved consumers in the settled east. Mountain men's colorful accounts of petrified forests, prairie fires that could outrun a horse, buffalo herds stretching across the horizon, streams littered with gold nuggets the size of a man's fist—who was to say that such things weren't possible? As far as most Americans were concerned, weaving through hoaxes and frauds to discover a kernel of truth was far less satisfying than embracing western stories as manifestations of America's grand narrative. And for culture producers with their hands on increasingly sophisticated levers of communication, one didn't have to travel to California to strike gold. "Through these narratives, and throughout the popular understanding of the West itself, coursed a powerful theme of democratic exploration, less of the trail itself—which was well marked even before the gold rush—than of the spaces between western reality and eastern fantasy" (Warren 2005: 71).

On his way back to New York, Judson stopped off in Fort McPherson, Nebraska, to visit with William Frederick Cody, a colorful son of the frontier whose storied career to date included stints as a scout for the Fifth Cavalry, Indian fighter, and buffalo hunter for the Kansas Pacific Railroad. By the time of their fateful meeting on July 24, 1869, Cody was acquiring fame as a guide for celebrity buffalo hunts. Judson quickly dubbed him "Buffalo Bill" and appropriated his persona as the hero for a serial novel, *Buffalo Bill, King of the Border Men*.[12] The first installment, published in the *New York Weekly* on December 23, 1869, captivated readers' imagination with its compendium of clichés praising Buffalo Bill's sterling character and frontier skills (Kasson 2000). Though crude, predictable, and shot through with generic adventures, the language didn't keep readers from snatching up serials and dime novels by the bushel. Eventually, Buffalo Bill's adventures in the Wild West found outlets in more than 550 published accounts (Goetzmann and Goetzmann 1986). Thanks to advanced printing technology and marketing acumen on the part of Judson and others in the forefront of mass communication, Buffalo Bill was on his way to stardom.

An entertainment genre blossomed as dime novelists scoured the West for inspirational heroes. Yet none approached Buffalo Bill's status as an embodiment of Western values. Anxious to find other media outlets, Judson lured his prize catch to Chicago where, on December 16, 1872, he launched his theatrical career at the Windy City's famed playhouse, the Amphitheater, in *The Scouts of the Prairie*. Sporting his trademark mustache and goatee, and with his curly locks spilling over his shoulders, Cody gave his audiences the authenticity they craved in lives increasingly defined by the rhythms of commerce and industry. Others in the cast included Judson, who had written the sappy melodrama in four hours; Texas Jack Omohundro, another favorite of dime novelists whose off-stage exploits included driving cattle along Texas trails and roping wild Longhorns with his signature rawhide lariat; and an exotic Italian dancer named Giuseppina Morlacchi (Kasson 2000). By all accounts, the crowd at the Amphitheater went wild as Buffalo Bill dispatched Indians with his six-shooter and Texas Jack used his trusty lasso to save a maiden from savages that had somehow eluded his sidekick's marksmanship.

Drawn though he was to the stage, Cody wasn't quite willing to give up his regular employment. In a bizarre juxtaposition of reality and fantasy that foreshadowed mass entertainment in the twentieth century, Cody devoted only the winter season to the theater. During the summer months, he continued to serve as a scout for the Fifth Cavalry. In the summer of 1876, Cody was riding with his old regiment when word came that the Seventh Cavalry under the command of General George Armstrong Custer had been wiped out by a contingent of Sioux warriors at the Little Big Horn River. This unthinkable disaster was very much on Cody's mind when he and his regiment moved against some Cheyennes who were attempting to flee their reservation. In a skirmish that was elevated in subsequent press accounts to mythic proportions, Cody, sporting a stage costume of black velvet slashed with scarlet and trimmed with silver buttons, was credited with shooting and killing a warrior named Yellow Hair (referenced in subsequent press reports as Yellow Hand).[13] Cody wound up with the slain warrior's personal effects, including his scalp, which he eventually shipped off as a window display to a store near his wife's home in upstate New York. Meanwhile, in an act of astonishing self-promotion, Cody commissioned a stage play to commemorate the event. Billed as *The Red Right Hand, or First*

---

[12] William Cody was not the only frontiersman who acquired this epithet. In the 1860s and 70s, any number of men named Bill were dubbed "Buffalo" as a means of distinguishing among them. See Warren 2005: 47.

[13] Not only did Cody's battlefield theatrics and subsequent embellishment of the facts enhance his own celebrity; they also raised the significance of a conflict that was so insignificant that army officers, notably General George Crook, accused the commanding officer of wasting military resources in seeking it out. See Warren 2005: 119-20.

Scalp for Custer, the performance mesmerized audiences with a ritualized duel to the death between Cody and his savage foe. Cody's autobiography, published in 1879, gave a whole new meaning to hyperbole in its depiction of Yellow Hair's final moments on the battlefield. As some two hundred warriors raced in for the kill and a contingent of soldiers showed up in the nick of time, Cody lopped off the chief's top-knot and bonnet and swung them in the air, shouting, *"The first scalp for Custer!"* (Warren 2005: 118-19).

Accustomed to tall tales from the West that blurred the boundaries between fact and fantasy, readers and theater goers couldn't get enough of Cody's act of vengeance for the fallen soldiers at the Little Big Horn, and his reputation skyrocketed (Kasson 2000). Whether or not he actually shot and killed Yellow Hair (a matter that remains in dispute to this day) is less important than the uses Cody and his publicists made of the event. "By the 1860s, no region could match the West as a venue for the staging of attractions and the invention of personas that appealed to popular desires and begged audiences to separate them from reality" (Warren 2005: 77). Even as Indian resistance to White settlement was sputtering to its tragic conclusion, Buffalo Bill Cody's dual career as actor and Indian fighter was pushing him ever closer to the summit of America's pantheon of cultural heroes.

Cultural productions celebrating the West, written and staged even as real battles were being fought and new uses were being found for Western resources, signaled that something new was in the wind. The public's remoteness from lived experience, together with cutting-edge technology and the magic of mass entertainment, were converging to transform popular culture. Building on the frontier myth, playwrights and novelists in the late nineteenth century were amplifying a theme dating back to colonists' first tentative steps into the wilderness: the West as a region of hardy and self-reliant individuals, and democratic to the core. Cody and his ilk were thus nothing less than manifestations of America's Homeric epic, peculiarly suited to transmitting social values across generations and supplying the collective unconscious with a means of resolving persistent conflicts that are endemic to any society. Never mind historical evidence to the contrary: the real West afforded scant rewards for speculators and loners, and corporations, buoyed by eastern and often European capital, had no compunctions about muscling small farmers and homesteaders to the sidelines. What mattered in the popular imagination, and what resonated in literary and theatrical productions of the time, was the rejuvenation to be found in resurrecting fragments of history and exploiting accumulated legend.

Like Arthurian stories, the Western myth suffused culture with the makings of self-identity. It encouraged Americans to explore their history for models of action and rely on the past to redeem the future (Murdoch 2001). As industrialization and state-building chipped away at traditional forms of memory, venues for cultural expression proliferated, and Americans became ever more adept at transcending their parochial lives and recognizing essential elements of the frontier myth that simultaneously symbolized the present and linked it to traditions of a sanctified past (Slotkin 1992). Simply put, modernity was rolling like thunder through traditions, and repressed Victorians had little choice but to rely on theater as a substitute for what was forbidden in real life. Desires for intimacy, recognition, and a connection to the past were all available for the price of a ticket (Lipsitz 1990). Seen in the context of a shifting cultural paradigm, *The Scouts of the Prairie* thus represented a genre whose significance far outweighed the fleeting value of a night on the town.

> "It was not educational, factual or informative. It played solely upon the fanciful imagination and the evolving mythology about the frontier. In doing so,

INVENTING TRADITION

Buntline's new show founded all of the archetypal features we now associate with the Western novel, the Western film and the Western television series: brave heroes fighting against overwhelming odds, using their skills at gunplay and roping to subdue the Indians and save the beautiful maiden" (Goetzmann and Goetzmann 1986: 290-91).

Judging from the popularity of P.T. Barnum's circuses and exhibitions of equestrian prowess, Cody was justified in thinking that the public was ready for a whole new adventure. In the summer of 1882, he assembled a cast of characters schooled in the arts of frontier survival at his hometown of North Platte, Nebraska, to celebrate the Fourth of July in what came to be known as the Old Glory Blowout. The extravaganza featured sharpshooters, trick riders, steer ropers, and reenactments of episodes torn from the pages of Western lore, including a famous attack on a stagecoach billed as *The Startling and Soul-Stirring Attack upon the Deadwood Mail Coach* (Kasson 2000). Thanks to celebrity participation and publicity orchestrated by seasoned professionals, Cody's foray into exhibition entertainment was a tremendous hit. The next year, he built on the lessons learned from the Old Glory Blowout to create what was to become one of the most successful traveling acts in showbiz history: Buffalo Bill's Wild West Show.

In an artful blend of stage acting and sportsmanship whose authenticity was purportedly beyond dispute, Cody and his partner, Nate Salsbury, invited an ever-changing retinue of frontier heroes to link epic events in the conquest of the West with demonstrations of skill.[14] Reality blended seamlessly with romance, and adventures familiar to audiences worldwide were accepted uncritically as the building blocks of America's grand narrative. Heavily publicized through nascent techniques of mass marketing, the show helped the West to shed its image as the Great American Desert that had discouraged earlier generations of settlers from venturing into the heartland and promoted the region as a green and leafy world of Indians, bison, and spirited horses. Journalists were unanimous in their praise for entertainment that was both riveting and educational. For some, there was even a quasi-religious dimension to Buffalo Bill's Wild West Show. "It is not a show," wrote journalist Brick Pomeroy in an article praising the Wild West's claims to historical authenticity.

> "It is a resurrection, or rather an importation of the honest features of wild Western life and pioneer incidents to the East, that men, women and children may see, realize, understand, and forever remember what the Western pioneers met, encountered, and overcame. It is in secular life what the representation of Christ and the apostles proposed to be in religious life, except that in this case there are no counterfeits but actual, living, powerful, very much alive and in earnest delegates from the West, all of whom have most effectively participated in what they here re-produce as a most absorbing educational realism" (p. 61).

In 1887, Cody gathered his following and set sail for Europe, where thrill-seeking fans with only the vaguest concept of the American West clamored for a glimpse of cowboys and Indians, arrayed in their finest regalia, acting out dramas that were even then seeping into the

---

[14] Later, Salsbury, who was Cody's business partner from 1884 to 1902, claimed that he envisioned a show of equestrian prowess as early as 1876 and that he, and not the Old Glory Blowout, was the inspiration for the Wild West Show. See Warren: 2005: 210.

common lexicon. Between performances, Cody met with aristocrats and members of royal families; during an appearance in Rome, he was granted an audience with the Pope. As Cody's publicist, John Burke, explained to a group of French reporters during a second European tour in 1889, the object of the show was not to present a circus performance, "but to give a true picture of American frontier life with real characters who had played their part in the history of a portion of the American continent which would soon be a thing of the past" (p. 85). One promotional poster, endorsed by the famous French painter Rosa Bonheur, depicted a morose and dejected Napoleon, designated as "The Man on Horse of 1796," juxtaposed with Buffalo Bill as "The Man on Horse of 1898"—erect, defiant, and scanning the horizon for signs of danger (p. 87; Warren 2005: 350). Such artful deceptions could not help but sear in the popular imagination this symbol of America's self-definition as the ultimate intersection of history, drama, and nostalgia. Through an illusion of time travel, viewers were persuaded that they had participated, however vicariously, in the great American narrative. Enamored of technologies capable of producing a credible simulacrum, audiences were ripe for reenactments that blurred the difference between imitation and the real thing (Orvell 1989). As he galloped out of the arena with his famed flourish of his hat, Buffalo Bill left little doubt that the military leaders of the Old World were no match for the knights of the American West.

But Buffalo Bill left at least one skeptic in his wake. Teddy Blue Abbott (1939), Montana's favorite son and as authentic a character as ever strapped on a set of spurs, knew showmanship when he saw it.[15] Like Charlie Siringo (1950) and Andy Adams (1903), Abbott wanted posterity to know something about the animate trinity of human, horse, and cow that received short shrift in staged productions where cowboys rarely had much to do with cattle. He was interested in the real West where seasoned men spent far more time tending their herds than shooting one another and whose moments of adventure were shoehorned between endless days in the saddle and nights huddled around lonely campfires. In his memoir, he recalled an incident back in Buffalo Bill's home town of North Platte that gives us a glimmer not only of Bill Cody's entrepreneurial bent, but more important, of what was on the horizon for American entertainment.

> "He was a good fellow, and while he was no such great shakes as a scout as he made the eastern people believe, still we all liked him, and we had to hand it to him because he was the only one that had brains enough to make the Wild West stuff pay money. I remember one time he came into a saloon in North Platte, and he took off his hat and that long hair of his that he rolled up under his hat fell down on his shoulders. It always bothered him, so he rolled it up and stuck it back under his hat again and Brady, the saloon man, says: 'Say, Bill, why the hell don't you cut the damn stuff off?' And Cody says: 'If I did I'd starve to death'" (pp. 59-60).

---

[15] Abbott's reluctance to exaggerate his and other cowboys' exploits almost cost him the opportunity to publish his memoirs. He tried for years to interest someone in collaborating on a book before securing the help of Helena Huntington Smith. Part of the problem was his refusal to sensationalize the cowboy life by adding phony gunfights and other contrivances aimed at satisfying the market for shoot-'em-up Westerns. See Slatta 1994: 48.

Abbott cut a wide swath across the West. In 1883, he ran into Calamity Jane after he'd helped to bring a herd to Montana. She graciously loaned him fifty cents and told him not to worry about paying her back. Their next encounter was twenty-four years later, in 1907, long after the trails had closed down forever and Calamity Jane had earned celebrity status as a favorite attraction in Buffalo Bill's Wild West Show. When Abbott asked her to reflect on her notoriety and experiences in the civilized East, the aging star allowed him a glimpse into a tortured soul, caught between the frontier culture that nurtured her and a kaleidoscopic world of mediated imagery that was just then coming into focus. "Her eyes filled with tears," recalled Abbott. "She said: 'Blue, why don't the sons of bitches leave me alone and let me go to hell my own route? All I ask is to be allowed to live out the rest of my life with you boys who speak my language. And I hope they lay me beside Bill Hickok when I die'" (p. 87).

Bill Cody was not the only one to exploit the market for vicarious western adventure. His imitators included Gordon "Pawnee Bill" Lillie, Nevada Ned, and "Mexican Joe" Shelley, all of whom dazzled their audiences with historical reenactments and emotionally-charged theatrics. But none could hold a candle to Buffalo Bill's Wild West Show. As early as 1884, newspapers were referring to the genre as "Buffalo Bill shows," and competitors tailored their performances to resemble the grand master's showmanship (Warren 2005). Cody's production enjoyed its zenith of popularity in 1893, when it attracted some six million viewers during the World's Columbian Exposition in Chicago (Murdoch 2001: 42). In one of those odd twists of history that makes us question the nature of coincidence, the audience included historians who had opted for a few hours of entertainment rather than sit through Frederick Jackson Turner's presentation of his frontier thesis at the annual meeting of the American Historical Society across town. Cody the showman and Turner the scholar were thus reacting, each in his own way, to the closing of the frontier. "Now that the rugged and adventurous frontier life as epitomized by the cowboy on the open range was jeopardized, it was natural that it be not only dramatized, but analyzed, as each man in his own way sought to clarify the nature of what it was that was disappearing" (Lawrence 1982: 48).

Between Two Worlds

By 1890, the real West and the West of the imagination were at a crossroads. Farmers had been muscling their way onto the Plains since the end of the Civil War, and the communities that sprouted in their wake could not long coexist with the nomadic culture that, paradoxically, was sowing the seeds of its own eclipse. Anxious to protect their crops, farmers were turning to barbed wire, "the devil's rope," as a last ditch defense against marauding herds of cattle. Cattlemen, too, were fencing their grazing lands, all the while adopting technologies that pushed the old ways ever further into obsolescence.[16] Yet as we have seen, Mother Nature had the last word, for the snows that came roaring onto the northern Plains in the late 1880s were more than an already weakened industry could withstand. In the spring of 1889, just a few years after the

---

[16] Celebrated events in the winning of the West tend to overshadow more gradual processes that undermined the nomadic way of life common to both cowboys and Indians. For a glimpse into the ingenuity that tamed the great prairies, visit the world class collection of barbed wire on display at the National Cowboy and Western Heritage Museum in Oklahoma City, Oklahoma.

northern herds were wiped out, settlers thundered onto the Oklahoma prairies to begin parceling up what was left of the open range. The sun was clearly setting on the range cattle industry. No stockman with enough sense to come in out of the rain needed to read the census of 1890 to realize that his freewheeling days were numbered.

A burgeoning entertainment industry determined to capitalize on fascination with the Old West certainly tapped into the *zeitgeist* of the era, but it did little to alleviate a sense of foreboding among academics and social critics. Among the first to sound the alarm over America's disappearing frontier was Henry George, a newspaperman and entrepreneur whose outlook was formed when his own businesses were crushed by monopolies. Deeply concerned with land speculation and puzzled by the unlikely relationship between poverty and material progress, George poured his passion into *Progress and Poverty* (1942), a work of political economy that "would set the tone for the frontier anxiety of the ensuing decades" (Wrobel 1993: 9). Originally published in 1880, George's book outsold most of the most popular novels of its time, was translated into several languages, and earned its author fame and respect enjoyed only by a select few. In his decidedly Malthusian estimation, land speculation led inexorably to poverty, and concentration of power exercised through taxes, monopolies, and cartels was robbing people of their sovereignty. George's conclusion, as impractical as it was radical, was that "nothing short of making land common property can permanently relieve poverty and check the tendency of wages to the starvation point" (George 1942: xix). Echoing a theme dating back to America's founding, George despaired over a vanishing Eden and what its loss might mean for future generations.

> "The child of the people, as he grows to manhood in Europe, finds all the best seats at the banquet of life marked 'taken,' and must struggle with his fellows for the crumbs that fall, without one chance in a thousand of forcing or sneaking his way to a seat. In America, whatever his condition, there has always been the consciousness that the public domain lay behind him; and the knowledge of this fact, acting and reacting, has penetrated our whole national life, giving to it generosity and independence, elasticity and ambition. All that we are proud of in the American character; all that makes our conditions and institutions better than those of older countries, we may trace to the fact that land has been cheap in the United States, because new soil has been open to the emigrant" (p. 326).

The census of 1890, together with social unrest and economic turbulence that signaled tough times ahead, seemed to confirm George's worst fears: the frontier had closed, and America was in danger of choking on the fruits of material success. His outlook resonated in the work of Frederick Jackson Turner, whose conviction that the frontier experience explained American development was matched by an equally strong belief that future generations were in peril (Wrobel 1993).[17] By examining the wilderness through the prism of a messianic idealism, Turner imbued wild country with new values. "Turner recast its role from that of an enemy which civilization had to conquer to a beneficent influence on men and institutions. His greatest service to wilderness consisted of linking it in the minds of his countrymen with sacred American virtues" (Nash 1967: 146). Turner's battle cry was taken up by the likes of Sir Robert Baden

---

[17] Henry George's *Progress and Poverty* (1942) was a foundational text for Turner's frontier thesis. See Jacobs 1994: 113.

INVENTING TRADITION

Powell, who founded the Boy Scouts in 1907 as a way of introducing urban children to the wilderness; John Muir, who pioneered wilderness preservation; Aldo Leopold, founding father of the Wilderness Society; and countless others who went beyond Romantic rhetoric to ensure, through whatever means they had at their disposal, that the loss of the frontier would not mean the end of America's grand narrative. An inclination to make the most of earthly existence through contact with nature was not lost on the philosopher and psychologist William James, who believed that hiking brought him into contact with nature's power. As a corollary, he found organized sports to be appropriate vehicles for experiencing the order, discipline, and sacrifice that the wilderness had bequeathed to its conquerors (Mrozek 1983). Thus, the aims and agendas of America's wilderness promoters differed widely. "But all were dealing with the same basic theme—the relation of the individual to society in postfrontier America" (Wrobel 1993: 85).

Still, the wilderness was, for the teeming millions beyond its reach who might never experience it first-hand, an abstraction. To ensure the preservation of time-honored values in the nascent age of modernity, culture producers needed heroes and symbols to weld the nation's heroic age into a coherent story that could be packaged and sold. They needed protagonists who had already taken up residence in the national consciousness, but whose exploits needed a bit of embellishment to make sure that the lessons they had to teach would hit their mark, and stick. Dime novelists, playwrights, and Wild West performers had paved the way, and they proved beyond all doubt that there was an enormous market for tales of high adventure in the West. It was left to their heirs in the twentieth century to harness new technologies and elevate one icon in particular, the lowly cowboy, to heroic status.

By all accounts, the cowboy was an unlikely candidate for stardom. As late as the 1870s, the cowboy was widely dismissed as an uncouth ruffian and, even worse, a thief and a murderer (Boatright 1964). "In this decade the term 'herder' was as likely to be used as the classic name of 'cowboy,' and it usually called up the image of a semi-barbarous laborer who lived a dull, monotonous life of hard fare and poor shelter" (Smith 1950: 109). In his first message to Congress in 1881, President Chester A. Arthur referred to disturbances by armed desperadoes known as "Cowboys." Accusing them of lawlessness and brutality in Arizona Territory and Mexico, he requested armed intervention (pp. 109-10).

Scoundrel that he was, the cowboy didn't have much time to mark his passing. His passage through history spanned no more than three decades after the Civil War, and his heyday, shorter still, was sandwiched between 1870 and 1885 (Munden 1958). Nor did his numbers compensate for the brevity of his era; as we have seen, no more than 40,000 of these dubious characters, and perhaps as few as 35,000, drove cattle from Texas to the northern railheads and ranges (Frantz and Choate 1955; Porter 1971). Moreover, in an age in thrall to social Darwinism, racial diversity on the trail didn't do much to elevate the cowboy's status. Nevertheless, his day in the limelight was coming. "The public's appetite for tales of wilderness exploration, great as it was, could not match its hunger for cowboy tales," wrote Wrobel (1993: 91-92).

> "In a sense the yearning was the same: The rugged wilderness served as a mental antidote to the supposed corrupting influence of civilization in the postfrontier age. And the cowboy, too, in all his mythic grandeur, served as a symbol of a simpler, more rugged frontier age. The image of the cowboy was a creation of the postfrontier mind, and incidentally, one that bore little resemblance to the grim realities of that character's existence."

The twilight of the Old West coincided with an explosion in communication technologies. Mass-market publishing, pioneered by the dime novel, had to make room for crude, silent films, and they in turn succumbed to movies, radio, and television—all firmly embedded in the web of free enterprise, and all desperate to provide content that could ensure a steady stream of consumers. Meanwhile, culture producers were reacting to the closing of the frontier with a determination to stem the decline of American values, a virtual certainty now that modernity and the consumerism that fed it were seeping into every nook and cranny of the continent. It was hard to deny the benefits of a consumer culture that brought the trappings of wealth within the reach of millions. Yet its acceleration after 1890, and particularly its penchant to substitute imitation for the real thing through the miracle of mass production, generated "a sense of the 'real' self as a remnant of one left behind, and that too would remain a consistent feature of American experience, a part of the national mythos, extending into the twentieth century" (Orvell 1989: 71). The dawning of the twentieth century thus witnessed two unlikely bedfellows standing between America and the abyss: an entertainment industry in thrall to Mammon, and self-appointed guardians of culture bent on rescuing a civilization in peril. Perhaps it was inevitable that they settled on the Western myth as the ticket to salvation, and the cowboy as their most promising messenger.

Chapter Four — Nostalgia, Collective Memory, and the Yearning for Cowboy Ways

"I grew up a-dreamin', of being a cowboy,
and loving the cowboy ways.
Pursuing the life, of my high-ridin' heroes,
I burned up my childhood days."[1]

Song lyrics
"My Heroes Have
Always Been Cowboys"

Inventing Tradition: America at a Crossroads, 1880-1920

Between 1880 and 1920, the radical economist Henry George's dire predictions seemed to be coming true with a vengeance. Signs of prosperity were everywhere: businesses were booming, cities were sprouting from barren prairies, and rags-to-riches stories were fueling unparalleled waves of immigration to American shores. Yet the price of progress was a series of crises that left many Americans wondering if the Apocalypse was at hand. Reconstruction had degenerated into partisan politics that doomed the South to decades of white supremacy and desperate poverty. Influenced by social Darwinism, legislators passed laws that left laborers at the mercy of an unforgiving capitalist system. Business moguls were steam rolling small competitors with impunity, and syndicates such as the infamous Tweed Ring in New York City were adding a whole new dimension to political corruption. A swelling tide of immigrants, largely from southern and eastern Europe, was eroding home-grown cultures with strange languages and customs. Industrialization, the crown jewel of modernity, pitted impoverished workers against employers who commanded *de facto* armies to protect their interests. Predictably, conflicts over working conditions usually led to violence. A steel strike in Pennsylvania resulted in pitched battles where strikers found themselves staring down the bore of the Gatling gun, the nineteenth century's weapon of mass destruction. In 1894, a strike at the Pullman Car Company near Chicago brought thousands of federal troops to the scene and claimed some thirty-four lives. From 1892 to 1917, Western mines were sites of some of the most extreme violence, complete with assassinations, massacres of unarmed laborers, mass deportations, and concentration camps (Jenkins 1997). Struggling to reconcile domestic troubles with their nation's increasing prominence of international affairs, Americans were plunging headlong into what can best be described as an identity crisis.

For many, the American Dream had fragmented into a welter of conflicting values and frustrated hopes. Forced into a tightening straightjacket of conformity and interdependence and

---

[1] Words and music by Sharon Vaughn. Copyright © 1976, 1980 Polygram International Publishing, Inc. International Copyright Secured. All Rights Reserved. See Hal Leonard, (1996), *Classic Country*, Milwaukee, WI: Hal Leonard Corporation: 112-13.

frightened by systemic class conflict, Easterners were susceptible to the lure of Western lore insofar as it reflected cherished values: "individualism, self-reliance and an instinctive commitment to democracy" (Murdoch 2001: vii). As politicians (none more advantageously than the late President Ronald Reagan) learned a long time ago, resurrecting the Western ethos all but guarantees a sympathetic hearing. Why? "The reason is simple: the vision of the frontier heritage recently so staunchly defended by politicians and press and the images so consistently presented by the Western movie are not history, not even romanticized history: they are myth and the power of myth is not to be gainsaid" (p. x).

Drawing on Rousseau's "natural man," Fishwick (1952) posited the cowboy as a romantic symbol of freedom whose exploits were in global circulation when American soldiers spread to the corners of the globe to combat fascism. Wherever they went, locals expected them to shoot from the hip, opt for horses over jeeps, and form posses to track down the enemy. Travelers to distant shores thus embodied a fictional ideal bearing little relation to historical reality, constructed more out of Western lore than everyday life on the cattle frontier. Weather-beaten and rough, this child of nature, along with his trusty horse, "form the most enduring team in American mythology, and incidentally help explain the growing horse cult in a highly mechanized America" (p. 81). From Buffalo Bill's showmanship and dime novels to more modern avenues of cultural expression and identity formation, the cowboy has never been at a loss for publicity. Rodeo, "the closest thing to a 'national institution' which has developed west of the Mississippi" (p. 87), has certainly played its part in propagating cowboy culture, as has America's entertainment juggernaut. The result is a typed figure that symbolizes freedom, individuality, and proximity to nature which, for most of us, have become all but unattainable. Just as Turner posited the frontier as a safety valve for an industrializing nation, so has the cowboy survived as cultural safety valve in our own time, never further away than the nearest movie theater, bookstore or, for those who prefer a more visceral experience, a rodeo arena. "The cowboy stories are morality stories," concluded Fishwick.

> "[L]ike his predecessor, the knight-errant, the cowboy travels the land making amends in an unbalanced world: and selling the American landscape and personality to the rest of the world. With so formidable and sound a function, he need not fear extinction. Even if the western range disappears forever, and the last doggie is put behind barbed wire, the memory and legend of the open-range American cowboy will follow that imaginary trail which winds its way through the unbroken sea of grass" (p. 92).

Coffin (1953) had high praise for Fishwick's (1952) inquiry into the cowboy's contributions to world mythology. At the same time, he believed that Fishwick failed to explain the forces in nineteenth- and twentieth-century culture that caused the fictional cowboy to acquire mythic status. Accordingly, Coffin (1953) suggested two forces that catapulted the cowboy to his exalted place in American mythology, both of which lead back to Rousseau's "natural man" by way of the hunter and plainsman: western local color and nationalism on the one hand, and the urge toward individual law and violence on the other. As a typed figure representing Rousseau's paeans to the primitive, the cowboy thus became a champion of the masses and an embodiment of the law unto himself, his trigger finger itching to dispense justice in the interests of traditional society. Forged in the crucible of democracy and nostalgia for the Old West, the cowboy reflected Americans' penchant in the late nineteenth century to explore their roots and, not incidentally, to expand their imperial reach. These forces heated up after World War I as British power waned and American power gained momentum. "Truly," wrote Coffin, "the cowboy legend developed as a natural result of the expansionist tendencies of our country" (p. 291). Thus we see the Byronic figure clad in chaps and spurs: independent, hell raising, and supremely interesting to boot. Like all mythic figures, the cowboy was thus a natural manifestation of his time and culture, reveling in nationalistic glory and prone to violence in defense of the common good.

To bridge the gap between folklorists interested in national level or mass culture studies and others who focus on small, face-to-face groups, Stoeltje (1987) sought to understand how folklore shapes myth, belief, ideology, and behavior on a national scale through mass media as well as traditional forms of communication. Perhaps the most important thing to realize is that folklore is deeply embedded in culture and reveals itself in both nationalistic tendencies and mass culture. Simply put, specialists in fields as diverse as history and film criticism have come to a consensus that folklore operates in a much broader universe than previous generations of scholars have acknowledged.

> "All agree that the world no longer functions in discrete units such as the folk, the popular, or the elite, or the primitive and the modern, but that folklore, like economics and politics and religion, thrives in a web of forces directly connected to the larger world as well as to the intimate relations of the family and the tribe" (p. 238).

As a primary metaphor for America's historical experience, folklore arising from the frontier and its heroes takes on sociopolitical functions. Preserved in a variety of communicative forms, the conquest and transformation of the unknown play out across generations in all dimensions of culture, including myth, history, warfare, art, literature, and film. The Old West may seem light years removed from the Space Age, but the underlying metaphors are the same. Covered wagons become space ships, and cowboys morph into astronauts.

The frontier myth flickered to life between 1880 and 1920, when labor unrest and immigration signaled chaos in the East and, as Turner argued in 1893, the Western frontier was dissolving in a sea of settlement. Ideologies that prevailed prior to the Civil War were of little use to a rapidly industrializing nation. For generations, Easterners had perceived the West through a cultural prism reflecting the frontier as a shapeless mass where fact blurred into fiction to produce a realm of the imagination. By 1885, however, the West was taking on distinctive characteristics. The Populist movement of 1890s, culminating with William Jennings Bryan's nomination to presidency, revealed a class structure in the making. Dime novels expressed values characteristic of life in the wide open spaces. Wild West shows and theatrical productions brought the West within reach of anyone who could afford a ticket, and Turner's frontier thesis leant academic credibility to experiences that were uniquely Western and intrinsically American. In short, the Western wilderness was becoming a region whose influence, both economic and cultural, was very much bound up with the fortunes of the nation, and the mythologies that it spawned were finding ever more ways to seep into the national consciousness.

For Stoeltje, three ideological themes dominated the emergent myth of the frontier: the romantic, which amounted to nostalgia for a lost time and place; the rational, which hinged on man's faith in science and reason to build a brighter future; and the reactionary, which praised the status quo and opposed social change. Besieged by conflicting claims to legitimacy, members of the social and political elites in the East relied on the frontier myth to preserve traditional values and impose a hierarchy upon complexity and diversity. As we will see, they also were nurturing a myth that validated existing social structures, thereby molding it to fit their own agendas. Aided by mass media, a national culture was emerging that looked to the myth of the frontier as its guiding light. "Only a timeless story derived from the familiar, complete with plot and national hero, could yoke the diversity of the late nineteenth century and transform it into unity again" (p. 243).

So who, specifically, were the mythmakers so bent on using their power and influence to harness American folklore to the purposes of postfrontier society? Frontier historians and folklorists (Boatright 1951, 1964, in Speck 1973; Fishwick 1952; Kuenz 2001; Lawrence 1982; Murdoch 2001; Slotkin 1981, 1992; Stoeltje 1987; White 1968) agreed that three men in particular were responsible for promulgating the frontier myth, and particularly its final chapter that played itself out between 1865 and the late 1880s, to a receptive nation: Theodore Roosevelt in literature and politics; Owen Wister in fiction; and Frederic Remington in art and illustration. White (1968) suggested that these scions of the Eastern establishment both reflected and reproduced the dialectic in American culture between runaway industrialization and nostalgia for a simpler, more primitive past. Born within three years of each other in the decade of the Civil War, they went West to recover from personal traumas and search for a sense of tranquility that was proving so elusive in the stratified East. Unsure of their professional destinies and suffering from what can best be described as crises of identity, they chose the West as the most promising route to manhood. "This sense, itself a manifestation of the rapid economic and social change which characterized late nineteenth-century eastern America, was to provide a jumping-off point for the large attraction Remington, Roosevelt, and Wister were to feel for the West, and their subsequent articulation of this attraction in original and imaginative terms" (p. 54).

Under the influence of these Ivy League aristocrats, the distinction between the hero of the frontier myth and the proletarian laborer on horseback blended in the cultural stew of late nineteenth-century America (Stoeltje 1987). Eschewing historical accuracy and even fabricating elements of the Western experience out of whole cloth, they drew on the resources of a market-driven society and honed in on the last and arguably most heroic phase of America's conquest of the continent. Although they bore little responsibility for changes sweeping through the West, there can be no doubt that the interaction between cultural transformations beyond the Mississippi and the attitudes that these men brought to bear on them helped to determine the kind of West that would blossom in America's collective memory. "All eastern men of social and financial prestige, they were heavily responsible for a sudden and dramatic restatement of the western theme and a reexamination of the American West in an industrial and urban context" (White 1968: 51). Through literature and art and even the rough and tumble arena of politics, they invented traditions, the essence of which had been germinating for centuries on the frontier and were therefore already embedded in American culture. "'Invented tradition'," wrote Hobsbawm (1983: 1), "is taken to mean a set of practices, normally governed by overtly or tacitly accepted rules and of a ritual or symbolic nature, which seek to inculcate certain values and norms of behaviour by repetition, which automatically implies continuity with the past."

Denied the luxury of falling back on ancient traditions gestated from unconscious depths, from time out of mind, Americans have tended to put their faith in the land or, more specifically, in the mythologies that America's magnificent vistas have propagated (Wright 1977). The frontier thus became an abbreviation for an entitling myth that has continued throughout the twentieth and early twenty-first centuries to impose an authoritative agenda deeply rooted in cultural expressions that, for the purposes of this inquiry, include cowboy sports. But before turning to sports, let us consider the cultural trinity that popularized the cowboy, the entertainment industry that lifted him to lofty heights of the imagination, and the collective memory of a nation that will probably always keep him on a range of his own.

The Cultural Trinity

Theodore Roosevelt (1858-1919)

As we have seen, Frederick Jackson Turner played a pivotal role in casting the West as a crucible of American character formation. His thesis was strongly endorsed by none other than Theodore Roosevelt, a celebrated outdoorsman in his own right whose multi volume *Winning of the West* was in its final stages of production when Turner made his splash in Chicago.[2] Like Turner, Roosevelt believed that the frontier had played a key role in forming the mystical entity that both men referred to as the "national character." As historians, each was wary of nationalistic rhetoric and sought to bring a rigorous methodology to the study of westward expansion. Yet they differed in their approaches to the dialectic between myth and ideology that continues to bedevil our interpretation of the frontier experience. Turner, safely ensconced back East in the halls of academe after accepting a position at Harvard in 1910, was drawn to the ideology of the yeoman farmer and its prospects for agrarian democracy. Roosevelt, by contrast, drew from personal experience to formulate a perspective of the West that was reflected not only in his writing, but also in the political style that leant shape and substance to his political career.

Grieving from the sudden deaths of his wife and mother and suffering from political setbacks, Roosevelt opted for hands-on management of a ranch that he had purchased in the Dakota badlands in 1883. Hofstadter (1977) suggested that Roosevelt's abrupt career change stemmed in part from the displacement he felt as members of a nascent *nouveau riche,* practically oozing wealth from expanding industries, muscled their way to political power and prestige at the expense of the old gentry. The upheaval in status that characterized the era fostered changes not only in leadership, but also "in the distribution of deference and power" (p. 135). Angst-ridden and anxious to test his mettle on the Western prairies, he jumped at the chance to ride to the beat of a hardy life—to tend cattle, hunt, and endure a loneliness that matched the desolation in his soul. His teachers were cowboys, a stoic and self-reliant breed whose qualities seemed the perfect antidote to anxieties over the closing of the frontier. "For these men severe experience had been a most demanding teacher, but for the most part they had stoically learned its grim lesson; in praising them, Roosevelt resorted to epithets many of his contemporaries had come to associate with success in the masculine world of industrial enterprise" (White 1968: 82).

Roosevelt's mythology was thus steeped in the exploits of Indian fighters, gunslingers, and buffalo hunters. "Whereas Turner would locate the crucial human dynamism in a democratic collectivity, Roosevelt would locate it in successive classes of heroes, emerging from the strife of

---

[2] The admiration worked both ways. One of Turner's prized possessions was a deluxe edition of Roosevelt's *The Winning of the West*. Turner was captivated by Roosevelt's idea that a frontier 'hunter type' emerged from the cultural melting pot of the woodlands, and the idea of a frontier type was a central theme in his writing. See Jacobs 1994: 25.

races to earn the right to rule" (Slotkin 1981: 613). His reverence for cowboy ways, and his conviction that they could mitigate the uncertainties of a nation hurtling headlong into modernity, lie at the heart of *Ranch Life and the Hunting-Trail* (1888). Illustrated by his friend and fellow aficionado of the wide open spaces, Frederic Remington, Roosevelt's account of ranching in the Dakota badlands tapped into the burgeoning interest in the Western genre and helped to propel the cowboy and his contrary ways to the forefront of the national consciousness. "Civilization seems as remote as if we were living in an age long past," he wrote wistfully of his experiences under Western skies.

> "The whole existence is patriarchal in character: it is the life of men who live in the open, who tend their herds on horseback, who go armed and ready to guard their lives by their own prowess, whose wants are very simple, and who call no man master. Ranching is an occupation like those of vigorous, primitive pastoral peoples, having little in common with the humdrum, workaday business world of the nineteenth century; and the free ranchman in his manner of life shows more kinship to an Arab sheik than to a sleek city merchant or tradesman" (p. 6).

Before the cowboy could be made acceptable to the genteel middle class, he needed to be presented on a slightly more sophisticated level. Even more important, he had to fit the contours of the reigning social mythology of an increasingly urbanized class. Among Roosevelt's lasting legacies to American culture was to foster this synthesis by interpreting the cowboy in terms of the dominant social philosophy of the period: social Darwinism. To counter the crises that seemed to stem from the closing of the frontier, Roosevelt reminded his countrymen that American history was simple, heroic, and firmly rooted in pioneer virtues. Within the rubric of a naive Darwinism, God smiled on those who helped themselves, and who was more self-reliant than the cowboy? Given his adolescent joy in vigorous physical activity, his impatience with speculative thought, and his racially tinged acceptance of the survival of the fittest, it is hardly surprising that Roosevelt found in his Dakota cowboys the manly virtues that could mitigate the decadence and disorder that were poisoning the land. In his estimation, ideals and action were inseparable, and the social good trumped all other considerations. "By precept and example he urged the American people to lead a strenuous life" (Boatright 1964: 170). The appeal of the strenuous life for Roosevelt and his ilk stemmed not only from their passion to triumph over demanding conditions, but also from their conviction that it refreshed the body and renewed the spirit.[3] In their rapidly modernizing world, experience and action were eclipsing religion as the

---

[3] Such sentiments were supported by the medical community, where the repressed sexuality of the era seems to have found a welcome refuge. Concerns about exhaustion in the machine age led some physicians to subscribe to the concept of "spermatic economy." According to this theory, the human male possessed a limited quantity of sperm, and its conservation for productive enterprises depended on the regenerative effects of exercise. Dr. Augustus Kinsley Gardner, a prolific author and innovator in gynecological surgery, advised boys and young men to eschew masturbation and channel their sexual energies toward athletics. Dr. George M. Beard praised the energetic type as a paragon of bodily health and sexual continence. Not surprisingly, moralists were eager to join the bandwagon. The Reverend John Todd, committed to eradicating the dreaded vice of masturbation, recommended bodily exercise and manual labor as remedies for a wide range of sexual dysfunctions brought on by exhaustion. Not surprisingly, Victorians

most promising route to regeneration (Mrozek 1983). At home and abroad, Roosevelt thus came to symbolize an increasingly secular America, and the cowboy, honed to the rigors of survival on the edge of civilization, shared the spotlight.

Turner and Roosevelt believed that their task as historians was not only to glean evidence from the historical record, but to go a step further and "apply historical knowledge to the ideological task of defining and projecting resolutions of contemporary crises" (Slotkin 1992: 32). Through his writing and from the bully pulpit of the presidency, Roosevelt—that damned cowboy, in the immortal words of Mark Hannah—was in an ideal position to extol cowboy ways to a troubled nation. In a century that began with America's first taste of empire in the Spanish-American War and ended with a triumphant West consigning Communism to the dustbin of history, Roosevelt's interpretation of the frontier experience seems to be the more salient of the two. Suffused with racism and unapologetic about America's right to rule, Roosevelt's origin myth has much to tell us about the formation of American values and their resonance throughout the twentieth century. "For Roosevelt," wrote Slotkin (1981: 636),

> "history was continuous and progressive; he could think of nothing better to say of our pioneers than that their work had produced ourselves. Nor was the most important part of the frontier unrecoverable. Since its true significance lay in its effects on racial morale, a disciplined program of preaching, myth-making, exercise, and conquest enabled the historically-selected new class of hero-leaders to reacquire the spirit of the frontier."

Frederic Remington (1861-1909)

"Evening overtook me one night in Montana, and I by good luck made the camp-fire of an old wagon freighter...I was nineteen years of age and he was a very old man. Over the pipes he developed that he was from Western New York and had gone West at an early age. His West was Iowa. Thence during his long life he had followed the receding frontiers, always further and further West. 'And now,' said he, 'there is no more West. In a few years the railroad will come along the Yellowstone and a poor man can not make a living at all.'

"The old man had closed my very entrancing book almost at the first chapter. I knew the railroad was coming—I saw men already swarming into the land. I knew the derby hat, the smoking chimneys, the cord-binder, and the thirty-day note were upon us in a resistless urge. I knew the wild riders and the vacant land were about to vanish forever, and the more I considered the subject the bigger the Forever loomed" (Samuels and Samuels 1979: 551).

So wrote Frederic Remington in an article for the March 18, 1905 edition of *Collier's Weekly* under the unassuming title, "A Few Words from Mr. Remington." His memory of the encounter with the wagon freighter was by no means fresh; Remington's first Western excursion was more than twenty years behind him as he reflected on the vanishing frontier from the comfort of his study. Hounded by occupational frustrations and craving a nonindustrial

---

had considerably less to say about the role of exercise in women's lives. See Mrozek 1983: 19-27.

environment, the young Remington left his home in upstate New York and, in the spring of 1883, poured his modest patrimony into a sheep ranch in southern Kansas (White 1968). After two years of mind-numbing work, plunging wool prices compelled him to seek his fortune elsewhere. In the summer of 1885, his wanderlust landed him in Arizona, where his dreams of cashing in on a gold mine turned to fool's gold. More gifted in sketching than business, Remington was compensated for his failed vision with an historic opportunity to capture Apache Indians on canvas at the very time that Geronimo and his followers were eluding the U.S. Army. He never saw Geronimo. In fact, he never even made it within two hundred miles of him. Yet he did manage to complete countless sketches of Apaches, soldiers, and cowboys. Upon his return to New York in the fall of 1885, the would-be prospector's portfolio was filled with more gold than he ever could have scratched out of the Pinal Range in Arizona Territory.

Remington wasted no time in approaching prestigious art markets with his sketches. His timing could not have been better. Weaned on a steady diet of Western tales, Easterners were primed for Remington's depictions of the Wild West in all its glory. *Harper's Magazine* and *Outing* were among the first publications to seize on Remington's sketches, and others quickly followed suit. Large canvases, suffused with the same verve and realism that characterized his sketches, made their way to exhibitions, where they garnered awards and high praise from art critics. His success prompted more Western ventures, and by the late 1880s, he was recording his impressions in words and bronze as well as on canvas. Between 1881 and 1909, Remington captured the last days of what he called "men with the bark on" in some 2,750 paintings and drawings, twenty-five bronzes, eight books, a novel, a play, and countless magazine articles. At one point in the 1880s, his work was appearing in nearly every mass circulation magazine (Goetzmann and Goetzmann 1986). As the curtain fell on America's final act in the conquest of the frontier, Remington's Eastern contemporaries looked to him and other articulate exponents of Western life to dramatize the meaning of a region that was so unlike their own and yet so firmly ensconced in the collective consciousness (White 1968).

Like Roosevelt, Remington believed that Western life was genuine—masculine and dangerous, fit only for people with the audacity to trade Eastern refinements for life "at its most real" (p. 107). Increasingly disgusted by waves of immigrants and urban squalor that were casting a pall across the East, Remington became ever more nostalgic for the vanishing West and ever more determined to record what was left of it. Noting the romanticism and even Christian allegories that made their way into Remington's art, Nemerov (1991) suggested that the artist, more embittered with each passing year, was committed not so much to faithful depictions of an historic process as he was with spinning out a morality play whose setting was epic in scope and whose actors were manifestations of a divine consciousness. A yearning for Old America was thus the central drama of his life. "For Remington, as for others at the turn of the century, metaphors of loss and distance were inextricably bound with what it meant to imagine a historical scene" (p. 39). Goetzmann and Goetzmann (1986) compared his existential world of tragedy tinged with chivalry to the literary world of Ernest Hemingway, where violence was a constant companion and tough-guy killers waited for the end.

Unwilling to witness firsthand the death throes of the Old West, Remington made no major excursions after 1895. From the sanctity of his studio on an island in the St. Lawrence River, he ballooned to three hundred pounds and settled into his role as a cultural entrepreneur, producing representations of a time and place that obscured as much as they revealed about their subject. He was not alone in his perceptions of a changing America, but he was certainly one of its most gifted chroniclers, and he had the talent to both reflect and reproduce the values of a culture that considered itself hopelessly dislocated from an idealized, sentimentalized, and pre-industrial era. Toward the end of his life, he was known to cry out, "'Cowboys! There are no cowboys anymore!'" (White 1968: 121). Such were the lamentations of a soul pining for the real thing under the crushing weight of modernity.

Owen Wister (1860-1938)

The third member of the cultural trinity was Owen Wister, easily the most prominent of the troubadours who exalted the cowboy to a readership with an insatiable appetite for Western lore. To escape memories of a detested childhood and the regimentation of a law practice in Philadelphia (White 1968), Wister made his first trip to Wyoming in the summer 1885, when the range cattle industry was riding the crest of a boom destined to collapse in the blizzards of the late 1880s. No sooner did he arrive in the West than he began to record the sights and sounds of his new surroundings that dramatized both his frustrations with the stultifying life he had left behind and the sense of freedom that greeted him. "This life has a psychological effect on you," he wrote to his mother during his first summer in Wyoming. "To ride 20 miles and see no chance of seeing human traces; to get up on a mountain and overlook any number of square miles...and never a column of smoke or a sound except the immediate grasshoppers—and then never to go upstairs. You begin to wonder if there is such a place as Philadelphia anywhere" (p. 123). On a subsequent trip in 1889, he put his sentiments into verse:

> Would I might prison in my words
> And so hold by me all the year
> Some portion of the Wilderness
> Of freedom that I walk in here (p. 124).

It wasn't long before Wister virtually abandoned his law practice for a writing career. When his first western story was published in 1891, the heroic age of the cattle drives was already fading into memory, and even dime novelists were beginning to abandon the cowboy as a waning mythology (Boatright 1951). In his copious correspondence with Frederic Remington, Wister echoed the artist's sense of foreboding over the passing of the Old West. Yet rather than sink into bitterness over forces beyond his control, Wister imbued his writing with aspects of the Western experience that seemed most hopeful for the future of the region and the nation (White 1968). His genius was to portray the cowboy neither as an Arcadian innocent nor a drunken trouble-maker, but rather as a gentleman, deeply imbued with a code of honor, more apt to rely on brains than brawn, and steeped in chivalry that harkens back to the aristocratic South—modified, of course, by the vicissitudes of Western life. By interpreting the cowboy through much the same lens as Roosevelt, Wister's "colonial romance" (Kuenz 2001: 99), written as a self-conscious political allegory about the state of the nation, made him respectable to publishers and readers alike (Boatright 1964).

By the time *The Virginian* (2002), arguably the most famous Western novel ever written (Murdoch 2001), was published in 1902, the cowboy type was embedded in American folklore. Readers couldn't get enough of cowboys. Again and again, they replayed the Horatio Alger story of the faithful apprentice against a Western panorama. It was the perfect antidote for an American Dream sullied by sectionalism, a yawning gap between rich and poor, and a socially irresponsible plutocracy. Like Roosevelt, Wister both reflected and reproduced elements of social Darwinism that prevailed at the turn of the twentieth century. "In Wister's fiction the best man wins, but in fairness to him it should be said victory is not the only evidence of the winner's superiority; it is manifest also in his physical appearance, his bearing and manner, and in his native intelligence" (Boatright 1951: 161).

The appeal of Wister's cowboys lies not only in their qualities, but also in their style: "their economy of speech and action, their laconic humour, and their minimalist approach to critical situations" (Murdoch 2001: 74). Ironically, what is missing in *The Virginian* are references to life on the range. Day-to-day cattle punching portrayed by the likes of Andy Adams (1903), Teddy Blue Abbott (1939), and Charlie Siringo (1950) is nowhere to be seen. Frantz and Choate (1955) suggested that the novel is not at all representative of Wyoming between 1874 and 1890, as it purports to be, insofar as its characters spend more time in love-making and playing pranks on one another than tending cattle. *Cowboy* is, after all, a job title rather than a state of being. Arguably, the freedom associated with the cowboy's West depended fundamentally on not seeing the work he did and perhaps not even regarding him as a worker. Hired to brand and castrate cattle in the spring, graze them in the summer, and drive them to market in the fall, cowboys were subject to the same kind of employment cycles that had long since ensnared their industrial counterparts back East (Kuenz 2001). But you'd never know it from the quixotic horsemen who roamed the vistas of Wister's imagination.

Like Remington, Wister filled his work with romantic qualities reflecting an Easterner's lament with the end of an era. The fiction that captured America's imagination at the turn of the century and helped set the stage for an entire genre of entertainment in the century to come thus had more to do with inventing new traditions to live by than depicting faithful representations of the past. Moreover, the manliness coursing through the veins of Wister's cowboys was code for whiteness and middle-to-upper class status, thus belying the cultural and economic realities of the range they rode. As worldly as they are adaptable, his cowboys seem perfectly compatible with an industrialized and mechanized world.

> "Americans have had different success models at different times in their history, and their cultural heroes are products of trends and changes in the social and economic structure of the nation. The interaction between the idealized traits of Wister's horseman of the plains and the aspirations of Americans at the close of the nineteenth century is particularly significant" (White 1968: 140).

Wister may or may not have been familiar with Turner's frontier thesis. Yet the notion that the frontier constituted the most important determinant in American history, and that the cowboy, the last of the frontier types, symbolized the American way, resonated in his fiction and influenced subsequent generations of writers, film makers, and playwrights. In his seminal article on the cowboy's contribution to the world's mythology, Fishwick (1952: 85) wrote that "Owen Wister performed the considerable service of making the little-known and much-maligned figure of the cowboy a respectable, and even intriguing, character for serious literature." From a cultural perspective, Kuenz (2001) cautioned us against accepting Wister's creations at face value. Hewn from hardy Anglo-Saxon stock, the Virginian and his ilk were embodiments of racial purity, and their representations in literature had less to do with faithful depictions of a vanishing way of life than with shifting discourses in postfrontier America. Boatright's (1951: 163) conclusion, certainly perceptive when he penned his article in the 1950s, might give us pause as we stand on the threshold of the twenty-first century:

"There must be popular amusement—release from the tensions of modern life—and the cowboy is a hero with many faces, most of them innocent. But it is not altogether reassuring that in a time of greater complexity and greater insecurity than Wister lived to see, the cowboy with his six-shooter, his simple ethics, and his facility for direct action is our leading folk hero."

Roosevelt, Remington, and Wister were by no means alone in easing America's frontier anxiety by extolling various versions of the cowboy myth. Yet they certainly played a vital role in raising the cowboy from proletarian to a paragon of American virtue. In the process, they blended historical facts with mythology to invent a tradition aimed at saving America from the perils of modernity—and, not incidentally, satiating a "culture industry" attuned to the rhythms of capitalism (Adorno and Horkheimer 2002). Together, they played a sort of regional round-robin: their Eastern heritage drove them West, where they found raw materials and shaped them in ways that were acceptable to their contemporaries back East, and they in turn came to envisage an integration of East and West that would imbue the new century with the best of both worlds (White 1968). Theirs was a social construction of the most obvious kind, and it bequeathed to future generations an heroic past that was perfectly suited to a yearning for authenticity (Kuenz 2001). In her anthropological study of rodeo, Lawrence (1982: 24-25) was similarly taken with the cultural trinity's success in honing cowboy ways to the contours of a new century.

"It was Easterners like Owen Wister (1902) with his literary creation of the archetypal horseman of the Plains, Frederick Remington with his painstaking artistic depictions of range life, and Theodore Roosevelt with his characterization of ranching as an invigorating and adventuresome life, who had gone West and, by means of heightened awareness to their new surroundings combined with special talent, were able to fix for all time the image of the American cowboy."

From Proletarian to Pop Star: The Resilience of the Cowboy Myth

By 1913, Buffalo Bill Cody was well past his prime as a showman, and financial losses exacerbated by an unsuccessful mining venture prompted him to look outside the Wild West arena for sources of income (Goetzmann and Goetzmann 1986). Given his unprecedented run as an entertainer, it is not surprising that he looked to the nascent motion picture industry as yet another potential gold mine. Moreover, there was precedent for success in producing films with a Western theme. Edwin S. Porter's *The Great Train Robbery*, released to great acclaim in 1903, featured nearly all the essential elements and conventions that would come to typify the Western genre: good guys versus bad guys, an affront to law and order, a chase, and a final showdown, all set against an epic backdrop.[4] Emboldened by this and other precedents, Cody set about

---

[4] *The Great Train Robbery* was the most commercially successful film of the pre-nickelodeon era. Yet its setting was far from epic. Porter, the father of the story film who was responsible for the one-reel, ten-minute film, shot the picture in New Jersey and Delaware rather than Wyoming. It was not until 1906 that Westerns were shot in the West rather than on the East Coast. For a succinct history of the Western genre, visit http://www.filmsite.org/westernfilms4.html.

producing *The Indian Wars Refought*, a documentary of the Indian wars that "won" the West. Although all but the final reel of this landmark production has been lost, *The Indian Wars Refought* set a precedent for a genre of entertainment that has captivated the imagination of movie-goers for more than a century.

Of course, neither *The Great Train Robbery* nor *The Indian Wars Refought* were without precedent in American popular culture. They must be viewed in the context of a tradition that dates back to folk tales of the colonial period and wound its way to Cooper's Leatherstocking Tales and Mark Twain's stories of life on the Mississippi frontier. In the waning years of the nineteenth century, Wild West Shows, dime novels, and melodramas vied for a share of Americans' disposable income. Yet it wasn't until technology caught up with myth that the Western genre coalesced into a distinct art form, complete with conventional plots, elements, and characters. Six-guns, horses, dusty towns and trails, and of course, cowboys and Indians, are the most prominent icons of the film industry's eulogy to the cowboy era. From silent films of the 1920s and singing cowboys of the 1930s to classic Westerns of the 1950s and beyond, the Western genre has had as much to say about prevailing attitudes toward the past as it has toward the frontier history it portrays.

It is of no small consequence to American culture that the Western exploded across the screen at the same time that culture producers were searching for ways to protect frontier values from the onslaught of modernity. Caring less about historical authenticity than the emotional jolt offered by fast-paced entertainment, audiences were only too happy to contribute their fare share to a film industry poised for unprecedented profits. For their part, film producers knew that audiences were interested not so much in real cowboys as they were in mythic heroes who could be counted on to save the town before riding into the sunset. Run-of-the-mill herdsmen along the lines of Andy Adams, Teddy Blue Abbott and Charlie Siringo who actually knew something about cattle need not apply. For audiences and culture producers alike, the myth made the movie, and the movie represented traditions forged in the nexus of postfrontier anxiety. With more money than peace of mind, audiences lined up at the ticket office to indulge their nostalgia for a bygone era that was fertile ground for entertainment as well as a source of moral rejuvenation.

Like listeners in another age enthralled by tales of Odysseus and Achilles, audiences came to feel the power of the gods as they experienced the ritualistic reenactment of the Western's classic themes: the triumph of good over evil, civilization over savagery, Christianity over paganism. Through the Western genre, we learn that our mythical hero is a superb horseman, lightening-quick on the draw, a dead aim with a Winchester, a champion of justice, a defender of virtuous women, implacable foe of the Indian, and brave in the face of danger. The Western blends symbolic, psychological, and moral elements that reduce audiences to a hypnotic state where familiar themes play out *ad infinitum* (Schein 1955). Thus the genre provides not so much an escape from reality as a bewitching strength that manifests itself in the magic of repetition. "The desire to deify the cowboy seems to infect even the most normally disenchanted observer," concluded Frantz and Choate (1955: 82). "But there is no denying that the cowboy myth does exist, that it is fundamental to an understanding of the cultural content of American life, nor that it is real." Using language reminiscent of Turner's (1977) frontier thesis, Fishwick (1952) suggested that the cowboy became a psychological safety valve for a culture whose yearning for freedom, individuality, and closeness to nature has been thwarted by mechanization and urbanization. Kuenz (2001) agreed, asserting that the Western's appeal lies in the hero's repudiation of Eastern forms of accumulation and productivity. It was a place Frederic Remington found not yet "cluttered up with office buildings" (White 1968: 59), and it served as a magnet, both literally and imaginatively, for people fed up with the alienating and exploitative working conditions shaping up back East.

In his study of Owen Wister, Boatright (1951) ascribed the cowboy's popularity to his prowess and cleverness, the latter encompassing his defense of the weak against the strong and the practical against the ideal. At a time when social Darwinism was fostering a contempt for the masses and legitimizing natural selection, it is perhaps not surprising to find in Wister's fiction an element of manifest destiny—a suggestion that God-fearing Anglo-Saxons were destined to rule the land. As we have seen (Slotkin 1981), Wister's sentiments were echoed in the life and writings of his contemporary, Theodore Roosevelt, whose multi-volume *Winning of the West*, informed by his experiences on the North Dakota range and suffused with racist undertones, did so much to color our collective memory of the cowboy era and shape the contours of our mythology.

Davis (1954) revisited America's connection to cowboy mythology through literature, music, art, and film. Recognizing that the harsh realities of range life bore little resemblance to the sanitized heroism popularized in film and literature, Davis suggested that a yearning for the cowboy's authenticity lives on in popular culture. "Despite the incongruities," wrote Davis,

> "the cowboy myth exists in fact, and as such is probably a more influential social force than the actual cowboy ever was. It provides the framework for an expression of common ideals of morality and behavior. And while a commercial success, the hero cowboy must satisfy some basic want in American culture, or there could never be such a tremendous market" (p. 112).

Lumberjacks, whale fishermen, railroad builders, and fur traders certainly left rich legacies, but none approach the cowboy as a source of mythology. Little boys rarely dress up like Paul Bunyan, and harpooners don't watch us eat breakfast from the backs of cereal boxes. The cowboy represents a synthesis of two American traditions that were fused in the 1890s: on the one hand, he stands in a direct line of descent from the Western scout immortalized in Cooper and the dime novel; and on the other, he symbolizes the golden myth of the antebellum South. Somewhere on the Great Plains, the traditions coalesced when Daniel Boone's progeny came face-to-face with the drawling Texas cowboy.

And what, exactly, are the qualities that have endeared this character type to posterity? Certainly, the cowboy's carefree lifestyle appeals to generations clamoring to escape the iron cage of modernity. Then, too, there is the cowboy's commitment to justice and honesty, twin pillars of a code that is perhaps best understood as a Western and democratic version of the Southern gentleman's "honor." As a timeless embodiment of freedom, the cowboy represents a natural reaction to civilization that demands increasingly monotonous work and, on a psychological level, an adolescent forever staving off the responsibilities of adulthood. Given the dearth of women on the trails and in Kansas cowtowns, the cowboy learned to get along just fine without feminine refinements, and sexual encounters were intermittent and unlikely to lead to the kind of settled lifestyle that would have doomed his way of life. His tenderness was reserved for his horse, his religion was best found under a canopy of stars, and his modes of relaxation remain the stuff of legend. "Above all," concluded Davis (1954: 124), "the cowboy is a 'good joe.' He personifies a code of personal dignity, personal liberty, and personal honesty."

Elkin (1950) approached the cowboy myth as a component of our national memory whose longevity is due in no small measure to the psychological appeal of the Hollywood

Western. Two characteristics common to Western films at mid-century were action and simplicity. Daring rescues, rearing horses, and fist fights kept audiences on the edge of their seats even though the story's outcome was never in doubt: the good guy, suffused with Christian values, invariably emerged as the hero. Other values that brought audiences back for more included rugged individualism and a brand of frontier folk equality suggesting that problems have less to do with social and economic issues than with the machinations of evil men. The fairy tale values embodied in early Western films have their antecedents in Bible stories as well as Greek and Teutonic legends. Yet instead of daring explorers and sailors plying unknown seas, the West produced the cowboy astride his horse, packing a six-shooter for all the world to see and itching for a show-down with some ne'er-do-well cattle rustler or train robber. Such continuity down through the centuries points to a human yearning for quick and decisive resolution to life's quandaries and a sense that justice will prevail and balance will be restored, no matter the odds or degree of hardship.

Western heroes in the old movie tradition shared basic Anglo-Saxon qualities. They were neat in appearance and never lost their tempers; they refrained from smoking, drinking and gambling; they were not prone to emotional expressiveness; and when it came down to a fight, they fought fairly. A subsequent generation of heroes, including Roy Rogers and Gene Autry, sported theatrical clothes and were inclined to smile and even sing when the occasion called for it. These two hero types were, of course, complemented by feminine counterparts. Early on, film makers introduced the gentle girl, steeped in traditional values, who accepted without question her role as a ranch housekeeper. Subsequent Western heroines were more independent. They were likely to hold down jobs, laugh at ribald jokes, and participate in activities that had once been reserved for men. Like the social milieu in which they were produced, Westerns reflected a society still enamored with old-fashioned values but, at the same time, increasingly tolerant of women who had the spunk to succeed in a man's world.

The appeal of the Hollywood Western, suffused with folklore far beyond the ken of most audiences, is sometimes explained in terms of psychology. It seems plausible to suggest that children have always been more susceptible to the Western allure than adults. Reared in a complex and confusing society, children naturally gravitate toward a world that is simple, clear-cut, and well ordered. Not only does identification with cowboy heroes alleviate children's sense of insecurity; it also provides them with an outlet for aggression and creative energy and satisfies their yearning to escape from enclosures forced upon them by an unforgiving world. Like the cowboy on the silver screen, the child has the freedom "to roam amidst the wide open spaces of the west, to choose his own direction and his own course of action" (Elkin 1950: 81).

Arguably, as we put away childish things and accept the responsibilities of adulthood, the voices of our inner child are never entirely stilled. Perhaps some of us weaned on the Western motif retain a longing for cowboy ways—for an age steeped in myth, its harsh realities softened by the patina of time, when adventure lurked around the next mountain pass and gunslingers dispensed justice from the business end of a Colt 44. As is the case with all media consumed during childhood, determining the lasting effects of Westerns on their audiences is fraught with difficulty. It is entirely possible that the Western's impact depends more on the characteristics of viewers than on the film itself. Moreover, one cannot escape the confounding effects of families, schools, neighborhoods, gangs, churches, and other media that compete at an ever-accelerating pace for our attention. Nevertheless, given its resilience in American culture and its popularity throughout the world, the Western clearly speaks to some deep longing in the human psyche that transcends age and a host of socially constructed boundaries.

INVENTING TRADITION

Then again, it is entirely possible that the cravings of our inner child tell only part of the story. In his inquiry into the Western's sociological symbolism, Nussbaum (1960 – 61) treated what he called the "adult western" as a folk art form expressing the emotions, fears, inadequacies, and psychoses of modern man. Like Elizabethan drama, Greek sculpture, Arthurian tales, and classical ballet, the Western arose in response to cultural questions that demanded resolution and perhaps even catharsis. Seen as an expression of a culture plunging headlong into modernity, the Western provided recurring themes that seemed to satisfy all segments of society. First and foremost was the spirit of adventure in new and exciting places that gave audiences the vicarious thrill of escaping their everyday lives of routine and predictability. Second, the excitement was mediated by a hero unique to the American landscape: the cowboy who, like the knight-errant of medieval legend, upheld the principles of law and order, remained cool and calm in the face of danger, and was reconciled to life's vicissitudes. The Western was also shaped by the protagonist's independence and uncomplicated contact with his magnificent environment. "He is a drifter," wrote Nussbaum,

> "a vanishing symbol of individualism in an age of togetherness and conformity. For the westerner can do what we can't, when the pressures and monotony of life become depressing and wearisome, he can 'saddle-up' and vanish into the setting sun. For us, who lead lives of stifled routine, identification with the westerner, via television, affords us a temporary escape" (p. 26).

Another recurring theme was the distinction between good and evil. In a world bedeviled by shades of gray, the Western posits a time and place where problems are reduced to their bare essentials and justice is meted out quickly and fairly. This brings us to what is perhaps the most compelling feature of the adult western: the hero's use of the gun. Without his gun belt, the western hero looks incomplete. What more degrading spectacle does the Western film offer than the protagonist caught by surprise and forced to surrender his firearms? But with his six-shooter strapped to his side, the cowboy stands before us as a complete man—uninhibited, decisive, fearless, and noble, ready to defend himself and dispatch his enemies calmly and without remorse. In an age when rationalism and reason may well be approaching their limits, as we find ourselves ever more confined in a world of machinery and managerial structures, the existentialist cowboy suggests "that there is a limit to reason, that the only way we can resolve our difficulties is by being men of faith, faith in the all-knowing and self-sufficient, earthy, western hero" (p. 28).

The literature reviewed thus far reveals two distinct approaches to explaining the cowboy's enduring appeal. Davis (1954) represented what amounts to a functional perspective. Borrowing analytical tools from Marx and Freud, he claimed that Westerns fulfill social needs insofar as they provide an outlet for psychic tensions and an escape, however fleeting, from neurosis. Western fans thus find relief from unmet sexual urges, release from repressed hostility, justification for resisting the demands of impending adulthood—in short, just about anything that social structures erect between modern man and satisfaction with his lot. Put simply, narrative patterns expressed in art become an outlet for impulses that are censored by our conscious minds because they are too disturbing for our egos to accept on a conscious level. By contrast, Elkin (1950) and Nussbaum (1960 – 61) provided what amounts to a thematic analysis. Employing the tools of literary analysis, scholars in this camp suggest that we look at the Western as a reflection of America's unique national culture and an expression of unique problems and aspects of the American experience.

For Cawelti (1971), both the functional and thematic approaches to the Western genre fail to explain its resonance across generations and, indeed, throughout the world. In his view, functionalism is too limiting because it compels us to focus with laser-like intensity on a single, dominant psychic purpose and ignore all other factors. Similarly, Cawelti rejects thematic analysis on three grounds: (1) it sidesteps the danger of ascribing special importance to one theme at the expense of all others; (2) it tends to distort the totality of the narrative insofar as it draws attention to isolated fragments; and (3) it lures us into equating works of art with real life. Adopting an interdisciplinary interpretation of the Western that embraces psychology, sociology, history, and film criticism, Cawelti sought a fit between artistic elements and psychological needs that allow us to bring psychological and sociological functions into a pattern of needs, interests, and values of the audience. This approach lets us consider works of art as autonomous structures arising from the possibilities inherent in unique kinds of human experience. Their detachment from the drama depicted on the screen or described in literature does not preclude audiences and readers from identifying with images and actions that resonate throughout the culture.

In Cawelti's view, the artistry involved in a single episode of say, *Gunsmoke*, or perhaps the plot of a Zane Grey novel, is far less important than "the cultural significance of the Western as a type of artistic construction" (p. 25). Individual works are ephemeral, but the setting, characters, and patterns of action that constitute the formula have much to tell us about dynamics and changes in the culture that produced it. To avoid meaningless generalities, Cawelti drew a distinction between formula, "a conventional system for structuring cultural products" (p. 29) that includes stereotyped characters, accepted ideas and metaphors; and myth, whose universality and multiple manifestations are ineffective guides to particular cultures and time periods. Oedipus and Narcissus may have a great deal to teach us about the human condition, but to unravel the mysteries of the American character, we need to pay particular attention to formulas that synthesize cultural functions and penetrate the collective consciousness through the miracle of mass media.

Clearly, the archetypal cowboy evokes a sense of nostalgia for a disappearing way of life. On a deeper level, the Western's resilience is best understood as an expression of the genre's three primary cultural dimensions. First, the formula has all the hallmarks of a game structure, complete with opposing players, rules, and a setting whose shape and characteristics point to the significance of particular actions. The goal of the game is to resolve conflicts between, say, the hero's alienation from the advancing tide of civilization and his commitment to townspeople. Although the formula has remained fairly constant, different time periods since the closing of the frontier have called for different plots and resolutions. Second is ritual—that is, the reaffirmation of cultural values, resolution of tensions, and sense of historical continuity afforded by the entertainment industry. "The Western," wrote Cawelti, "with its historical setting, its thematic emphasis on the establishment of law and order, and its resolution of the conflict between civilization and savagery on the frontier, is a kind of foundation ritual" (p. 73). Finally, the Western genre provides an arena for expressing troubling ambiguities in American history and culture. Manifest destiny and its dire consequences for traditional ways of life, America's role as a redeemer nation and the nightmare of nuclear annihilation, and the rhetoric of democracy and the persistence of oppression at home and abroad are just a sampling of conflicts whose resolution seems always to exceed our grasp. The Western has thus responded to our longing for a fictional pattern of legitimate violence carried out by a reluctant hero steeped in the moralistic code of the West. Its capacity to accommodate different kinds of meaning, and its flexibility in responding to changing cultural themes and concerns, "have made the formula successful as popular art and entertainment over many years" (p. 85).

Wright (1977) provided what may be the most systematic analysis of Western films. The author began his study by citing anecdotal evidence of the popularity of the Western motif, ranging from literature, advertising, and theme parks to film and apparel. Ubiquitous though it may be in the popular culture, the Western genre has attracted little attention from academics. Rejecting the stereotype of the Western as a barren wasteland, Wright conducted a content analysis of top-grossing Western films produced between the 1930s and the early 1970s. His analysis revealed four historical periods that correspond with variations on the Western theme: 1930 to 1955 and the classical plot, featuring lone gunfighters bent on saving farmers or townspeople from the machinations of evil men; the 1950s to 1960 and the vengeance variation, in which an ill-used hero, unable to find justice, seeks revenge as a gunfighter; the early 1950s and the transition theme, in which a hero and perhaps a heroine defend justice only to find themselves rejected by society; and 1958 to the early 1970s and the professional plot, where heroes join somebody's payroll as professional gunfighters interested solely in making money. Wright's thesis is that, within each period, the structure of the myth corresponds to the conceptual needs of social and self-understanding required by dominant social institutions and that historical changes in the structure of the myth correspond to changes in the structure of those dominant institutions.

Wright's analysis provides an alternative to theories that address the Western's resilience in terms of satisfying social and psychological needs. For Wright, each of these approaches to myth is based on assumptions that limit their ability to grasp the Western as an experience; that is, they assume that myth reflects a shared concern with a specific conflict in attitudes or desires and that failure to resolve conflicts leads to tension and emotional disturbance. Borrowing from such diverse fields as anthropology, philosophy and literary criticism, Wright suggested that we look at cultural forms, attitudes, and conflicts as problems in communication rather than as consequences of specific and assumed tensions. "The central concern of social man," asserted Wright, "is seen to be the establishment of meanings and the communication of these meanings" (p. 10). The bottom line is that people *do* establish symbolic meanings and they *do* communicate. The key, then, is to make symbolic sense of ordinary experience. Interpreting myths in terms of social or psychological tensions might confirm the existence of those tensions, but it falls short of explaining the social meanings of myth. Wright's interest was in cognitive rather than affective psychology. Rather than focusing on how we inherit, express, and resolve emotional disorders, Wright sought to explain how we understand, organize, and communicate our experiences.

> "Like language, myth exhibits an unconscious, formal structure through which its elements have meaning; whereas the elements of language–words–analyze human experience, the elements of myth synthesize experience. Words classify and separate, images and stories interrelate and unify. For this reason, myth–together with ritual, art, kinship, and politics–can be seen as a necessary symbolic strategy to reintegrate the experience that language makes detached and problematic. Through their stories and characters, and their unconscious, structural significance, myths organize and model experience" (p. 12).

Wright's seminal study of Western movies has much to teach us about the structure of myth and its applicability to real experiences. Yet his analysis falls short of explaining the active role that audiences play in decoding mediated messages and constructing meaning. Shively (1992) redressed this imbalance in her exploration of the meaning that audiences impute to cultural works. She, too, set her sites on Western films, a genre that has been shown to provide audiences with a vehicle for escape and fantasy and, insofar as it taps into mythic structures, provides viewers ensnared in capitalism with a guide for navigating the shoals of an unforgiving economic system. Using this framework, Shively chose a sample of Anglos and Indians and examined the ways in which they appropriated and found meaning in the Western genre.

Armed with the assumption that people's understanding of movies is based on their cultural backgrounds, Shively asked matched samples of twenty Indian males and twenty Anglo males living on a reservation in the Great Plains to respond to *The Searchers*, a Western film featuring John Wayne. Surprisingly, Indians and Anglos experienced the film in much the same way. They generally liked the Western genre and agreed that Hollywood should produce more of them. Differences between the groups showed up in the ways they interpreted and valued characteristics of the film once they immersed themselves in the narrative. Indians tended to hone in on the cowboy's freedom and independence and were particularly taken by the majestic scenery. Anglos, too, appreciated the setting. Yet they believed that the film accurately portrayed America's pioneer heritage, whereas their Native American counterparts were reluctant to accept celluloid Indians as authentic depictions of their ancestors. Moreover, Indians were more likely to appreciate humor than Anglos, whose fixation on historical authenticity precluded an appreciation of comedic scenes. "Thus," concluded Shively, "for Anglos, the Western resembles a primitive myth. But it is not a myth in this sense for Indians—Indians do not view the Western as authentic" (p. 733).

As is the case in so many classic Westerns, *The Searchers* embodies messages that lie at the heart of the cowboy mystique. Yet those messages are far from uniform, and their effects are by no means immediate and direct. It is up to audiences to use their experiences and cultural backgrounds to filter media messages as a first step toward arriving at a meaningful experience. In the context of Shively's study, Indians and Anglos were not passive recipients of whatever Hollywood was dishing out. Rather, they constituted culturally distinct audiences and, as such, were active participants in the construction of meaning.

Old Worn Out Saddles and Old Worn Out Memories: Cowboys in Collective Memory

Oklahoma historian Edward Everett Dale (1965: 250) combined his own experience as an accomplished cowhand with his skills as a researcher and storyteller to reflect on the emergence of what he called Cow Country psychology, which amounts to "the development of a state of mind or cultural heritage which has persisted long after the conditions and the life which produced it have passed away." He characterized the range rider as a type whose attributes, forged by months of solitude in remote line camps and endless hours of eating dust on the trail, included initiative, courage, resourcefulness, loyalty, and a sense of humor. In essence, he was a man of action, but long, lonely hours spent in the saddle gave him plenty of time for reflection. Sooner or later he developed an attitude toward life that put a premium on prompt and decisive action, a disdain for pomp and ceremony, and an upbeat spirit that was often the only defense against sleet, snow, droughts, floods, and all the other challenges that simply went with the territory. "All these characteristics of the range riders," wrote Dale,

> "when taken in the aggregate eventually served to give to the regional society which they formed a certain intangible quality that might be designated as the Spirit of the Cow Country...Moreover, as the range cattle industry declined and many men formerly engaged in it scattered throughout the country to enter new vocations, they carried this spirit with them wherever they went. Its influence upon others must not be overemphasized but they could hardly fail to pass it on in some degree to their children as well as to spread its ideals among their neighbors and associates as a leaven which in time came to affect the points of view and attitudes of people in every walk of life" (pp. 253-54).

As the dust slowly settled on the cattle trails that snaked across the Great Plains, the cowboy was already on his way to becoming a sociological type that has provided fodder for historians and social scientists ever since. Yet cowboy ways—a collage of characteristics ranging from workaday skills to cultural attributes peculiar to his nomadic existence—exhibit a duality that transcends the American experience. Even though the tools of the cowboy's trade were simple, they were instrumental in taming the frontier, and they draw attention to America's predilection for progress. Yet progress, either as an expression of optimism or an historical guidepost into remembered time, tells only part of the story. An equally vital dimension of American culture is nostalgia, "a deep-seated, heartfelt, romantic longing for the yesterday that is gone but is never to be forgotten" (Dudden 1961: 516). In a sort of psychological balancing act, Americans over the centuries have charged Hell-bent-for-leather toward an elusive utopia that seems always to recede over the horizon and, simultaneously, yearned for some golden age that exists more in the imagination than in the historical record. It is no coincidence that, as railroads and telegraphs spread their tentacles across the continent and factories dotted a once-pristine landscape, the cowboy emerged as a symbol of all that was right about America. He also came to represent everything that was threatened with extinction in a culture mesmerized by visions of progress. Generations of moviegoers thus gravitated toward Westerns as nostalgic phenomena of everyday dimensions. "In these modern morality plays," wrote Dudden,

> "where heroic good is stalked unsuccessfully by cowardly evil across an unbelievably primitive landscape, even the simplest-minded onlooker can grasp the message. Human problems are capable of attaining just solutions, or at least they were once upon a time in the good old days when men were men and women were glad of it" (p. 528).

If media have been a port of entry for Western themes to infiltrate culture, then collective memory is their natural repository. Until about 1980, the social dimensions of memory were fair game for sociologists, historians, literary critics, anthropologists, and other academics interested in practices of commemoration. Lacking a firm foundation in theory and methodology, social memory research was, at best, a centerless enterprise. To bring coherence to this disparate field, Olick and Robbins (1998) identified scholarly threads that constitute the fabric of social memory studies. As is so often the case, all roads lead to Durkheim and his focus on rituals and symbols as sources of social bonding and historical continuity. In terms of collective memory, however, there was a detour through his celebrated student and collaborator, Maurice Halbwachs, who placed memory at the center of his work during the interval between the two world wars. For him, "studying memory was not a matter of reflecting philosophically on inherent properties of the subjective mind; memory is a matter of how minds work together in society, how their operations are not simply mediated but are structured by social arrangements" (p. 109). In a direct challenge to psychology, Halbwachs (1992) suggested that an individual's memory cannot be disentangled from its group context. Individuals remember by placing themselves in the perspective of their group, but the memory of the group realizes and manifests itself in individual memories. Moreover, there is a difference between history and memory. Whereas the former aims to reveal truth, the latter is drastically selective insofar as it relies on recollections of events that we ourselves experience rather than abstractions reflected in historical records. The meaning embedded in memory, therefore, casts doubt on history's epistemological claims. We are left with a notion of collective memory, not necessarily as an alternative to history or historical memory, but rather as a rubric to conceptualize the myriad ways that we are shaped by external stimuli and interpersonal communication.

Collective memory has been highly susceptible to the juggernaut of technology. As orality practiced in primitive cultures gave way to literacy, societies inherited a heightened capacity for abstract thinking, and memory was transformed from a private to a public affair (Ong 1988). With the onset of modernity, new technologies such as film have been incorporated into the accepted cultural construct of memory and have changed not only the way we remember, but have also given us new ways to conceptualize memory (Olick and Robbins 1998; Olick 1999). Lipsitz (1990) went a step further to assert that electronic media have created a crisis for collective memory insofar as they legitimate exploitative social hierarchies, colonize the body as a site of capital accumulation, and foster consumerism, thus threatening subcultures that rely on shared constructions of the past to shape their identities. Lipsitz claimed that his book was neither a celebration of nor a jeremiad against popular culture. Yet Collins (1991) recognized the author's antipathy toward mass media and suggested that Lipsitz's book is both a condemnation of mass culture and a celebration of folk cultures. Whatever one's stance vis a vis technology, it seems clear that media have altered the ways that cultures construct meaning. Sociologically speaking, media have become key variables in the relationship between cultural traditions rooted in the past and the formation of identity in the present. "Rather than signaling the death knell for historical inquiry, electronic mass media make collective memory a crucial constituent of individual and group identity in the modern world" (Lipsitz 1990: viii).

New technologies notwithstanding, membership in a human community requires us to situate ourselves in an historical context. Hobsbawm (1972) reflected this sociohistorical perspective in his characterization of the past as "a permanent dimension of the human consciousness, an inevitable component of the institutions, values and other patterns of society" (p. 3). Yet situating oneself in the flow of history does not imply immobility. Progress, even within traditional societies, constantly pulls us from the comfort of tradition into untested waters. Bewildered by changes we can neither control nor understand, many of us yearn for a restoration of old law, morality, religion, and whatever else has been lost along the march of civilization. In some instances, restoration can be literal, as is the case in the preservation of an architectural style. Yet restoration can also be symbolic insofar as it attempts to summon the ethos or mythology of a bygone era. "History," concluded Hobsbawm, "the unity of past, present and future may be something that is universally apprehended, however deficient the human capacity to recall and record it, and some sort of chronology, however unrecognizable or imprecise by our criteria, may be a necessary measure of it" (p. 16).

These days, events unfold at such a rapid clip that our connection to history is under siege. Nora (1989) distinguished between memory, "social and unviolated, exemplified in but also retained as the secret of so-called primitive or archaic societies" (p. 8), and history, which is the way modern societies organize the past. Swept up in a maelstrom of accelerating change, we have come to rely on *lieux de mémoire*, or sites of memory, to provide an anchor to a past that is increasingly dissociated from lived experience. Museums, archives, and monuments have become substitutes for the collective consciousness that kept primitive societies in tune with their traditions. Moreover, technology has fostered a world awash in mediated imagery. In contrast to the days when storytellers kept customs alive and socialized children into traditional ways, cultures now rely on retinal and televisual memory. *Lieux de mémoire* leave us with devotional institutions that seem cold and beleaguered. They signify the rituals of a society devoid of ritual and celebrate moments of history detached and subsequently returned to the flow of history. Like shells washed up on the seashore, institutional repositories of memory are neither life nor death, but rather ghostly reminders of what happened before the tide of living memory receded.

Nora's *lieux de mémoire* provide more than focal points for collective memory; they also give us opportunities to indulge in nostalgia. Its etymology reveals that, in the seventeenth century, nostalgia was seen as a pathology with dire consequences for people unable to resist its seductive embrace (Vromen 1993). As the age of Enlightenment approached, the meaning of the word shifted to indicate a manifestation of a desire to return to a specific place. The *anomie* wrought by modernity stripped nostalgia of its geographical specificity and transformed it into a sociological complaint. Dissatisfied with the present, people began to look to the past for models of morality and conduct. Not surprisingly, reliance on history—or, to be more precise, distorted and often idealized interpretations of the past—to alleviate current stress has been analyzed in both positive and negative terms. Raymond Williams (see Vromen 1993) defined nostalgia as a kind of opium of the people insofar as it discourages rational critiques of the present. In their pessimistic and decidedly elitist reflection on modernity, Horkheimer and Adorno (2002) stepped into the realm of nostalgia by contrasting the pre-consumer era, when life and art were supposedly integrated and attuned to one another, with the cultural vacuity fostered by mass society.

Boym (2001) distinguished between restorative and reflective nostalgia. Like Hobsbawm's (1983) notion of invented tradition, restorative nostalgia is fodder for nationalist sentiment; it builds on the loss of community and cohesion and offers a collective script for individual longing (Boym 2001). Insofar as it signifies a "return to the original stasis, to the prelapsarian moment" (p. 49), restorative nostalgia serves as a panacea for temporal distance and displacement. Reflective nostalgia, by contrast, is less oriented toward the national past than individual and cultural memory. It seeks not to recover what is perceived as absolute truth, but rather to meditate on history and the passage of time. Neither form of nostalgia explains the nature of longing or its psychological make-up and unconscious undercurrents. "Rather, they are about the ways in which we make sense of our seemingly ineffable homesickness and how we view our relationship to a collective home" (p. 41). Ultimately, nostalgia mediates between our individual memories and collective memory. Messy and unsystematic though it is, nostalgia opens a window onto cultural myths and forms the glue of common intelligibility.

When nostalgia was diagnosed as a disease in the late seventeenth century, treatments ranged from opium and leeches to trips home. In the postmodern age, technology has become the opiate of the people whose allure lies in speed, ease of use, and oblivion of everything except technology itself. It is perhaps ironic that technology and nostalgia have merged in our wired world to build bridges between times and spaces and form relationships between distance and intimacy. Indeed, to be nostalgic is to gaze through sepia hues, soft and deceptive, at the past. The mimesis underlying cowboy sports certainly comes to mind as we reflect on Boym's understanding of nostalgia and the wild and Western action displayed by the animate trinity.

> "Nostalgia is never literal, but lateral. It looks sideways. It is dangerous to take it at face value. Nostalgic reconstructions are based on mimicry; the past is remade in the image of the present or a desired future, collective designs are made to resemble personal aspirations and vice versa" (p. 354).

Halbwachs' (1992) studies in collective memory led him to suggest that nostalgia is not without its merits. In a Durkheimian sense, it might even serve a function by rendering the present bearable and providing people "with an entirely different vantage point, a privileged position, from which aspects missed in the haste and the intensity of the present may be uncovered" (Vromen 1993: 77). Given their perennial fascination with adolescence, it is not surprising to find Americans waxing nostalgic toward the carefree days of their youth, when adulthood had yet to limit their modes of expression. Strengthened by generational ties and compounded by the effects of mass media, nostalgia has become a special aspect of collective memory. It helps us adjust to fragmented lives, triumph over routinized existence, and retreat, however briefly, from the tensions inherent in the real world.

With due deference to Freud's work on the construction of identity and Halbwachs' insights into memory as a collective enterprise, Klein (2000) credited Nora for his role in bringing memory into the historical discourse. For far too long, specialists with a bias toward written documentation have dealt with such phenomena as oral history, autobiography, and commemorative rituals without connecting them under an all-embracing rubric. All that has changed now that scholars are beginning to employ memory as a metahistorical category that subsumes a variety of cultural expressions. "*Memory* is replacing old favorites—*nature, culture, language*—as the word most commonly paired with history, and that shift is remaking historical imagination" (p. 128). Buoyed by authenticity and even religiosity that are often missing in document-based interpretations of the past, memory invites us to consider the ways that cultural practices emerge from a fusion of subjective experiences and material artifacts. Freed from the shackles of individual psychic states, memory becomes a subject in its own right, and it enables us to roam freely across time and culture. Secure in its embrace, we conjure up distant memories as a prerequisite to revealing group consciousness and its implications for contemporary cultural practices. Klein further suggested that memory might well be the most appropriate discourse for postmodernity insofar as it allows for the kind of fragmentation and transience that characterize our chaotic times. Moreover, given our culture's obsession with therapy and the increasing prominence of identity politics, memory stands the best chance of breathing life into Nora's *lieux de mémoire*. "It is no accident," concluded Klein, "that our sudden fascination with memory goes hand in hand with postmodern reckonings of history as the marching black boot and of historical consciousness as an oppressive fiction. Memory can come to the fore in an age of historiographic crisis precisely because it figures as a therapeutic alternative to historical discourse" (p. 145).

Enmeshed though it is in contemporary historical discourse, collective memory remains mired in ambiguity. To mediate between competing conceptions of collective memory as a prerequisite to reconciliation, Olick (1999) identified two radically different approaches to social memory studies: "one that sees culture as a subjective category of meanings contained in people's minds versus one that sees culture as patterns of publicly available symbols objectified in society" (p. 336). For the most part, political culture theorists have attached themselves to the former interpretation. Relying largely on survey research, they try to discover and then aggregate the hidden sources of social patterns that have taken up residence in people's heads. In recent years, collective memory scholars have broadened their horizons to conceive of culture not simply as an aggregate of subjective memories, but rather "as the symbolic dimension of all social situations" (p. 337). Thus we find ourselves in a seemingly arcane dichotomy between *collected memory*, where individuals do the remembering and psychology supplies the research methodologies; and *collective memory*, where social frameworks provide the setting and context for remembering. Olick's path to clarity lies in jettisoning the term collective memory and replacing it with social memory studies, a rubric that does not cause confusion about its objects of reference, and one that focuses on the social dimensions of remembering. "The real point," concluded Olick, "is to open our thinking about the variety of mnemonic processes, practices, and outcomes and about their interrelations...There is no individual memory without social experience nor is there any collective memory without individuals participating in communal life" (p. 346).

Schuman and Scott's (1989) study of the generational effects of memory suggested a need to distinguish between two meanings of collective memory. In its most general sense, collective memory is the property of large segments of the population. Yet this kind of memory tends to be personal and particular, lacking a sense of grand themes or narratives that transcend individual experiences. An entirely different kind of collective memory emerges when part of a generational cohort agrees on the meaning behind historical events. A clear illustration of this kind of memory is found in the Vietnam generation's recollection of the 1960s as a period of distrust and division. Regardless of its precise manifestation in the population, it seems clear that collective memory cannot escape generational influence. What is less clear are the implications that collective memory has for future behavior.

With specific reference to American history, Thelen (1989) looked into the ways that cultures establish myths and traditions to guide the conduct of their members. People construct memories in response to changing circumstances, and understanding the ways that memories are constructed can illuminate how individuals, ethnic groups, political parties, and even entire cultures shape and reshape their identities. Clearly, storytelling is one means of creating and perpetuating memory over time insofar as storytellers and their audiences become partners in the process. Herein lies a key to the social dimensions of memory: people depend on one another to decide which experiences to remember and how to interpret them, and by identifying, exploring, and agreeing on memories, shared identities are created. The historical study of memory thus becomes an inquiry into the ways that people negotiate their collective identity from smaller pieces plucked from the past, often as a means of recovering feelings and memories that meet current needs. Social history is a promising field for the study of memory precisely because it reveals common patterns in the ways that people construct memories in response to change. "Instead of dismissing the construction of imagined pasts as romantic, escapist, inaccurate, or neurotic," wrote Thelen, "we should try to understand why it is so common" (p. 1125). Drawing on Hobsbawm and Ranger's (1983) pathbreaking work on the invention of traditions, it seems plausible to suggest that cultural entrepreneurs such as Roosevelt, Remington, and Wister succeeded in popularizing their versions of the cowboy era because their publics, beset by turn-of-the-century anxieties, were desperate for new myths and traditions to pave the way to a more coherent future. Myths of America as a new Eden, the yeoman farmer, the machine in the garden, the unresolved conflict between the wild and the tame, and certainly the cowboy's role in identity formation and cultural expression, might well be interpreted as products of the struggle over memory.

Like Olick and Robbins (1998) and Olick (1999), Confino (1997) decried the fragmentation that has plagued memory studies. Beginning with the premise that memory is best understood as a manifestation of culture, Confino suggested that the resurrection of memory as a field of inquiry has produced an embarrassment of riches and a dearth of critical reflection on both theory and method. Part of the problem lies in the fact that representations of the past, whether in museums, films, or commemorations, usually lie outside the symbolic universe available to society. Memory thus finds itself in symbolic isolation, disconnected from everyday life and lacking intermediaries that might bridge the gap between representation and reality. Simply put, memory cannot speak for itself, and it certainly cannot be abandoned to the political realm, where official history devalues collective mentalities that emerge from social practices. Memory is first and foremost a cultural concept; it is bigger than the sum of its parts, and it is "subsumed within a culture that is constituted by common practices and representations" (p. 1399).

In their inquiry into the links between collective memory and cultural identity, Assmann and Czaplicka (1995) came to the conclusion that groups tend to conceive their unity and peculiarity through a common image of the past. They distinguished between two kinds of memory: communicative memory, which emerges from everyday communications and tends to fade over the course of three or four generations; and cultural memory, transcendent, distant from the everyday, and impervious to the passage of time. Drawing on both dimensions of memory, collectivities derive their consciousness of unity and specificity from knowledge steeped in culture that has been objectivized through texts, images, rites, buildings, monuments, cities, and even landscapes. Memory as the contemporized past, culture, and the group thus come together in a seamless web. Societies thus become visible to themselves and to others through their cultural heritage. "Which past becomes evident in that heritage and which values emerge in its identificatory appropriation tells us much about the constitution and tendencies of a society" (p. 133).

In terms of the current investigation, cowboy sports emerge as a dimension of objectivized culture and an ideal intermediary between America's frontier narrative and contemporary social contexts. "The beauty of memory," concluded Confino (1997: 1403) "is that it is imprecise enough to be appropriated by unexpected hands, to connect apparently unrelated topics, to explain anew old problems." Somewhere at the intersection of history and culture, cowboy sports flourish as a product of everyday communication and the deep cultural memory they both reflect and perpetuate. To the extent that they commemorate the frontier, cowboy sports are a treasure trove of rituals and symbols that help competitors make sense of their lives. Although popular culture has thrust up a bevy of alternative means of identity formation and cultural expression, the Western myth, in one incarnation or another, hasn't ceded much territory without a fight.

Their resilience notwithstanding, cowboy ways have certainly receded to what Nora (1974) referred to as *lieux de mémoire*: monuments and museums that glorify the past even as they forfeit their connection to lived experience. The Old West has also retreated to the twilight of nostalgia, where fantasies can be indulged in the privacy of the mind. And yet, even though time has done its part to distance us from our frontier heritage, the Old West remains very much alive as a source of identity formation and a site of cultural expression. For reasons that lie beyond the scope of this investigation, most people attracted to cowboy ways satisfy themselves through entertainment. People who participate in cowboy sports, however, have more at stake than visits to art galleries and high-dollar trips to dude ranches. Ethnographic evidence indicates that Old Dominion cowboys relish the chance to play their part in the animate trinity of human, horse, and cow. For them, the West isn't just a pretty picture or a visit to the high country of the imagination. It's a fast-paced and often dangerous contest to see who's the best at penning, sorting, and cutting cattle.

Beyond the Imagination

Like the aquifers that have transformed much of cow country into lush farmland, the Western myth percolated through America's consciousness and left its indelible stamp on the national character. Its earliest manifestations were evident in colonial times as pioneers sought to reconcile the settled lives they left behind with the savagery that surrounded them. Yet the most resilient dimension of the Western myth is not to be found in the eastern woodlands or mountains of Appalachia, but rather on the great prairies, where Longhorn cattle, mustangs, and young, agricultural laborers coalesced into a culture that was obsolete practically before it began, but that survived as a repository of values that can be summed up simply as *cowboy ways*.

When the great cattle trails closed for good in the late 1880s, some cowboys drifted off to more predictable employment on ranches, while others hung up their spurs altogether. Meanwhile, the values they embodied were appropriated and modified by Roosevelt, Remington, Wister, and like-minded cultural entrepreneurs bent on maintaining a connection with the frontier in a nation hurtling headlong into modernity. Increasingly divorced from the reality of life on the trail, the cowboy type, still embryonic at the turn of the twentieth century, went on to become fodder for an entertainment industry whose depictions of the frontier, usually exaggerated and often fabricated, delighted readers and film goers who were more than happy to empty their wallets if it meant relief from their increasingly regulated lives. "Thus," wrote Lipsitz (1990: 11) in his polemic against popular culture, "commercialized leisure both facilitated the triumphs of industrial capitalism and focused attention on their psychic and emotional costs. Commercial culture sought credibility with its audiences by promising at least the illusion of connection with the past."

It is perhaps significant that the cowboy myth was never encapsulated in a single person; that is, cow country never produced the likes of King Arthur or Roland or, a bit closer to home, Daniel Boone or Paul Bunyan and his faithful ox, Babe. Rather, the myth resided in the cowboy as an ideal type, a composite of characteristics that was flexible enough to evolve with the times, yet specific enough to withstand a century of bewildering change. Whatever its manifestations and the ends to which it leads (and, not incidentally, the mischief that it has fostered)[5] there can be little question that the cowboy myth survived as a repository of entertainment themes and metaphor and continues to occupy a preeminent position in America's collective memory. "Perhaps," wrote Lawrence (1982: 267) in her anthropological study of rodeo, "in an age when personal autonomy is rare, and as the earth becomes increasingly over-civilized, we visualize the cowboy riding over the range in a world uncluttered by the restraints that have tamed and domesticated us."

At the same time, it would disingenuous to suggest that the Western myth has been unaffected by social and cultural change. The same forces that have tamed and domesticated us have compelled us to revisit America's favorite sandbox and search for new ways to shore up our identities and express our cultural longings. For Wright (1982), the demise of the Western was apparent as early as the 1970s, when mass audiences began to gravitate away from frontier imagery because it no longer reflected social conditions. As long as people still believed that individual strength and skill counted for something, Western themes remained unchallenged in their representation of a just and decent social order. All that changed when ghettos went up in flames, Vietnam revealed the limits of American power, and Watergate exposed the seamy underbelly of politics. "The western could not be made relevant, either mythically or historically, to this experience, for its very landscape was too imbued with the promise of success and victory through individual effort" (pp. 122-23). In its stead, audiences were left to choose between space sagas such as *Star Wars* that favored fantasy over history and films of paranoia such as *The Godfather, Jaws, The Marathon Man,* and *Dog Day Afternoon* whose main message was a sense of powerlessness in a world given over to forces and institutions beyond our control. Simply put, the frontier brand of rugged individualism seemed hopelessly out of place, and audiences could no longer relate to cowboy ways. The Western calls on us to believe in ourselves; its successors appeal to frightened and desperate viewers more at ease with technological make-believe than trail-hardened cowboys, and who need a higher power to look after them because they lack the self-confidence to look after themselves.

Thus has the cowboy myth loosened its grip on the cultural imaginary while postmodernity, "volatile, illogical, kaleidoscopic, and hedonistic" (McQuail 2000: 114), has given us new stories to live by. Yet as we have seen, the myth remains alive and well as a source of metaphor, and in spite of competition from new myths fostered by changing social structures, it continues to provide a source of shared meaning. Nowhere is it more tangible than in its power to inspire weekend warriors to load up our horses and travel to the nearest penning, sorting, or cutting competition, where nobody needs a movie screen to remind us who we are and where we come from. Cowboy sports provide compelling evidence that the Western myth has retained an outpost not only in collective memory, but also in social practices, where it is celebrated in the arena, maintained through communication, and mined for its rich store of symbols that still have the power to shape identity and express longings embedded deeply in American culture.

---

[5] In her investigation of the ranching industry, Russell reminded us that the myth has its dark side insofar as contemporary ranchers, steeped in Western lore and tradition, have sometimes been insensitive to environmental concerns such as overgrazing and degradation of rangeland. See Russell 2001.

Chapter Five — From Custom to Ritual: Identity Formation and Cultural Expression through Rodeo and Cowboy Sports

> "I believe I would know an old cowboy in hell with his hide burnt off. It's the way they stand and walk and talk. There are lots of young fellows punching cows today but they never can take our place, because cowpunching as we knew it is a thing of the past. Riding fence and rounding up pastures ain't anything like the way we used to work cattle in the days of the open range."
>
> E. C. "Teddy Blue" Abbott
> *We Pointed Them North:*
> *Reminiscences of a*
> *Cow Puncher (1939)*

The Sociology of Sport

As early as the 1870s, scholars seeking to unravel the intricacies of social organization and relationships began to set their sights on sport and leisure activities. For the most part, they were not so much independent units of analysis as they were components of more holistic research projects, and theories reflected little more than their function, motivation, and content. Common themes included character formation, group solidarity, and the development of fortitude on the playing field. Fostered in the tradition of Judeo-Christian morality, the prevailing attitude visualized sport as a crucible of manly virtues and, not incidentally, a vehicle for military preparedness. Many a prep school student was weaned on the belief that the battle of Waterloo was won on the playing fields of Eton (Edwards 1973).

Victorian-era scholars tended to address sports as a manifestation of *play*, thus revealing a propensity for psychological and philosophical explanations. Spencer (1966: 95-96), concerned with the state's responsibility to educate children, made reference to the dearth of attention paid to physiology, "as is abundantly proved by the ill-health written in so many faces." Borrowing from Schiller's literary imagination, Spencer extended and qualified the concept of play as a consequence of surplus energy that arises when a given species is secure in its environment and is no longer preoccupied with day-to-day survival (Lehman and Witty 1976).[1] In a study ranging from philosophical biology and animal psychology to the genetic study of art, Groos (1898) suggested that play is an instinct whose function is to prepare all sentient creatures for the tasks of later life. Hall (1907: 73) disagreed, asserting that Groos' "partial, superficial, and perverse" conclusions failed to account for the mimetic nature of play activities. Falling back on

---

[1] Both Schiller the poet and Spencer the social scientist recognized similarities between play and art insofar as neither contributes directly to life processes. See Lehman and Witty 1976: 11.

the biological mantra that ontogeny repeats phylogeny, Hall's recapitulation theory emphasized the ways that play facilitates the transmission of heritage from one generation to the next. "In play every mood and movement is instinct with heredity," wrote Hall. "Thus we rehearse the activities of our ancestors, back we know not how far, and repeat their life work in summative and adumbrated ways. It is reminiscent, albeit unconsciously, of our line of descent; and each is the key to the other" (p. 74). Firmly in the classical tradition, Hall lauded the ancients' reverence for the body and its presumed symbiosis with the mind. *Valare est philosophari* (to be well and strong is to be a philosopher) resonated in Victorian sensibilities much as it did among the students at Plato's Academy. Turning to the competitive aspect of play, McDougall (1926) recognized in play a primitive expression of combative instincts, an impulse of rivalry that catapulted Europe, and especially England, to the pinnacle of world power. Stripped of all intellectual complications, the will to conquer is thus a modified form of the combative impulse that seems to underlie playful fighting among young animals. "[I]t constitutes the principal motive to almost all our many games, and it lends its strength to the support of almost every form of activity" (p. 117).

To reflect a more social scientific perspective of collective and goal-oriented pastimes, subsequent scholars subsumed sport and leisure activities under the rubric of *games*. "To them 'game' apparently meant social activity carried out within the context of a network of rules, roles, and relationships and guided by the desire to accomplish a defined goal" (Edwards 1973: 12). According to Simmel (Wolff 1950), the aggregation of isolated individuals into specific forms of interaction constitutes the basis of human societies. Like art, play and the structured activities it fosters emerge from the realities of life to produce autonomous enclaves that become impervious to the very realities that created them. "It is from their origin," wrote Simmel, "which keeps them permeated with life, that they draw their depth and strength. When they are emptied of life, they become artifice and 'empty play,' respectively" (p. 43). The connection between sociability and play had deep implications for the games that were coming into vogue in the late nineteenth century. Even when money was at stake, sportsmen were drawn more to the social dimensions of their leisure-time activities than the prospect of financial gain.

Like Simmel, Weber (Bendix 1977) was interested in the prevalence of games throughout the ages. Imbued with a sense of loyalty to their rulers that transcended contractual obligations, the vassals of Europe and *samurai* of Japan were steeped in the arts of hand-to-hand combat. The kind of mass discipline that produced the Greek phalanxes and Roman legions of Antiquity was of less use to feudal warriors than the skillful handling of weapons. As a result, feudal society incorporated the game as a means of training that inculcated not only life-sustaining skills, but also qualities of character. "The game was not a 'pastime' but the natural medium in which the physical and psychological capacities of the human organism came alive and became supple" (p. 364). Games were thus serious business, and they had an affinity with spontaneous expressions of art insofar as they eschewed utilitarian rationality in favor of the pomp and circumstance that are decisive in the struggle for power. Contemptuous of businesslike approaches to economic matters, the aristocracy of medieval Europe bequeathed to posterity an ideology built on the conventions of chivalry, a pride of status, and a sense of honor. Stripped of bloodlust and territorial aggrandizement, games evolved into self-contained activities that are as important to modern athletes and their fans as they were to the knights of Crécy and Agincourt.

More interested in playgrounds than battlefields, Mead (1934) recognized the significance of games as vehicles of socialization and identity formation. His pioneering work in symbolic interactionism led him to emphasize language in analyzing the social world. Bridging the gap between sociology and psychology, Mead suggested that language provides a symbolic universe that allows us to become self-conscious beings—that is, creatures who become aware of their individuality through interaction with others. Moreover, just as children outgrow simple play activities and adapt themselves to structured games, so do primitive people evolve from a vague relationship with the natural world into complex societies based on rules and regulations that can only be sustained through the medium of language. In both cases, the key variable is the development of a sense of what Mead called "the generalized other": a recognition and internalization of the general values and moral rules of the culture that nurtures us. In the absence of such awareness, people would be hard-pressed to build cooperative enterprises and regulate their own behavior in a social context. As activities with definite goals and a need for relational clarity, games offer an ideal milieu for the development of the generalized other. Mead's conclusions would have a familiar ring to physical education teachers in our own day:

> "The game is then an illustration of the situation out of which an organized personality arises. In so far as the child does take the attitude of the other and allows that attitude of the other to determine the thing he is going to do with reference to a common end, he is becoming an organic member of society. He is taking over the morale of that society and is becoming an essential member of it" (p. 159).

More recent scholarship has probed into the ritualistic and structured dimensions of game activity. Goffman (1959) posited social systems as human creations and people as actors whose identities are formed through interpersonal communication. Like other micro sociologists, Goffman believed that face-to-face interaction through symbols and rituals has more to tell us about social phenomena than the unseen forces underlying structural functionalism. He was more interested in the meanings that people impute to their actions than the functions that their actions fulfill. In short, Goffman was convinced that lived experience rather than sociological abstractions hold the key to understanding.

Goffman is perhaps best remembered for his dramaturgical perspective. Using the stage as a metaphor, Goffman studied people's use of symbols in performing their roles in society. As actors on the stage of life, all of us perform roles according to scripts that lie in wait for us, to be donned like a suit of clothes. As the basic units of socialization, roles are nothing less than virtual selves awaiting realization. Through give and take between people as actors and everyone else that make up the audience, we acquire "tactical repertoires" (Calhoun 2002: 29) that enable us to manage our identities and defend ourselves from excessive scrutiny and criticism. Our performances contribute to the smooth functioning of society in an ongoing process of integration.

No role, of course, is entirely deterministic. No matter what roles we take on, from professional identities to positions in families and communities, our creativity and individuality give us leeway to carve out unique niches and ensure at least a modicum of human agency. At the same time, society sees to it that we play our hour upon the stage within circumscribed parameters that limit our capacity to threaten communal values. Under the rubric of Goffman's dramaturgical perspective, games become situated activity systems, or focused gatherings, that compel participants to obey rules and interact in prescribed ways. "In the end," wrote Goffman, "our conception of our role becomes second nature and an integral part of our personality. We come into the world as individuals, achieve character, and become persons" (p. 52).

As a social psychiatrist, Berne (1964) was also drawn to games as vehicles of socialization and models for adult interaction. He posited intimacy and games as the most gratifying forms of social contact. Yet prolonged intimacy is rare, and even in the best of circumstances, it is primarily a private matter. Games, defined as ongoing series of complementary ulterior transactions that lead to well-defined and predictable outcomes, thus provide the primary matrix for social intercourse. From this perspective, virtually all forms of human interaction can be construed as game situations. Contexts change as we progress from childhood to adulthood and perhaps assume the responsibilities of raising children, and cultural differences remind us that our species is remarkably creative when it comes to building and adapting to social structures that span generations. Nevertheless, somewhere along the continuum between idle pastimes and intimate relationships, games in all their guises constitute our principal means of socialization.

Twentieth-century sociology eventually made room for a third conceptualization of structured leisure-time activities: *sport*. Veblen (1994) warrants attention as the first scholar to use the term extensively in his classic work, *The Theory of the Leisure Class*. First published in 1899, Veblen's critique of Victorian society reflected his era's ambiguity toward games and sports insofar as he failed to distinguish between the two. His assessment was decidedly pessimistic, particularly where impressionable young men are concerned. Anxious to prove their mettle through competition, boys revert to barbarism when they succumb to their fighting impulse. Sports, according the caustic and uncommonly verbose Veblen, are thus the mark of an arrested spiritual development.

> "Sports of all kinds are of the same general character, including prize-fights, bull-fights, athletics, shooting, angling, yachting, and games of skill, even where the element of destructive physical efficiency is not an obtrusive feature. Sports shade off from the basis of hostile combat, through skill, to cunning and chicanery, without its being possible to draw a line at any point. The ground of an addiction to sports is an archaic spiritual constitution—the possession of the predatory emulative propensity in a relatively high potency. A strong proclivity to adventuresome exploit and to the infliction of damage is especially pronounced in those employments which are in colloquial usage specifically called sportsmanship" (p. 255).

Sumner's (1940) *Folkways*, first published in 1906, pushed the envelope a bit further by including an entire chapter on popular sports, exhibitions, and drama. Like Veblen's, Sumner's terminology was unclear and nebulous, and his analysis ranged from Athenian drama and Roman gladiatorial contests to pagan festivals across time and culture. Whatever their origins and degree of brutality, Sumner believed that public amusements, including sports, reflected the prevailing mores of the cultures that produced them and served as a means of socializing children into the values of their society. His assessment of amusements mirrored Veblen's dim view of sporting activities. In reference to the savagery inflicted on man and beast under Rome's imperial mantle, Sumner suggested that "amusements and mores react on each other to produce social degeneration. The whole social standard of 'right' moves down with the moral degeneracy, and at no stage is there a sense of shame or wrongdoing in the public mind in connection with what is customary and traditional at the time" (p. 584).By the mid 1930s, play, games, and sport were deemed sufficiently important to warrant comprehensive analysis. European scholars took the lead in attempting to bring order to the disorganized field of sport sociology (Edwards 1973). Dutch historian Johan Huizinga's *Homo Ludens* (1968), originally published in 1938, explored the role of play in nearly every aspect of culture, from war to religion. The originality of his analysis lies in his conception of play as free activity, occurring within an area designated as sacred and therefore separate from everyday life. Even though Huizinga's work has been consistently cited by subsequent researchers, his suppositions and hypotheses have gone relatively unchallenged. Caillois (1961), a French sociologist, credited Huizinga for the fruitfulness of his research and reflection even as he criticized his shortcomings, particularly his propensity to minimize the diversified forms of play and the needs they serve and his failure to account for games of chance. Caillois' main contribution to sport sociology was to develop a typology of play on the basis of which the characteristic games of a particular culture can be classified and its basic patterns more clearly understood. His typology included four categories of play and games: *agôn* (competition); *alea* (chance); *mimicry* (simulation); and *ilinx* (vertigo). For an activity to fall under Callois' rubric of play, it had to be *free* (not obligatory), *separate* (circumscribed within limits of space and time, defined and fixed in advance), *uncertain* (the course of events cannot be determined, nor the result attained beforehand, and some latitude for innovation is left to the player's initiative), *unproductive* (it creates neither goods, wealth, nor new elements of any kind), *governed by rules* (conventions suspend ordinary laws and momentarily establish new legislation which is determinant) and *make-believe* (accompanied by a special awareness of a second reality or of a free unreality, as opposed to real life).

Its respectable lineage notwithstanding, the institutionalization of sport sociology as a subdiscipline dates back only to the 1960s, when an International Committee for the Sociology of Sport was established in Geneva and Warsaw (Luschen 1980). Drawing on theoretical perspectives and methodological approaches from sport science, psychology, anthropology, political science, philosophy, and social planning, a few hardy sociologists turned their attention to sport as a manifestation of social and political phenomena. Loy and Kenyon's (1969) collection of essays stands out as a seminal attempt to embrace sport as a legitimate object of scholarly attention. Their effort to systematize this disparate field led them to posit two major approaches to sport that were coming to the fore in the 1960s: normative oriented sport sociology, which assumes that certain social goals are implicitly established and that consensus exists as to their nature[2]; and nonnormative sport sociology, a perspective that draws deeply from Western social science insofar as it promotes objectivity (value neutrality) as its mantra. Acknowledging the points of convergence between these two approaches that were bringing scholars under the same tent, Loy and Kenyon concluded their introduction on an optimistic note: "Regardless of their orientation, they meet together, plan cooperative research projects together, and generally agree that the sociology of sport, although in its infancy, shows promise of becoming an established subdiscipline of social science" (p. 11).

Although scholars in the 1960s and 1970s made substantive contributions to the sociology of sport, their body of literature and the number of journals dedicated to their subject remained disappointingly small. Mired in functionalism and conflict theories, researchers neglected relationships between sport and other institutions and were only minimally aware of

---

[2] Scholars who adopted this perspective tended to visualize sport and exercise as vehicles to character formation in the tradition of Judeo-Christian morality, as is reflected in the expression, "The battle of Waterloo was won on the playing fields of Eton." See p. 92 above and Loy and Kenyon 1969: 9.

the epistemological concerns of sociology in general. In essence, the sociology of sport was hamstrung by a dearth of theory and a propensity toward methodological vagueness. Edwards (1973), whose own commitment was to promote sports as a critical dimension of cultural sociology, cited five reasons for the disconnect between sport's privileged status in contemporary culture and its banishment to the periphery of scholarship: (1) the people who are most involved in sports typically lack the training and credentials to conduct social scientific research; (2) sociology's unfortunate standing as a soft science has hindered career-minded researchers from risking their reputations on allegedly frivolous pursuits; (3) sport professionals often resist intrusions from outsiders; (4) organized athletics suffer from the fun-and-games image of sports; and (5) research funds rarely make it into the coffers of sport sociologists.

Birrell (1981) did her part to fill the breach with her suggestion that sport's importance lies in its ritualistic overtones. Combining Durkheim's (1995) observation that art and games originated in religious observations and Goffman's (1959) understanding of social systems as crucibles of identity formation, Birrell claimed that, even though sports have lost the religious fervor that animated our premodern ancestors, they have retained their form and are therefore capable of accepting new meanings fostered in modernity. Seen in this light, sport lends itself to examination from two perspectives: (1) as a social situation that facilitates communication and clarifies role expectations; and (2) as a social ceremony with parallels in religious observances. Either way, Birrell's study supports the notion that sports reaffirm the values of the social order. Moreover, like Weber's (1946) charismatic leaders,[3] athletes raised to celebrity status stand out as mediators between individuals and the social order insofar as they symbolize what Goffman posited as four motifs around which character contests in the United States revolve: courage, gameness, integrity, and composure—all key ingredients on the field of play as well as in the context of daily life (Birrell 1981). In his philosophic inquiry into the perennial allure of sport, Weiss (1969: 153) was unequivocal in his characterization of the athlete's elevated status: "The athlete and those who attend to him are content to accept the fact that he is an unusual man, exhibiting and achieving what most men do not." Sport's affinity with religion was also a central thesis in Edwards' (1973: 90) sociology of sport: "If there is a universal popular religion in America, it is to be found within the institution of sport."

Sport's privileged status in the American mind crystallized between 1880 and 1910, when brutish contests along the lines of boxing, cockfighting, and bullbaiting were eclipsed by organized sports characterized by institutional permanence and autonomy. Buoyed by middle class respectability and promoted by elites interested in fostering habits commensurate with America's burgeoning industrial and military might, sports came to be seen not so much as a way of passing leisure time as solutions to pressing societal concerns. As we have seen, the closing of the frontier in 1890 coincided with social, political, and economic disturbances indicating moral degeneration on an unprecedented level. With an eye on the ameliorative effects of education, traditionalists "thought that, through participation in well-managed sport, students might gain habits of efficiency that were needed for victory in business, politics, and international relations" (Mrozek 1983: xvi). The emergence of a national consciousness after the Civil War, the changing role of women, and a rising disposition in favor of an energetic and dynamic style in all aspects of life were the main contributors to America's love affair with sports. Through the medium of sport, Americans were able to satisfy their quest for greater power over the forces of nature, much as raw ores are converted to steel. The emphasis, of

---

[3] For an account of Weber's theory of charismatic leadership, see Gerth and Mills 1946: 245-52.

course, was on team sports such as football and baseball, rather than more individualistic mountain and equestrian sports, insofar as they served as building blocks for organizations and society. Valued as a source of regeneration and a means of connecting ideas and action, sports came to occupy a middle ground between explosive athleticism and the restraints demanded by civilization. As Mrozek concluded,

> "The imagery of sport provided ties of its own between nature and civilization. For example, sport linked man and machine by suggesting parallels in the workings of both. At a time when man's 'feel' of his own society and his relationship to nature on the grand scale had altered, the emergence of sport suggested a reconciliation of man and nature—of man's quality as an animal and his placement in a large natural context, even though it had been modified by the machine. In this respect, the complexity and fluidity of sport resembled the complexity of American attitudes toward nature and represented turn-of-the-century man's hope to have the best of all worlds simultaneously" (p. 234).

In a volume of previously published essays on the sociology of sport, Elias and Dunning (1986) posited the development of athletic contests as part of a civilizing process in which sports were gradually winnowed from their genesis in warfare. The origins of this development can be traced most clearly to medieval England. By the sixteenth century, a social consciousness was coming into focus that was both cause and effect of such factors as state formation, tightening bonds of interdependency between socio economic classes, democratization, and an elaboration and refinement of manners and social standards. "The learning of self-control," wrote Elias, "is a human universal, a common condition of humanity. Without it people as individuals would not become human, as societies would quickly disintegrate" (p. 45). The more people learned to regulate their aggressive and sexual inclinations, the more their sport and leisure activities took on a tone of civility. Foxhunting, for example, lost its focus on killing and eating the prey and evolved into a ritualistic activity in which the thrill of the chase became an end in itself rather than the requisite prelude to bloodshed. Ultimately, the formation of social clubs in England facilitated the organization of sports teams and the codification of rules. Elias and Dunning's work represents a milestone in our understanding of the sociogenesis of sport insofar as it avoids the compartmentalization of work and leisure and breaks through the disciplinary divide that bedevils so much scholarship. By examining sport as a developmental process and treating humans in the round, their synthesis reveals how societies cope with the routinization imposed by the civilizing process.

Like Weiss (1969), Edwards (1973), and Birrell (1981), Frey and Eitzen (1991) adopted a Durkheimian perspective in their characterization of sport as an institution whose appeal most closely approximates that of religion. Across time and culture, structured conflicts in controlled settings have revealed the complexities of social life insofar as they provide an arena for patterned activities, social structures, and relationships between institutions. Such linkages have eluded sociologists biased toward structural functionalism and conflict theory. For Frey and Eitzen, these theoretical constructs come up short insofar as they are too deterministic—that is, they tend to ignore the role of human agency in social change. Moreover, there is little room in functionalism and conflict theory for cultural imperatives, where sport emerges as an expression of culture. As an alternative to the social scientific lenses represented by functional structuralism and conflict theory, Frey and Eitzen suggested that a cultural approach stands the best chance of dismissing sport simply as a reflection of the capitalist mode of production and embracing it as a dimension of cultural life. Seen in the context of cultural studies, people are not simply passive responders to the exigencies of socioeconomic systems; rather, they are arbiters of their destinies whose creative energies make sport into an activity commensurate with their interests and needs.

Culture in Action

To approach rodeo and cowboy sports as manifestations of culture, we need to recognize the shortcomings of competing theoretical constructs and proceed to tackle such thorny issues as structure, agency, and action. Since the publication of Max Weber's *The Protestant Ethic and the Spirit of Capitalism* (Kalberg 2002), cultural sociology has wrestled with the connection between culture and action. In terms of Weber's seminal study, capitalistic economic behavior that enveloped the West in the sixteenth and seventeenth centuries was presumed to grow out of Calvinist doctrine founded on rationalism and asceticism. Yet if ideas shape ethos, then why did the ethos of ascetic Protestantism outlive its ideas? The resilience of his sociology notwithstanding, Weber failed to provide compelling evidence that culture affects action through values that direct it toward some ends at the expense of others, or, to put it more simply, that culture shapes action by defining what people want. Nor did his disciple, Talcott Parsons, make much headway in his application of Weberian principles to the problem of human action. Dissatisfaction with Parsonian orthodoxy mounted in the 1960s as libertarian social movements and protests undermined the analytic subordination of actors to an environment of functional requirements and highlighted the role of human agency in social life. Since then, social science methodologies positing social actors as passive bearers of sociological and psychological attributes have given way to an emphasis on "the cognitive bases of action and a focus on the situation of action as a means of resolving previously intractable research dilemmas" (Heritage 1984: 2).

Applied to contemporary social problems, functionalist reasoning has produced misleading and, in terms of policy making, dangerous assumptions about culture's role in shaping action. Witness the culture of poverty thesis, an increasingly discredited shibboleth based on the notion that people remain mired in poverty because their values prevent them from choosing middle class avenues to success. Such simplistic reasoning ignores the obvious: to pursue some version of the American Dream, one needs an image of the kind of world that lies in wait, a sense that one can determine his or her degree of success, and an ability to choose among alternative courses of action—in short, a sense of ease with social and economic reality. "Action is not determined by one's values," concluded Swidler (1986: 275) in her seminal critique of cultural sociology. "Rather action *and* values are organized to take advantage of cultural competences." The key variable is not the ends of action, but rather the way that action is organized.

For Swidler (1986), a more plausible link between culture and action emerges when we see culture not so much as the entire way of life of a people (Geertz 1973), but rather as a force that shapes the capacities from which strategies of action are constructed. Using a metaphor that has gained currency in recent years, Swidler (1986) posited culture as a tool kit of habits, skills, and styles that people use to devise strategies for action that incorporate, and in turn depend upon, habits, moods, sensibilities, and views of the world. Culture, then, is a repertoire brimming with items that actors can pick and choose according to their perceived needs. Thus,

"People do not build lines of action from scratch, choosing actions one at a time as efficient means to given ends. Instead, they construct chains of action beginning with at least some pre-fabricated links. Culture influences action through the shape and organization of those links, not by determining the ends to which they are put" (p. 277).

Swidler went on to suggest that culture's influence on social action depends on historical circumstances, and specifically, a society's degree of settlement. As the designation suggests, settled cultures are characterized by organizational structures imbued with relatively unquestioned authority of habit, normality, and common sense. "Although internally diverse and often contradictory, they provide the ritual traditions that regulate ordinary patterns of authority and cooperation, and they so define common sense that alternative ways of organizing action seem unimaginable, or at least implausible" (p. 284). Unsettled cultures, by contrast, are beset by social transformations that force people to adopt new cultural models and reorganize their collective lives. "Culture has independent causal influence in unsettled cultural periods because it makes possible new strategies of action—constructing entities that can act (selves, families, corporations), shaping the styles and skills with which they act, and modeling forms of authority and cooperation" (p. 280).

Postmodern theory suggests that we live in decidedly unsettled times. In the welter of confusion that defines postmodernity, a case can be made for adopting Swidler's perspective and focusing less on cultures as unified wholes than on "chunks of culture, each with its own history" (p. 283). Seen in this light, rodeo and cowboy sports provide a cultural tool kit loaded with symbols and rituals tailor-made for constructing a collective identity. Armed with skills forged on the cattle frontier in the late nineteenth century, sport enthusiasts have appropriated cultural capacities created in one historical context, internalized the invented traditions that they spawned, and honed them to fit entirely new circumstances far removed from their place of origin, where they occupy what one scholar has referred to as "that country that might be called our unofficial fifty-first state: the Western State of Mind" (West 1997: 131). Cultural symbols derived from the frontier are thus best understood in terms of the values that they reflect and the strategies of action that they sustain. In terms of this investigation, those values and strategies of action are evident in penning, sorting, and cutting cattle. As Swidler (1986: 284) concluded,

"Strategies of action are cultural products; the symbolic experiences, mythic lore, and ritual practices of a group or society create moods and motivations, ways of organizing experience and evaluating reality, modes of regulating conduct, and ways of forming social bonds, which provide resources for constructing strategies of action. When we notice cultural differences we recognize that people do not all go about their business in the same ways; how they approach life is shaped by their culture."

If culture as a causal variable has muddied our thinking about prerequisites for action, then so, too, has the relationship between social structure, agency, and culture produced what Hays (1994: 58) decried as "a quagmire of conceptual confusions." Typically, social structure is associated with constraining systems; agency conjures up vague notions of freedom and randomness; and culture, agency's "weak-kneed cousin" (p. 58), is treated as a free-floating sphere of tradition, impervious to rigorous analysis. Much of the blame for this conceptual ambiguity lies in America's simultaneous and perhaps irreconcilable commitment to individual freedom and its antithesis, social order. We celebrate the free-ranging cowboy even as we seek patterns and generalizations to assure us that the universe is a coherent place after all.

To untangle these confusions, Hays claimed that social structure and agency might not be diametrically opposed after all. For her, social structures are not necessarily rigid and determinant, and agency doesn't always imply pure will or absolute freedom. Social structures "are simultaneously constraining and enabling," and even though they preclude the possibility of making certain choices, "they also provide the basis of human thought and action, and therefore offer the very possibility of human choice" (p. 65). A less polarized perspective of structure and agency opens new possibilities for tackling the sticky problem of culture, which is a subjective, endlessly malleable, and decidedly anti-materialistic rubric that, like a Seurat painting, loses its meaning when examined too closely. Conceiving of culture as a social structure with an underlying logic of its own, Hays argued that social structure consists of two essential and interconnected elements: (1) systems of social relations and (2) systems of meaning. "If one wants to understand the resilient patterns that shape the behavior of any individual or group of individuals, *both* the cultural and the relational milieu must be taken into account" (p. 66).

The bottom line is that culture—subjective, private, non-material, abstract, and inaccessible—is not reducible to mere thought. It is not arbitrary, it is remarkably resilient, and it is perpetuated through social relationships as well as individual, subjective experience. It is a short step from recognizing culture as social structure to realizing that agency is not so much a threat to relationships and meaning systems as it is a factor in reproducing social structures. Changing jobs, adopting new patterns of speech, and forming a trade union are certainly reflective of agency, but none of these bursts of individual freedom are likely to alter the underlying form of either culture or social relations.

> "Culture is, in fact, both external and internal, objective and subjective, material and ideal. Not reducible to systems of social relations, culture has a logic of its own. Transcending individuals, constraining and enabling, produced in interaction and producing the form of interaction, culture is a resilient pattern that provides for the continuity of social life. A focus on culture, then, is no more voluntaristic than a focus on the mode of production. Culture is a social structure. Like systems of domination, it confronts us ready-made" (p. 70).

Swidler's (1986) theory of culture in action, together with Hays' (1994) conception of culture as social structure that is simultaneously constraining and enabling, provide the most appropriate lens for developing a sociology of cowboy sports. Both cowboy sports and their close cousin, rodeo, draw on competencies forged in a time and place where fact blurs with fiction to produce a reservoir of symbolic meaning that is reflected both in the heart-stopping action unfolding in the arena and the values that sustain cowboy culture. To borrow from Swidler's (1986: 277) lexicon, these sports are "pre-fabricated links," available to Old Dominion cowboys as they construct their "chains," or strategies, of action. In response to her challenge, the current investigation seeks not to estimate how much culture shapes action, but rather, to determine how culture is used by actors—in this case, Old Dominion cowboys—the extent to which cultural elements constrain or facilitate patterns of action, which aspects of cultural heritage affect action, and what specific historical changes undermine the vitality of some cultural patterns and promote others.

At the same time, we need to be aware that cowboy culture as it is reflected in rodeo and cowboy sports constitutes a social structure built on the twin pillars of social relations and meaning systems. As Hays (1994) insisted, it doesn't do much good to wallow in dichotomies between scientific rationalism and fuzzy-headed theorizing that have done little to advance our understanding of either social structure or culture. Rather, we need to realize that all social life is fundamentally structured, and that social structures facilitate the choices we make in everyday life. In the absence of rules to regulate competition, organizational structure to systematize relationships, and arenas to constrain movements, Old Dominion cowboys would be hard-pressed to the exercise the freedom and independence, or agency, which they lack in their day-to-day lives but that constitute the defining features of cowboy culture and, arguably, the *raison d'etre* for cowboy sports.

Rodeo: Cultural Expression through Symbols and Rituals

For the most part, sport sociologists have set their sights on conventional team sports. Yet there is ample room within the rubric of cultural studies to embrace rodeo and cowboy sports as reflections of America's obsession with athletics whose origins lie in the ethos and practices of a premodern era. As we have seen, the pastoral life did not long survive the closing of the cattle trails in the late 1880s. Yet it left its legacy in the tradition of the annual spring round-up, when cowboys fanned out across the range to gather, sort, and brand cattle on behalf of the cattlemen who employed them. From a practical standpoint, there was little alternative to rounding up each man's mobile property and marking them with distinctive brands, a process that signified the "nature-to-culture transformation" (Lawrence 1982: 78) and constituted the Western version of harvest festivals that are no doubt as old as agriculture. Perhaps it was inevitable that cowhands who prided themselves on their skills with livestock would face off to see who could stay on a bucking horse the longest or rope a steer the fastest. Before long, impromptu contests evolved into social events, and the term "rodeo," taken from the Spanish word, *rodear*, meaning "to encircle or surround," became a popular form of entertainment. "After the open range cattle industry gave way to fenced ranching," wrote Lawrence, "the cowboy skills of the roundup came to be practiced—and exhibited—for their own sake" (p. 80).

Competitions were common from the 1870s on, so much so that it is difficult to determine a date for the first rodeo. Precedent-setting honors have been claimed by Deer Trail, Colorado (1869) and Cheyenne, Wyoming (1872) (Lawrence 1982). Buffalo Bill's Old Glory Blowout near North Platte, Nebraska, on July 4, 1882, was certainly a milestone in the evolution of rodeo (Boatright 1964; Slatta 1994). In subsequent years, community leaders exploited Americans' fascination with a vanishing way of life by offering prizes and charging admission at cowboy competitions. Such was the case on July 4, 1883, when ranch hands in the vicinity of Pecos, Texas, had an opportunity to settle a dispute about which outfit had the best ropers.[4] News of the impending showdown spread quickly, and the small West Texas town soon found itself under siege from curious onlookers.

---

[4] *Outfit* is a generic term that cowboys use to describe everything from tack and equipment to the ranches that employ them.

"Cash prizes were posted, and the leading ropers from each ranch were selected. Morgan Livingston of the NA ranch took first money, and Trav Windham second. There was a barbecue, and the town was crowded with people. Business was booming, especially around the saloons" (Boatright 1964: 197).

Slatta (1994) cited a Grand Cowboy Tournament held in Caldwell, Kansas, in May, 1885 as a prototype of the rodeo form. Westermeier (1987) credited Prescott, Arizona, with the oldest continuous annual rodeo performance on record, beginning with the Frontier Days Celebration on July 4, 1888. Regardless of which community deserves the honors, there is no doubt that America in the late nineteenth century was secure in its independence, well on its way to recovering from the trauma of the Civil War, and primed for a new national hero to represent the unique experience and spirit of the country (Boatright 1964; Fishwick 1952; Stoeltje 1989). The Fourth of July emerged as the most propitious date to celebrate American exceptionalism, and the cowboy, made famous in dime novels, melodramas, and Wild West shows, and interpreted to an eager public by the likes of Roosevelt, Remington, and Wister, was the ideal embodiment of national values.

In its early days, rodeo failed to attract much attention from the scholarly community. That began to change when Westermeier (1987), a freshly-minted college graduate in the 1930s poised for a career in art, set out from his native New York to tour the American West. Sketchbook in hand, he attended a rodeo in Sidney, Nebraska. He left with a fistful of sketches and a fascination with the sport that became a lifelong obsession. Over the next decade, Westermeier logged 100,000 miles, from Canada to Mexico and New York to the Pacific, to investigate the origins of rodeo, its growth, its relation to the cattle industry, and its popularity in a nation reeling from the effects of the Great Depression. Relying on interviews, statistical questionnaires, and published materials, Westermeier eventually produced *Man, Beast, Dust: The Story of Rodeo*. Published in 1947, his book represents the first serious treatment of the rodeo game and the first book-length study of any kind. More anecdotal than scholarly and told from the perspective of an Easterner who had stumbled across an alien culture, Westermeier's book nonetheless gives us a glimpse into professional rodeo culture and provides a touchstone for its counterpart in cowboy sports.

Through his research and endless bull sessions with rodeo contestants, Westermeier was drawn ineluctably to the nineteenth century cowboy prototype. He was a human being, to be sure, with all the vices and virtues common to humanity, "but because he was reared in an atmosphere of absolute freedom and unusual hardship, his life was perhaps more individualistic" (p. 40). Wary of settled ways, cowboys on the open range "were perhaps closer to their God than they ever could be within the four walls of an unpainted, weather-beaten, uninspiring church" (p. 41). Such character traits certainly contribute to rodeo lore, but like all things modern, sports demand a degree of professionalization commensurate with business enterprise. By mid-century, rodeo cowboys of both genders thus represented a beguiling blend of old and new. They were mostly young (certainly under 40 years of age), proud of their Western heritage,[5] enthusiastic about their work, and drawn to prospects of fame and prize money, so

---

[5] Westermeier was quick to point out that some of rodeo's most illustrious competitors and ardent supporters have come from eastern states. "Although there are not many contestants from the East, the Easterner is, nevertheless, an important contributor to the development of rodeo as a

much so that many had trouble extricating themselves from a way of life that becomes more hazardous with each passing year. Perhaps paradoxically, Westermeier found that people in rodeo were not conscious of the fact that they were maintaining traditions from the Old West. "Rodeo is a business and livelihood for them; they make the best of it" (p. 58). Nevertheless, contestants were alike insofar as they exhibited a gracious independence that made the world seem like their corral. Suspicious of outsiders, reluctant to divulge too much to the uninitiated, and hounded by superstitions that provided scant protection from injury and death, rodeo cowboys in the mid-twentieth century made poor copy and poor theater, but were genuinely sincere.

Lawrence (1982), an anthropologist by training, updated Westermeier's impressions of rodeo culture by following the Professional Rodeo Cowboys Association (P.R.C.A.) circuit from 1975 through 1978 throughout the Great Plains states of Montana, Wyoming, Nebraska, Oklahoma, Texas, and the Canadian province of Alberta. She acknowledged that access to her subjects was not always easy: her Eastern ways marked her as an outsider, and cowboy superstitions stood between her and the bucking chutes, both literally and metaphorically. Perhaps to compensate for the social distance between her and her earthy companions, Lawrence delved into her tool kit of anthropological theory to identify the dichotomy between the wild and the tame as fundamental to the range cattle industry and, consequently, the modern sport of rodeo that it fostered. Within the rubric of interpretive theory, the cowboy on the trail was constantly at war with forces of nature that threatened to destroy him. Emboldened by a Judeo-Christian ethic placing man at the center of the universe, cowboys were caught between the romantic allure of the wild and a practical need for tameness and predictability. "Although the cowboy at times saw beauty in nature, he was usually less in harmony with it than he was lord of it" (p. 63). Whether roping calves or hanging on to raging bulls for the requisite eight seconds, rodeo cowboys thus participate in a ritual that would be familiar to their trail-blazing predecessors by demonstrating over and over again man's capacity to control his environment and exert mastery over nature. Boatright (1964: 202) agreed, insisting that rodeo's survival in the machine age can be attributed to Americans' longstanding search for a key to their history, "for a concept that would make America more than an appendage of England."

> "Within this century, thanks to the mass media, the cowboy would become the popular symbol of the American frontier. The rodeo would survive. It would survive by becoming a ritual in which, on the obvious level, the last frontiersman, the cowboy, or, more accurately, a man in ceremonial garb representing him, re-enacts the conquest of the West, and on a deeper level symbolizes man's conquest of nature" (p. 202).[6]

---

sport" (p. 55). As a cowboy sportsman in Virginia, I'd have to agree with Westermeier that eastern origins are no barrier to ability and enthusiasm.

[6] To emphasize Americans' need for their own cultural expressions, Boatright (1964) cited tournaments in the Old South that failed to make the transition to modernity. Modeled on tournaments of Elizabethan England, these displays of horsemanship called on competitors, or "knights," to ride along a two hundred yard course with their lances at the ready, spearing metal rings approximately two inches in diameter that were suspended from posts with horizontal arms. Knights and their mounts wore elaborate costumes and participated in pageantry that would have been familiar to the dandies in Queen Elizabeth's court. The tournament lives on in the modern

Lawrence's (1982) background in equestrian sports and veterinary medicine sensitized her to perhaps the most obvious feature of rodeo: the peculiar relationship between man and animal. In a constant reenactment of the frontier experience, rodeo contestants personify the struggle between culture's ongoing dialectic with nature, a taming process that is ultimately resolved by man's primacy over the natural world. "It is my assertion," wrote Lawrence, "that rodeo picks up the main themes from the pastoral life of the cowboy, both past and present, identifies and exaggerates them, and makes them explicit through patterned performances" (p. 5).

In her review of Lawrence's book, Green (1984) praised the author for turning her critical lens on a much neglected and widely misunderstood subculture even as she criticized her conclusions. Skeptical that contradictions and conflicts are the essence of rodeo culture, Green perceived in Lawrence a genuine inability to see and hear the West, both on its own terms and on theoretical levels. Perhaps, wrote Green, hanging around New England farmers and stylish gentlemen in jodhpurs blinded Lawrence from the beginning. For Green, Lawrence lost credibility the minute she stepped into the rodeo arena with the air of an "Eastern – liberal – S.P.C.A. member" (p. 232), utterly unsure what to make of Western bronc busters and their unpolished ways. Probing deeper, Green took issue with Lawrence's reliance on clichés that obscured more than they revealed about rodeo culture and that exposed the author's reluctance to confront social facts that simply cannot be ignored. Lawrence's ambivalences between fascination and aversion, approval and disapproval, liking cowboys and damning them for their propensity to violence, come across as strongly as the cowboy's precarious perch between nature and culture. In essence, Green was suggesting that Lawrence should have spent less time pondering the similarities between rodeo and Geertz's (1973) Balinese cockfight and more time listening to what the cowboys had to say.

McNutt (1986), who identified relationships between man and animal as Lawrence's main focus, was far more positive. He particularly appreciated her carefully maintained stance as an outsider and claimed that her ethnological perspective, together with frequent cross-cultural comparisons, have added significantly to our understanding of rodeo. McNutt's major caveat was that Lawrence would have benefited from a dose of Geertzian thick description to alert readers to the emotional intensity of rodeo events, much as rookie journalists record the emotional lives of their subjects. He was also left wondering about the effects of global media and their potential to tap into the multivocality of rodeo, thus disseminating cowboy symbols beyond American shores.

Stoeltje (1989) recognized in the rodeo form an evolution from custom to ritual. Like other scholars, (Boatright 1964; Lawrence 1982; Slatta 1994; Westermeier 1987), she perceived the origins of rodeo in the twilight of the range cattle industry, when economic changes collided with environmental factors to sound the death knell of the cowboy's freewheeling days. As

---

sport of jousting, but its enthusiasts constitute a tiny subculture that pales in comparison to both rodeo and what I have designated as "cowboy sports." One of my fellow cowboy sport competitors and his family have participated quite successfully in jousting contests for many years. At a team cattle sorting competition in the Shenandoah Valley, I asked him about the origins of jousting. He was vaguely aware of the sport's popularity in England, but he was dismissive when I questioned him about its origins in Elizabethan England and the medieval pageantry that surrounded it. "I guess we've pretty much gotten away from all that kind of thing," he said as he rode away.

sporting contests became a basis for both athleticism and social bonding, operational customs constituting the cowboy's way of life were transformed into ritualized customs that were restricted to an arena and incorporated the essential elements of competition, humor, and danger. Between the 1870s and World War I, elaborate performances that appealed to Victorian sensibilities gave way to participatory ritual celebrations. The main attraction in rodeo was, and remains, the cowboy performance, "which emphasized the familiar, paid homage to the past, and fused the local and western with the national and American" (Stoeltje 1989: 250). The formation of professional cowboy associations, codification of rules, and elaboration of pageantry in the early twentieth century signified the maturation of rodeo as a cultural form. In 1929, the twin pillars of modernity, rationalization and bureaucratization, came to rodeo with the creation of the Rodeo Association of America. A governing body, the Cowboys Turtle Association, came into existence in November 1936. After several years of organizational bickering that left many cowboys with a bitter taste in their mouths, the group christened itself the Rodeo Cowboys' Association in 1945 and was renamed the Professional Rodeo Cowboys Association (P.R.C.A.) in 1975 (Lawrence 1982; Westermeier 1987). Clearly, the rodeo form was crystallizing, and the West was sufficiently settled that it could contemplate its history and honor it with cowboy reunions and celebrations of heritage. This stability of context thus completed rodeo's redefinition from custom to ritual.

Committed to unraveling the sociological significance of rodeo, Stoeltje (1993) later proposed a model for the study of ritual genres that identified the interaction of power with the performance of ritual. Eschewing simplistic conceptions of power as a manifestation of domination and subordination, Stoeltje recognized that "power also resides in the capacity to create, transform, or otherwise make things happen" (p. 140). Her model embraced both the creativity of power and the inequality of social relations insofar as it posited three sources of power: *form*, a term used to describe the performance of the ritual; *discourse*, which includes all dimensions of communication, oral and written, that contribute to the ritual performance; and *production*, the organization of forces, energies, and materials that constitute the actual production of the event. The basic elements of the form of rodeo were forged on the cattle frontier, and the discourse evolved as Western lore sifted through the ideology of late nineteenth century expansionism and social Darwinism to produce the cowboy type. As we have seen, nobody was more influential in transforming the American cowboy into a white, Anglo-Saxon, Protestant hero, and the West into a haven for rugged individualists, than the cultural trinity: Theodore Roosevelt, Frederick Remington, and Owen Wister. "They blended the dominant political discourse of the era with American identity and defined its natural home as the West of the imagination and the cowboy as its hero" (p. 148). Popularized through mass entertainment and ensconced in collective memory, the discourse that became so central to the nation also informed the array of logistical and organizational challenges that constitute the production of rodeo. Moreover, as Wild West shows made way for rodeos, power struggles shifted from groups of contract performers and their producers to local communities, where business leaders took on the task of rounding up cowboys and livestock, putting them in an arena, and staging ritual competitions under the shadow of Old Glory and the blare of the national anthem to commemorate America's foundation myth. Familiar icons—or, more accurately, the invented traditions that they inspired—thus "linked the place identified as the West with the West of the imagination, created familiarity with the cowboy through performance, and provided an historically based symbolic hero to represent both the conquest of North America and national unity" (p. 150).

For Errington (1990), rodeo's unresolved tensions don't end at the arena gate. Like Lawrence (1982), Errington approached rodeo from an anthropological perspective. Yet he was less interested in the contestants than the committees responsible for staging rodeos. Specifically, Errington conducted a qualitative study of the forty to fifty men in Rock Creek, Montana, who come together each Fourth of July to organize the Home of Champions Rodeo. As Geertz (1973) found in his study of the Balinese cockfight, human experience is "the process of affective and intellectual interpretation, which necessarily takes place within—in terms of—a specific cultural context, a particular framework of meaning" (Errington 1990: 628). Rock Creek's annual celebration gave Errington an appropriate setting to explore the values and attitudes of community leaders, some of whom were former ranch hands and regulars on the rodeo circuit, who had long since given up their boisterous ways, married, and settled into lives of tameness and predictability. Their opportunity to revisit the glory days of their youth came in the run-up to the rodeo as they participated in the minutiae of pulling off a community-wide event. Like men in similar situations, they patted their beer bellies, recounted exploits that no doubt became more daring with each passing year, and complained about wives whose romantic appeal had surrendered to the ravages of time. In the stories they told of their younger days and their responses to mournful cowboy songs, Errington discerned "a troubled preoccupation with the passing of life" (p. 631). Arguably, such ruminating reflects a dilemma that lies at the heart of America's cultural assumptions, particularly in Western towns like Rock Creek, where the can-do spirit that carved civilization out of a wilderness has given way to a social compact based on interdependencies and complex social structures. Personal history is thus mirrored by social history; life choices made on an individual level are manifest in the broader culture. According to Errington,

> "To the extent that Rock Creek men assume that society is, at least in some measure, based on choices made by individuals and that those choices involve a sacrifice of individuality, they may be all the more conscious that they *could* have decided to live other lives. They would, then, be all the more likely to ponder whether they have chosen well the turns their lives have taken. Yet, regardless of whether assumptions about the social compact affect the lives of these Rock Creek men in this way, these men do encounter an existential dilemma focusing on choices they have made" (p. 632).

Herein lie some disturbing questions. Is ambivalence about community life inevitable? If individualism is natural, is community problematical? And if so, then what are we supposed to do about it? Frustrated with their lots in life, the men serving on Rock Creek's rodeo committee found at least temporary relief from their angst-ridden lives in the weeks leading up to the Home of Champions Rodeo. For a brief moment, these men are "able to relive and transcend their pasts in such a way as to conclude that they, as responsible citizens, have *appropriately* controlled but not *significantly* relinquished their vitality as men" (p. 632). Drawing on wisdom tinged, perhaps, with a hint of resignation, committee members dismissed rodeo contestants as irresponsible drifters, thereby confirming their own commitment to family and community. Errington suggested that their annual catharsis is based not so much on a perception of culture's triumph over nature, as Lawrence (1982) would have it, but rather on their recognition that they are distinct in subtle but nonetheless important ways from the unruly contestants in the arena. Through the ritual of rodeo, their values are confirmed, and after the last steer has been roped and the last bull rider has tasted dirt, they can return to their homes and places of business with the conviction, however fleeting, that their manhood is intact and they have made the right choices.

Cowboy Sports: Amateurs in the Arena

Rodeo's evolution from custom to ritual has given us what is arguably the only sport to evolve from an industry as well as an activity that ranks as one of America's most popular forms of entertainment. Although many rodeos are staged as purely local affairs, the most prestigious and lucrative events are held under the auspices of the Professional Rodeo Cowboys Association (P.R.C.A.). Lawrence (1982) based her anthropological study of rodeo on her observations of P.R.C.A. – sanctioned competitions, and Stoeltje (1989) cited the P.R.C.A. as the crystallization of rodeo's redefinition as a ritual celebration. Based in Colorado Springs, Colorado, staffed by seventy full-time employees, and boasting a membership of some ten thousand contestants, the P.R.C.A. is far and away the largest and oldest rodeo organization in the world.[7] Each year, the organization sanctions nearly seven hundred rodeos nationwide and offers some $34 million in prize money, thus providing communities across the country with an opportunity to garner millions of dollars in downstream economic benefits.[8] To foster the progression of athletes from youth and collegiate competition to the big leagues, the P.R.C.A. has established partnerships with the American Junior Rodeo Association, the National Little Britches Rodeo Association, the National High School Rodeo Association, and the National Intercollegiate Rodeo Association.

---

[7] The P.R.C.A. staff swells to nearly a hundred during the peak summer season. In addition to a state-of-the-art communications system and computerized records and marketing departments, the P.R.C.A. headquarters has included, since its establishment in 1979, the Pro Rodeo Hall of Fame and Museum of the American Cowboy. See the P.R.C.A. website, http://www.prorodeo.org/history/.

Another commemoration of what is reputed to be America's favorite sport can be seen at the National Cowboy and Western Heritage Museum in Oklahoma City, Oklahoma. The American Rodeo Gallery, a colorful and dramatic interpretive gallery encompassing 6,500 square feet and some 450 artifacts, combines a replica of a 1950s rodeo arena with audio-visual and interactive programming to impart a visceral sense of excitement. The Gallery presents six thematic areas: The History of Rodeo; Women in Rodeo; Trick Riders, Fancy Ropers and Clowns; Trophies and Regalia; The Rodeo Historical Society; and The Main Events. See the National Cowboy and Western Heritage Museum website, http://www.nationalcowboymuseum.org/g_rode.html.

[8] The P.R.C.A. cites "widely accepted economic principles" to claim that every dollar a rodeo brings to a community is multiplied five to seven times in the local economy. It is interesting to note that the Prescott, Arizona Frontier Days, already cited as a contender for the world's oldest rodeo, has grown to an eight-performance extravaganza that generates between one and two million dollars and draws approximately 85,000 spectators annually in a community of 30,000. Lodging is commonly sold out six months in advance. See the P.R.C.A. website, http://www.prorodeo.org/members/.

Stock contractors fulfill rodeo's need for livestock, makers of everything from blue jeans to horse trailers line up for a piece of the action through advertising and sponsorships, and qualified judges receive the training they need to ensure that all P.R.C.A. rodeos comply with the rules of the Association. For every child who dreams of growing up to be a cowboy or cowgirl, there are plenty of opportunities to live the fantasy vicariously in the grandstands. And the few whose dreams turn to reality are the beneficiaries of a highly rationalized system that would be all but unrecognizable to their proletarian forebears who didn't need a digital clock to prove who was the best hand.[9]

Similarities in provenance and athleticism notwithstanding, cowboy sports lay claim to a somewhat less illustrious pedigree. Livingston (1991) traced team cattle penning to California in the mid 1950s, when ranch cowboys made a contest out of separating and corralling cattle. Instead of roping, riding broncs, or simply cutting cattle, they decided that sorting a designated number of yearlings from a herd and hazing them through a gate, standard operating procedure back at the ranch, would make for a lively sport. After years of trial and error, the number of cattle was fixed at thirty, and teams of three riders were given a designated time to complete their rides. Two minutes in the early days has since been reduced to seventy-five seconds. In 1993, enthusiastic penners gathered in Fort Worth, Texas, to promote penning as a national sport. Their goal was two-fold: (1) to standardize methods and rules; and (2) to attract more people to penning and educate them about the sport. In September of that year, fifty-three penners from across the United States met to charter what was to become the United States Team Penning Association, or U.S.T.P.A. Seasoned professionals in the horse and cattle industries, legal professionals, business owners, and just regular folks who established the U.S.T.P.A. were united in their determination to advance penning as a serious competitive enterprise. Today, the Fort Worth-based organization boasts a membership of more than 6,000 team penners in 3,500 households scattered across twelve regions, thus constituting the largest and only national not-for-profit team penning organization in the world.[10] An offshoot of team penning, team or ranch sorting, has been gaining in popularity, in part because it requires less space and fewer cattle than a full-blown penning.[11] Perhaps reflecting more enthusiasm than accuracy, the

---

[9] A comprehensive guide to the P.R.C.A. is available at the association's website, http://www.prorodeo.org.

[10] Regions are organized as follows: Region 1: Western Sunbelt—southern. CA, southern NV, and AZ; Region 2: Lonestar—TX; Region 3: Arkla Valley—AR and LA; Region 4: Sunshine—NC, SC, GA, and FL; Region 5: Great Northwest—WA, OR, northern CA, and northern NV; Region 6: Rocky Mountain—WY, UT, CO, and NM; Region 7: Great Lakes—MI, WI, IA, IL, and IN; Region 8: Northeast—VA, WV, OH, PA, MD, NJ, DE, NY, and New England; Region 9: Wilderness Region—ID and MT; Region 10: Heartland—KS, OK, and MO; Region 11: Great River—KY, TN, MS, and AL; Region 12: Badlands—ND, SD, NE, and MN. See the U.S.T.P.A. website, http://www.ustpa.com/subpages/aboutus/regionmap.aspx.

[11] Less space and fewer cattle translates into less financial risk and not as much wear and tear on herds. Since I have been participating in cowboy sports, I have learned that hosts often prefer to stage a team or ranch sorting. Like any athlete, cattle need a chance to rest, particularly during the summer heat. Herds of thirty head each are therefore rotated over the course of a day's penning, and because a single ride in a standard team penning requires thirty head of cattle, at

INVENTING TRADITION

association's website claims that no organization in the equine industry, and indeed no sport, has grown as quickly as team penning. The website is also unequivocal in its mission statement: "The purposes of the United States Team Penning Association are to engage those with an affinity for the western lifestyle in the sports of team penning and ranch sorting and to develop resources and services for the benefit of U.S.T.P.A. members and growth of the sport." Promoting a blend of athleticism and camaraderie, the website elaborates on the sport's deeper purpose.

> "The U.S.T.P.A. is a National Team Penning Association formed to educate and promote team penning. It is not the cows that make penning, not horses, not numbers, gates or pens, but it is the interaction between people, and most importantly, family that makes penning work both in the arena and out. The camaraderie that we share before the first foul line is crossed and after the dust has settled on the last ride is what has made this Association and team penning what it is today."[12]

Responding to complaints that the U.S.T.P.A. rating system was unfair, the National Team Penning Championships (N.T.P.C.) sprang into being. Based in Wellington, Colorado, the upstart organization promised members that they would have opportunities to participate on a level playing field in an arena with their peers. Sanctioning and affiliate programs have been established, and a magazine was launched to keep members informed and, not incidentally, to raise money for rewards and prizes. The association website, perhaps reflecting the Western proclivity for exaggeration to drive home a point, asserts that 100,000 people participate in team penning and that 320,000 team penning websites are available at the click of a mouse. Invoking a mantra that clearly reflects dissatisfaction with the status quo, the website announces its mission: "That's why we believe 'It's about time' that an organization stepped up to allow people to compete in a first class competition with more money, prizes and opportunities than your sport has ever seen."[13]

Like the U.S.T.P.A., the National Cutting Horse Association (N.C.H.A.) goes back to the early days of cattle ranching, long before anyone thought about separating cows from a herd under the watchful eye of a judge and the tyranny of a digital clock. From its grassroots beginnings in 1946 to the 16,500-member organization that it is today, the N.C.H.A. has promoted cutting competition, standardized contest rules, and done its part to preserve the heritage of the cutting horse, those scrappy little Quarter Horses whose ancestors boarded Columbus' ships when they weighed anchor in Cadiz and set out for parts unknown. Based in Fort Worth, Texas, the N.C.H.A. sanctions hundreds of shows and limited-age events each year and offers millions in prize money. That's a far cry from the days when cowboys and their horses

---

least ninety cows need to be available. A team or ranch sorting, on the other hand, requires ten cattle per ride. Assuming that three herds are on hand, only thirty cattle, with perhaps a few substitutes, are required for a day of sorting.

[12] The history and mission statement of the U.S.T.P.A. are available on the association's website at http://www.ustpa.com/subpages/aboutus/ustpahistory.aspx.

[13] For more information on the N.T.P.C., see the organization's website at http://www.ntpc.us.

distinguished themselves simply by getting the job done. Through partnerships, the Association produces six major events: the World Championship Futurity, the World Finals, the Eastern National Championships, the Western National Championships, the Super Stakes and Super Stakes Classic, and the Summer Cutting Spectacular. The economic impact in cities fortunate enough the host these events is estimated at $70 million.[14] As is the case with penning and sorting, cutting horse competition offers seasoned pros as well as rank amateurs the chance to experience the adrenaline rush of cowboy rituals in the company of others who, as the U.S.T.P.A. website proclaims, share an affinity for the Western lifestyle.

Toward a Sociology of Cowboy Sports

On all levels of competition, rodeo and cowboy sports are practically kissing cousins. They share a sociogenesis on the cattle frontier of the late nineteenth century, tap into an affinity for the Western lifestyle, and provide structured opportunities to mimic, historically and emotionally, the animate trinity's role in defining America's frontier experience. Practically speaking, they are lucrative enterprises, not only for contestants and host communities, but also for businesses that serve the horse and cattle industries. And as we will see, cowboy sports have followed rodeo on its journey from custom to ritual insofar as they incorporate the essential ingredients of competition, humor, and danger, and reflect the same sources of power—form, discourse, and production—that have kept rodeo alive well into the postmodern age. From tiny crossroads across rural America to high-tech urban arenas, rodeo and cowboy sports both reflect and reproduce traditions that lie somewhere between fact and fantasy. Served up as an antidote to the frontier anxiety that accompanied the closing of the cattle trails, celebrated in mass entertainment, and planted in the collective memory of a nation that refuses to relinquish its connection to a mythic past, cowboy ways and the sports that commemorate them have never quite lost their allure. To borrow from Swidler's (1986) lexicon, they constitute what is arguably the most tangible tool kit that the frontier has left us to facilitate identity formation and cultural expression.

Yet the similarities between rodeo and cowboy sports fade as one rides into any number of equestrian arenas in Central Virginia to pen, sort, and cut cattle. Perhaps the most obvious distinction is that rodeo includes up to seven competitive events and presents enormous logistical challenges in terms of production. Cowboy sports, by contrast, are simple. Landowners who host events, many of whom are already in the cattle business, need only assemble enough cattle to stage a competition, affix numbers to their flanks, and keep their arenas dry. Sometimes picnic food is available, either from a vendor or by arrangement with the host; otherwise, competitors bring their own refreshments. Plumbing requirements are met with a porta-potty, and hoses are always available for riders and their horses to slake their thirst and wash off the dust. Moreover, penning, sorting, and cutting events are never staged simultaneously. Competitors know in advance what to expect and plan their days accordingly.[15] Competitions thus take on a

---

[14] The history and mission statement of the N.C.H.A. are available on the association's website at http://www.nchacutting.com/about.htm.

[15] For people who own more than one horse, advance planning includes knowing which horse to bring to a competition. Predictably, opinions are mixed: Some people insist that a penning and

festive atmosphere as cowboys socialize, soft drink or hot dog in hand, on the backside of our horses, anxious for our turns in the arena and pleased to be in the company of friends, family, and our four-legged companions.

Even though all equestrian sports are fraught with risk, rodeo clearly poses the most danger, not only to competitors, but also to their horses and the rodeo stock used for saddle and bareback bronc riding, team steer and calf roping, steer wrestling, and the ever-popular bull riding. Given the perils of rodeo, it is not surprising to find that contestants are typically young and seemingly invincible. Cowboy sports, however, are considerably less dangerous and are open to all ages. Since I began competing, my teammates and competitors have ranged in age from twelve to seventy. And although we accept the prospect of injury, we do what we can to minimize risk, including the requirement that contestants under the age of eighteen wear crash helmets.

Perhaps the most glaring difference has to do with gender. As anyone who has attended or participated in rodeos can attest, women can be fierce competitors, not only in the traditional female venue of barrel racing, but also in all-girl rodeos that signify the extent to which gender distinctions have faded in the realm of sport. Yet rodeo at all levels of competition remains largely a man's world, with women restricted to barrel racing, perhaps watching a husband or boyfriend test his mettle, and sometimes vying for the title of Rodeo Queen in the Western equivalent of a beauty pageant. Cowboy sports, by contrast, are gender neutral. Men and women ride on the same teams and compete head-to-head, with no quarter given, and certainly no quarter asked.

No effort to distinguish between rodeo and cowboy sports would be complete without reference to finances. As we have seen, rodeo's evolution from custom to ritual has produced yet another opportunity for contestants and service providers to cash in on a money-making sport, particularly in the context of P.R.C.A. – sanctioned events. To be sure, penning and sorting events sanction by the U.S.T.P.A. and the N.T.P.C., and cutting events sanctioned by N.C.H.A., offer the prospect of winnings that are commensurate with their levels of competition. I have had the opportunity to ride with Virginia cowboys whose success in the big leagues has earned them trips to national championships in Fort Worth, Amarillo, and Oklahoma City, and they are treated like rock stars whenever they compete closer to home. Top hands often supplement their winnings by training horses and offering clinics to beginners and novices. Inevitably, all this activity leads to what might be the murkiest dimension of equestrian sports: the buying and selling of horses. Although I hesitate to paint with too broad a brush, it would surely be disingenuous to assume that horse trading is always on the level. I have been on the receiving end of more than one dubious sales pitch, and I have even had the unpleasant experience of being swindled by an unscrupulous trader. Suffice it to say that business is business, and when it comes to horses, there's more than one way to turn a dollar.

Whether buying horses or saddling up for a day of competition, few Old Dominion cowboys have either the skills or the financial means to compete at the highest levels. This is particularly true when it comes to cutting horse competition. Prime cutting horses are often valued in the tens of thousands of dollars, far more than most middle-class competitors are able to spend to pursue their passion. Moreover, most cowboy sporting events in Central Virginia are

---

sorting horse should never be used for cutting, while others claim that horses are smart enough to figure out what they're being asked to do, as long as their owners know how to ask. In all likelihood, this is one of those debates that will never be settled.

not even sanctioned by the U.S.T.P.A., the N.T.P.C., or the N.C.H.A. For the most part, they are purely local affairs whose adherence to official rules and regulations in no way makes riders eligible to compete for the kind of prize money available at sanctioned events. With few exceptions, Old Dominion cowboys battle for a share of the jackpot that, even on a good day, barely compensates for entry fees, let alone the costs of maintaining horses and equipment and filling up the gas tank.

Our kinship with rodeo contestants notwithstanding, Old Dominion cowboys are unique. Far from the limelight and with scant prospects for monetary gain, we keep showing up at arenas, horses in tow and day-to-day concerns in the dust. Most of us have responsibilities, both at home and on the job, that preclude the level of dedication, let alone financial means, to be more than weekend warriors. Yet amateurism seems to be no barrier to enthusiasm. Fame and fortune clearly take a back seat to something less tangible, yet no less real, and certainly no less meaningful in terms of identity formation and cultural expression. Teddy Blue Abbott (1939) had a point about the vanishing cowboy, but he might be surprised by the resilience of his descendants in the postmodern, mimetic cowboys of Central Virginia.

Chapter Six — Showtime[1]

> "A bad day of penning is better than a good day at the office."
>
> Old Dominion cowboy
> North Garden, VA

Run Up

The sun was already creeping above the horizon when I turned off the two-lane highway and pulled into the farm where my wife and I stable our horses and maintain a small herd of cattle. I sped by the owners' modest, two-story home and drove directly to the barnyard. Relieved that none of the other boarders were around to engage in idle chit chat, I glanced at my watch. By my calculations, I had just under an hour and a half to hitch up my trailer and load my horse, retrieve my saddle and blanket from the tack room, make sure that I had enough hay and feed on board to last until nightfall, and drive over the mountain to Golconda Farm for a penning competition. Regretting my decision to have one more for the road only a few hours before, I took a swig of coffee and backed my Nissan Xterra until the rear end was less than a foot from the trailer hitch. After a few minutes of deft maneuvering, I was rewarded with a resounding metallic *clink*. I walked to the back of the truck, connected the electric cable and safety latches, and got back behind the wheel to position the rig for easy loading.

Satisfied that all was in order, I selected a halter and lead rope from the trailer and set out for the pasture where Colfax was no doubt grazing contentedly, oblivious to what was in store for her on this warm summer day. A loud honking noise drew my gaze skyward, where a flock of Canadian geese, perfectly arrayed in V-formation, was speeding toward a destination known only to them. The hair on the back of my neck tingled as a breeze from their wings, gentle as an angel's breath, washed over me. As they receded into the early-morning shadows, I wondered what it must be like to experience that kind of freedom—the exhilaration of soaring through the

---

[1] This chronicle of cattle penning day represents a composite of many such experiences that I have had as a cowboy sport competitor and member of the Blue Ridge Team Penning Association (B.R.T.P.A.) in Virginia. The location of the competition, Golconda Farm, is fictional. With the exception of my horses' names (Colfax, Haskell, and Caroline), I have avoided identifying my fellow participants, either by name or profession, in order to protect their confidentiality. Quotations are as accurate as I could make them, given the challenges of scribbling notes on horseback between rides and coping with Mother Nature's bag of tricks. Although I describe a cattle penning competition, sortings follow much the same routines and protocols. Cutters are to some extent a breed of their own; I have actually detected a not-so-subtle undercurrent of condescension that cutting horse competitors exhibit toward penners and sorters. Sociologically speaking, however, penners, sorters, and cutters are cut from the same cloth. We are all Old Dominion cowboys, and as near as I can tell, cultural enlightenment would be ill-served by slicing with too fine a blade.

skies with a flock of like-minded comrades, unencumbered by earthly cares and guided only by instinct.

Such musings weren't going to get me over the mountain any sooner. With some effort I redirected my gaze to the far side of the pasture. Colfax and our two other horses, Haskell and Caroline, their coats glistening and manes flowing, were galloping toward the creek, where they  proceeded to frolic and splash one another like unruly children. For the briefest of moments, I felt like an intruder into sacred space, spying on a ritual packed with wild, raw energy. At the same time, I realized that Colfax's playfulness was bound to cost me precious time in catching her. Cursing her contrary ways, I picked up speed and descended the hill to the creek below. She saw me coming, and we played our usual game of cat and mouse until I managed to throw a lead rope around her neck and secure her halter. Not for the first time, I paused to admire her confirmation and color, and especially the brilliant white blaze that is surely her most striking feature. We exchanged looks, and I reached up to scratch behind her ears. "Good girl," I muttered as we set off for the barnyard.

No sooner had we crossed the creek than her pace quickened. Within seconds, I was running to keep some slack in the lead rope. Was it my imagination, or had she spotted the open trailer and figured out what was going on? Surely her eagerness was due to more than a realization that we were heading for the barn, the source of good things to eat. Struggling to keep pace with her graceful strides, I couldn't help but wonder if she was actually *looking forward* to strutting her stuff in the arena. More and more, I was coming to agree with Ike, a former rodeo cowboy who co-owned the stable with his wife, Jane, that horses enjoy working with cattle. "She *enjoys* it," Ike said each time he watched Colfax and me pen, sort, or cut cattle. "She's got Doc Bar in her, she *can't help* it," he often intoned in reference to her breeding. Whatever her bloodlines, I found it hard to avoid the conclusion that Colfax and, for that matter, all of the horses that we would see later that day, were athletes in perpetual training, anxious to play their part in the animate trinity of human, horse, and cow.

Willie Nelson and a second mug of strong coffee kept me company on the way over the mountain. Every few minutes, I adjusted my rearview mirror to make sure that Colfax was behaving herself. Sure enough, there she was, the top of her head framed in the front left window of the trailer, wiggling her ears and chomping on hay from the vinyl feed bin in front of her. She'd loaded in seconds, barely giving me enough time to get out of the way so I could close the back door. For the second time that morning, I wondered what was going on behind that magnificent white blaze of hers. Resigned to the mystery of it all, I turned up the music and gazed at the valley below, where another flock of geese was slicing through the mist. It took an act of will to concentrate on the road. There was so much to see, and so much to be aware of, that driving seemed unbearably mundane. Mindful of my precious cargo, I took another gulp of coffee and turned my full attention to the highway.

Thankfully, the trip was uneventful. I arrived at Golconda Farm shortly after 9:00. As one of the early arrivals, I was able to park my rig anywhere I wanted in the pasture just south of the arena. After passing through the front gate, I swung my truck in a wide arc so that I would face the arena, and I drove a few extra feet to make sure that my truck and trailer were perfectly aligned. Later arrivals would line their rigs up with mine, and I didn't want to set a poor precedent in what would soon be a parking lot. My SUV and modest two-horse trailer would soon be dwarfed by elaborate rigs, complete with sleeping quarters and tack rooms, which would arrive shortly.

I killed the ignition, got out, and stretched. A few clouds drifted beneath a brilliant blue sky, and the stillness, broken only by the chattering of birds and muffled drone of traffic from the distant highway, was palpable. The trailer shook, indicating that Colfax was thrusting her muzzle ever deeper into her feed bin. A huge rig, partially obscured by ground mist and the dust that I had churned up, was pulling into the pasture and heading my way. I nodded in the driver's direction, and he nodded back.

I took a moment to survey what was, for me at least, a brand new venue for penning. Squinting in the bright sunlight, I noticed a lone rider just east of the arena, loping gently through grass that was more than likely ready for the first cutting of the season. I recognized him as John, one of the more accomplished cowboys in the Blue Ridge Team Penning Association. He tended to segregate himself from novices and rode only with his coterie of open riders—mostly mustached and weather-beaten men, often hard on their horses and always determined to finish in the money.[2] I recalled the time when I'd stopped on a highway to help John fix a flat tire on his trailer after a penning. Turned out I had just the right tool, and with a bit of jerry-rigging and help from other penners who were traveling with him, we were able to get him back on the road. He warmed up to me after that, at least enough for us to exchange pleasantries in the arena and congratulate one another on successful rides. But he was never quite willing to risk an entry fee on a rookie.

More rigs were starting to show up. Given the lack of rain in recent weeks, I wasn't surprised to notice that a fine layer of dust was already softening the sunlight. I waved at new arrivals, most of whom I knew (at least by their first names) as they maneuvered their cumbersome trailers in the alignment that I had established a few minutes before. I polished off what was left of my lukewarm coffee and opened the trailer door to find Colfax on full alert, head held high, oblivious to the perfectly good hay left in her feed bin.

"Showtime, sweetheart," I said as I untied her lead rope from its hook and tossed it over her neck.

As if she didn't know. With her ears jutting forward like daggers, nostrils flaring and upper lip quivering, Colfax was a sight to behold: nine hundred pounds of primal energy set to explode. I stepped quickly to the back of the trailer, removed the safety latches, and lowered the platform to allow her to back out on her own. The prodigious pile of manure at her back feet was

---

[2] Penning and sorting competitions typically include three divisions: novice (beginners and relatively inexperienced riders); mixed (open to novices and more experienced riders); and open (highly skilled riders with lots of experience under their belts). Children under sixteen years of age ride in a separate division. My best efforts notwithstanding, I remained a novice rider throughout the ethnographic phase of this project.

no impediment. She was out within seconds, intermittently snatching mouthfuls of grass and lifting her head to take in the surroundings. I let this ritual continue for several minutes, knowing full well that it was too soon to tie her to the trailer for grooming and saddling. If I didn't let her settle, she'd more than likely spook and leave me with a busted halter and a hefty repair bill at Blue Ridge Trailers.

I looked at my watch and realized that I had less than an hour to saddle up and line up my penning teams. With trepidation, I led Colfax to her accustomed hook on the left side of the trailer and secured her lead rope with a slip knot that could be undone at the first sign of trouble.[3] I then reached inside the trailer for my gloves, spurs, and leather chinks[4], strapped them on, and set about cleaning Colfax's hooves and brushing her coat. Satisfied that she was as ready as she'd ever be, I swung my blanket and saddle onto her back, secured the girth and flank cinch, and replaced her halter with a bridle and bit specially designed for the rapid-fire twists and turns that I would be asking her to make later on. Moments later, we were ready to head toward the arena and form up some penning teams. All I needed from the truck was my wad of cash for entry fees and a notepad that would double as a score sheet and repository of ethnographic scribbling. With those stuffed in my shirt pocket, I locked the truck and tossed my keys in the trailer, right next to my water bottles and miniature tape recorder.

I was mounted and halfway to the arena when I noticed that several women were starting to unload folding tables and picnic food from their vehicles. One of them, clad in flip flops and gym shorts, was setting up a card table where we'd soon plunk down our entry fees and sign up our rides. I recognized her as Barrett. She and her husband, Andy, owned the place, and he was a top competitor as well. A slight and very welcome breeze blew sign-up sheets and dollar bills off the table. With a few terse commands that I couldn't quite hear, Barrett sent children scurrying to collect them. Nearby, several older people were staking a tent and setting up camp chairs so they could enjoy the action and each other's company without subjecting themselves to the blistering sunshine that would soon be upon us.

---

[3] My fears of a mishap were not unfounded. At a practice penning near Culpeper, Virginia, Colfax pitched a fit when I tied her to the trailer and left her momentarily unsupervised. While I was strapping on my spurs on the other side of the trailer, I suddenly felt the entire contraption lurch. I ran to the other side (a difficult maneuver in spurs and chaps, to say the least) to find her loose and a bit shaken up. For reasons known only to the horse gods, she had reared back, broken a metal piece on her halter, and pulled the steel hook to which she was tethered completely out of the trailer frame. It was dusk, and it took me a few minutes of groveling in the dirt to locate the broken pieces. Then there was the matter of calming Colfax down so I could ride her. Ever since, I've been reluctant to secure her too tightly, and I try not to get very far from her side until she's saddled and ready to go.

[4] Chinks are ¾-length chaps which normally secure to the upper leg with buckles and straps. It is an "open" design which allows the best circulation of air. Chinks are the most versatile chaps and offer good upper leg protection from trees, brush, and other elements while offering freedom of movement. I rarely ride without chinks because they provide traction and thus lessen the risk of coming out of the saddle when things get wild and Western.

INVENTING TRADITION

Colfax flinched as the outhouse door slammed shut some twenty feet away. Reflexively, my leg muscles contracted around her ribs. "Easy, girl," I crooned as I stroked her withers, hoping she'd behave herself in the rising hubbub. "Time for a little warm-up before we get our penning teams together."

She nodded and lunged forward. It took some doing to temper her enthusiasm as we approached the arena.

Knowing that horses have a habit of holding their breath when they're being saddled, I paused near the arena gate to dismount and tighten Colfax's cinch. She eyed me warily, no doubt annoyed that I was on to her tricks. No more than ten feet away, several cowboys were engaged in a spirited discussion.

"I wouldn't any more keep a horse in a stable than I'd keep someone in prison," one of them said. I glanced over the top of my saddle and recognized the speaker as Greg, one of B.R.T.P.A.'s founding fathers. During the week, he managed a farm for a wealthy man who I knew to be traveling in Italy with his family. "Gives them an attitude," he said as the others nodded in agreement. Except for occasional swishes of their tails to keep the flies at bay, their horses stood stock still, oblivious to their riders and even the other cowboys who were careening around the arena. Neither horses nor riders batted an eye as the dust welled up around them.

We're like fish in the ocean, I thought as I swung myself into the saddle. *The dust is just part of our natural habitat.*

"Yeah, you know, people think horses are dumb." I knew the speaker without even looking up. It was Mitch, a middle manager of an international construction company whose New Jersey accent was so thick you could cut it with a knife. "Take mine," he continued. "He hates baths. One day I'm giving him a bath. I been around horses for thirty years and I've never seen this. All of a sudden, he purses his lips and squirts water, full of bits of grass and slobber, in a perfect arc, right in my face. I later figure out he'd been sucking down water that was trickling down his face the whole time I was bathing him. Son-of-a-bitch was thinkin', 'Take that, buddy!'"

A round of laughter followed. I didn't even try to fathom the smug look on his horse's face. *Probably just my imagination anyway.*

I spurred Colfax into a gentle trot and ventured into the billowing dust.

After several laps and a few near misses with other contestants, Colfax and I paused on the far side of the arena to practice roll backs, a thrilling maneuver that calls on the horse to stop on a dime, squat back on its haunches, and lunge in the opposite direction. We'd performed several of these vertebrae-rattling exercises when Tray, a horse trainer from somewhere near the coast, beckoned to me.

"Try shifting your weight more," he said even before Colfax and I came to a complete stop. "You need to move with her, not against her."

"Thanks, Tray," I said, always grateful for any advice that came my way. "I appreciate that."

"Well, I could see you're trying," he said. "As long as someone's working at it, I'm glad to help. Some people won't take advice or ask questions. I've been instructing this one girl who wouldn't say 'shit' if she had a mouthful of it!"

He paused, eyeing my horse and equipment. I braced myself for a lecture, hoping that nobody would plow into us in the increasingly crowded arena and cut this little lesson in horsemanship short. What came next surprised me.

"You can't do this alone," said Tray thoughtfully as he brushed his hand through his goatee and adjusted his hat to block out the glare. "Everyone needs a coach. Tiger Woods has a coach. Michael Jordan has a coach. I don't know how many of these people are NBA fans or watch sports, but the point is, you have to be ready for change. Change is inevitable. And," he said with emphasis, fixing his eyes on mine, "there are two ways to do something: a right way, and a wrong way."

Hanging on Tray's every word, I was startled to look around and see several other competitors, equally split between men and women but virtually indistinguishable in their cowboy hats and Western boots, gathered in a semicircle around us, eager to pick up hints from this renowned trainer.

"The other thing is," he said, a bit louder now so that others could hear, "you really ought to get yourself a trained horse. A horse is basically a piece of equipment. Say, one guy has a push mower, someone else has a gas-powered mower, and someone else has a deluxe riding mower. Now, who's going to get the job done?"

His question was rhetorical, answered only with bobbing cowboy hats. Defensively, I gave my decidedly untrained horse a pat on the rear.

"That's right," said Dan, a bearded fifty-something who was employed as a middle manager for a large company near the Chesapeake Bay. I tried to picture him in a suit and tie, sitting in front of a computer screen or strutting down some corridor in a glass and steel tower, then gave up and listened to what he had to say.

"Do you play sports?" he asked, looking in my direction.

"Sure, I run, play golf..." I trailed off, anxious for him to make his point.

"OK, so what kind of golf clubs do you play with?" Apparently running wasn't at the top of his list.

"Well, to tell you the truth, they're practically antiques," I said. "A friend of mine back in Tulsa once told me that I'm about fifteen hundred dollars shy of a good golf game."

Dan smiled, and several others chuckled, making me wonder how many golfers were in our midst. "Well, there you have it," he said with finality. "The better the equipment, the better you're gonna perform. Penning cattle's no different."

I let my comrades' words of wisdom sink in as I reached into my shirt pocket for my notepad and pen, preparing to form up some penning teams. Others had the same idea, and with cowboys hurtling by and dust swirling around us, we spent the next few minutes forming teams and exchanging wads of cash that we would eventually turn in at the sign up table. Several cowboys handed money over the railing to their wives and significant others, along with instructions pertaining to the divisions they wanted to ride in and the number of rides they wanted. Dutifully, they walked off toward the sign-up table. Predictably, the accomplished hands drifted off to themselves to form their own teams for the open division, a category reserved for the best riders.

"Hey, I need a third. Anyone have an opening?" George, one of the open riders, was riding his sleek chestnut gelding, already dripping sweat and sporting a Circle Y brand on his left flank, in our direction. Word was that he'd bought her at an auction in West Texas, and for a pretty penny, too.

Without hesitation and certainly without thinking, I hollered, "Sure, I'll ride with you!"

My offer fell on deaf ears. Without so much as a backward glance, George wheeled his horse and rode in the other direction, clearly looking for someone closer to his skill level and utterly disinterested in nurturing my novice skills.

"You'd better let him pick his own teams." Greg, who'd been warming up his horse nearby, had arrived just in time to witness my embarrassing rebuff. "He's one a them open riders," he said. I shrugged and exchanged knowing looks with him and the other novices who'd been listening to Tray's tutorial and Dan's paean to four-legged machines. It wasn't the first time, and it certainly wouldn't be the last, that body language and facial expressions carried more meaning than mere words ever could.

"Yeah, there's a lot of politicalness in this," said Mary, a seasoned rider who seemed to straddle the divide between factions. Her comment was directed to a newcomer who still had that deer-in-the-headlights look about him, anxious to be involved in the organization, but not sure how to fit in.

I pondered Mary's comment as George rode off to find a team mate who was up to his standards. We all knew the background to the little drama that had just played out: George and his ilk were threatening to tear the association apart with their competitive drive and lack of interest in bringing in new blood and nurturing youth. Clearly, the times were changing, and the stakes were nothing less than the goals, purposes, and ultimately the meaning of the Blue Ridge Team Penning Association.

⊥⊤

Dan and I rode out of the arena and visited about the chasm that was developing between recreational and competitive riders. His main concern at the moment was not so much organizational goals as it was equality among participants.

"You know, there's talk about setting up another association," he said. "We have to keep this equal. We can't treat a rich man one way and a poor man another way. Everybody's the same."

I looked around and realized that several others had ridden up beside us and were nodding their heads in agreement. Clearly, dust wasn't the only thing in the wind.

A buzz from the loudspeaker got our attention. "Mornin', everyone. Glad you all could make it." Andy, owner of Golconda Farm and our host for the day, was getting things started. I loosened my reins and spurred Colfax toward the judge's booth. Within seconds, cowboys who had been galloping and spinning their horses in random and potentially dangerous patterns in the arena gathered in front of Andy. A few stragglers were riding toward us from the parking area so they could participate in the opening ritual. Not far from the booth, cowboys milling around the sign-up table put down their pens and looked in our direction. My watch read 10:45. Not bad. Fifteen minutes before the open competition, and I already had three mixed rides and my quota of five in the novice division. All I needed to do was register them at the sign up table and fork over my cash, and I'd be through with logistical hassles and ready for action.[5]

---

[5] The reader is referred to the beginning of Chapter One, "Old Dominion Cowboys," where I outline the rules and protocols of cattle penning competition. Over time and with experience,

"As most of you know by now, we lost one of our own earlier this week."

A stillness settled over the gathering. I wasn't sure what was coming, but it didn't sound good. Andy fiddled with his microphone and continued.

"Details are kinda sketchy, but from what I gather, Glenda was riding near her home when her horse spooked and threw her. The guy she was riding with said she hit her head pretty hard, but she didn't complain and went off by herself to visit a friend. Musta had a hemorrhage or something. When her horse came back by himself, some friends went looking for her. Found her a half mile from home."

Andy paused. A few cowboys shifted slightly in their saddles, but not a word was spoken. "Anyway," he continued, "we've been asked to make contributions to the Northern Virginia Firefighters Association. Glenda was one tough lady, and I know we'll miss 'er."

In the moment of silence that ensued, I summoned a picture of a diminutive Glenda, no bigger 'n a cake of soap after a hard day's washin', sporting her signature purple cowboy hat and batwing chaps, and hollering like a band of Indians at uncooperative cattle and team mates who couldn't match her intensity in a month of Sundays. My recollections of a spirited, fifty-something redhead and, as I understood, one of Uncle Sam's career bureaucrats, were cut short when Andy closed his eyes, raised his right arm, and asked us to bow our heads. In what seemed like a single motion, cowboy hats went from heads to saddle horns. Horses stood like statues, and the few people who were afoot stopped dead in their tracks. The only sound was the flapping of an American flag that had been hung above the judge's booth. As I shed my own hat and fixed my eyes on a patch of weeds near Colfax's feet, I tried in vain to remember who had put the flag there, and when.

"Lord," Andy intoned gravely, "we thank you for bringing us together on this glorious day as friends and competitors. We hope you'll welcome Glenda to Paradise, and we ask for safety as we ride these horses and pen these cattle. These things we ask in the name of your Son, Jesus Christ, our Lord and Savior. Amen."

Andy lowered his right arm. With his left, he pulled the American flag from its holder and handed it to Cindy, wife of one of the open riders and a fierce competitor in her own right, who had just ridden up to the booth. In silence, she hoisted the flag above her head and spurred her horse to a full gallop. Just as she was reaching her stride, the loudspeakers high above the arena crackled to life with a scratchy rendition of the national anthem. I stole a glance at my comrades. Only a few lips were moving, but all eyes were riveted on Old Glory as she popped and cracked her way around the arena. Amazingly, none of our horses so much as flinched when Cindy sped past us. Toward the end of a recording that clearly had been played a few too many times, I could make out lyrics, familiar to all but sung by few, emitting from cowboys and cowgirls with the self-confidence to voice their patriotism. Cindy and her precious emblem were on their fifth lap when loudspeakers and cowboy accompanists sputtered into silence.

---

penners and sorters earn ratings ranging from one (novice) to six (expert). Divisions are thus based on skill level: riders with higher ratings compete in the open division; novices and more accomplished riders compete in the mixed division; and riders with little or no experience compete in the novice division. Children compete separately, but in my experience, there are rarely enough children to warrant a separate division. The rules for cutting are entirely different and lie beyond the scope of this narrative.

"Good luck, folks," said Andy good-naturedly, a bit louder now that the spell was broken. "Give the judge a minute to test the clock and we'll get this show on the road. We'll start with open riders, then go to mixed, and wrap up late this afternoon with novice."

Andy paused. I saw him exchange glances with his wife, Barrett, who was still manning the sign-up table. She shrugged. He nodded and raised the microphone to his lips.

"I guess we don't have enough kids for a youth division. Money goes to the top three teams in open, mixed, and novice. Ride hard, and take lots of chances!"

As if we needed to be told.

Gettin' Western

"The cattle are ready. Your number is..." Barrett, who'd migrated from the sign-up table to the judge's booth, paused and waited for a signal from the flagman perched in a pickup bed on the far side of the arena. As soon as the lead horse's nose crossed the imaginary barrier in its approach to the herd, he'd drop his flag, thus signaling the beginning of the first ride in the open division. Thirty head of cattle, five to six hundred pounds each and sporting vinyl numbers from zero to nine on their flanks, were milling warily on their side of the barrier. Between the flagman and the judge's booth, three cowboys were riding from the entrance gate toward the herd, their eyes fixed with laser-like intensity on the cattle, and their horses already glistening with sweat.

Suddenly, the flagman dropped his flag, and the two cowboys who had volunteered to *hold the herd* wheeled their horses and exited the arena at a dead gallop. "Seven, your number is seven," Barrett announced tersely. With that, the public address system fell silent, and the digital clock mounted above the window of the judge's booth sparkled to life.

Now that the barrier had been breached, the first team of open riders had seventy-five seconds to separate the three number sevens that Barrett had designated by random selection from the herd and drive them into a small steel pen situated near the entrance gate, all the while keeping the other twenty-seven cattle from crossing the barrier. For the duration of the ride, all cows without the number seven pasted on their flanks would be branded as *trash cows*, and their unwelcome forays beyond the barrier were grounds for disqualification. Many an entry fee, mine no doubt included, would be sacrificed that day to trash cows and their contrary ways.

Within seconds, all three cowboys were past the barrier, and the tightly packed herd was dissolving into a chaotic tangle of jittery cows. About a dozen of them were moving to the cowboys' left; another eight or nine were evading their pursuers by flanking to the right, while the rest stayed more or less in the center, increasingly panicked, unsure which way to go. The lead rider, John, was in the thick of it, scouring the herd for the three sevens, while his two team mates, Brad and Gloria, hung back, one on each side of the arena, to prevent trash cows from slipping by.

"There, John, on your right! Two sevens!" screamed Brad above the rising din. "One black cow and a baldy![6] Cut 'em off! I'll peel back the trash!" From where I was mounted on

---

[6] In cow country vernacular, a *baldy*, or *black baldy*, is a black cow with white markings and is usually a cross between an Angus and Hereford. Normally, young cattle would be referred to as either steers (castrated males) or heifers (females), depending on their gender. When the genders are mixed, cattle are known generically as cows.

Showtime

Colfax, I could hear the three riders shouting at one another as they jockeyed for position. Like players on any sporting field, penners need to communicate constantly and monitor one another's positions. The challenge is compounded with three horses and thirty cows thrown in the mix. In the common vernacular, penners must learn to multitask, simultaneously ferreting out designated cattle and keeping the trash at bay under the tyranny of the clock. "Come on, John, ride that son-of-a bitch!" yelled Gloria as she maneuvered her horse closer to the fence to intercept the trash. Seconds later, John managed to separate two sevens from the herd and push them across the barrier and toward the steel pen. "Finish 'em, Brad, I see the other 'n!" screamed John as he disappeared into the dust to separate the third number seven from the herd. Brad obliged by furiously spurring his mount toward the two number sevens that John had cut out. He arrived at their heels not a moment too soon; instinctively, they were already running in a wide arc in an attempt to rejoin the herd. Brad cut them off and, thanks to some brilliant sidestepping on the part of his horse, drove them further from the herd and in the direction of the pen. Meanwhile, John and Gloria peeled off the third number seven and emerged, beaming, from the whirlwind.

"We got the little bastard, Brad! Now ride!" screamed Gloria. As though guided by a single mind, the riders took their positions behind the three number sevens and drove them, Hell-bent-for-leather, toward the steel pen. In keeping with bovine instinct, the rest of the cattle clustered behind the barrier, pleased, in some primal way, to be left alone, utterly oblivious to the three ill-fated cows that had been torn from their midst. With ten seconds and change left on the clock, John, Gloria and Brad closed ranks behind the cattle and forced all three, almost simultaneously, into the pen. John's right arm shot into the air as his horse ground to a halt at the pen's entrance. The flag dropped, and the clock stopped at 67.831 seconds.

"Nice job, guys," announced Barrett over the public address system. "That's three head in 67.831 seconds. Next up are Larry, James, and Ashley. On deck are Earl, Phyllis, and Tom." As Barrett announced the lineup and reset the clock, the team that had just ridden nodded to one another and went their separate ways. According to regulations, two of them could, and no doubt would, team up in another open division ride. But not all three. Gloria, fully recovered from the broken arm that she had suffered a year earlier when her new horse had bucked her off, loped to the arena entrance and was met with a round of congratulations from those of us who were nearby. Meanwhile, John and Brad herded the number sevens out of the pen and back across the barrier to rejoin the herd. Soon, they had the cattle settled and were waiting for their cue to exit the arena.

"Gloria, that mare's got some cow in her," said Jason, a forty-something cowboy who drove long-distance rigs for a local trucking company. Gloria and her horse, a bay mare with black stockings, had joined a half dozen of us along the side of the arena. Predictably, we were already in debriefing mode. Our horses cooperated by standing still, eyes on the arena and tails swishing to ward off the flies, and seemingly oblivious to our weight on their backs.

INVENTING TRADITION

"Damn right she's cowy." Gloria, a high school teacher in her fifties from the eastern part of the state, removed her hat just long enough to rake her fingers through her hair. She settled it firmly back on her head and continued. "She's a little soft in her side, and for a while I wasn't sure she'd make a horse. But she's from West Texas. She was raised on a ranch, and she got some training from one of the big boys out there before she came east."

I stole a glance at Gloria's mount. *Yes, she's West Texas cow pony, alright. Not too tall, compact head, muscular neck, stout legs, and a brand bigger 'n Dallas on her left flank. Nice saddle, too. Billy Cook out of Sulphur, Oklahoma.*

I reached into my shirt pocket for my pen and notepad and backed Colfax a few paces so that my note taking would go unnoticed.

"So, yeah, she's got plenty of cow sense. She's got more cow in her than that roan gelding of mine," continued Gloria. "Did you see that number four Longhorn?" She paused as all eyes turned admiringly to the herd. "That little bastard can slip through anything. I just need to remember to warm this horse up plenty after I throw a bridle on her, to get the buck out of her. After that, this horse is real fast, real smooth, and real cowy."[7]

Marvin, a horse trainer from Tennessee with several national titles under his belt, chose that moment to gallop into our midst, spin his horse on its hind legs a few times like a four-legged corkscrew, and come to an abrupt halt. I figured he was going to give us his take on horse training. His specialty was cutting, and I was somewhat surprised to see him at a penning. I rarely saw much interaction between penners and cutters. But no matter: I just wanted to hear what he had to say about his field of expertise.

"There's three things you need in a cow horse," said Marvin with characteristic simplicity, "a horse that's broke, showmanship, and an ability to work cattle. But if a horse don't have a lot of handle on him, he won't work a cow. He needs to be soft in his face, and soft in his shoulders. You know, not rigid."[8]

---

[7] In cowboy vernacular, there are various ways to express a horse's eagerness and skill in handling cattle. A horse can *have some cow in him / her*, be *cowy*, and be *full of cow sense*. A horse that is *soft in its side* is overly sensitive to spurring and prone to misbehavior when spurred too vigorously. *Making a horse* is simply training one to perform well in competition. Texas cowboys, referenced herein as *the big boys*, are held in reverence not only because of their legendary skills, but also because of their iconic status as symbols of the Old West. No self-respecting cowboy would simply put a bridle on a horse; he'd *throw it on*. Finally, *to get the buck out of a horse* is to warm up enough prior to competition so that the horse is disinclined to act up. But of course, that's not a guarantee. Sometimes it's not much more than wishful thinking.

[8] Back to cowboy vocabulary: If a horse has *a lot of handle on him*, he is receptive to his rider's commands. Horses that are *soft in their face and shoulder* are supple enough to respond to

Marvin paused, probably for dramatic effect, and I poised my pen for another bout of scribbling. "The other thing is, if you want your horse to do somethin', you do it first or you do it with him. You're partners. Ride your horse with respect. Always *ask* a horse to do somethin'. If you don't get a reaction, then tell him."

He pointed at his spurs and drew knowing smiles from his listeners. "But always *ask* first. And the other thing is, if I can get a horse mentally, I'll have him the rest of the day. The number one goal is gettin' a horse to work with me mentally—get control of his mind."

Marvin started to ride away, then turned around to offer one last comment. "'Course, I'm no computer whiz or book junkie. I'm just a stupid horse trainer." And with that, he was off in a cloud of (what else?) dust.

"Trainers, huh? I'm not so sure about trainers, either." Donny, a renowned horseman from the northern part of the state who had been in the horse business for pretty much all of his seventy-plus years, had just ridden into the group and was adding his two cents to the discussion. All eyes turned in his direction to hear what pearls of wisdom he had to offer.

"You know," said Donny, clearly reveling in the attention he was receiving, "a horse trainer is about this far" (he dropped his reins in mid-sentence and placed his hands some eight inches apart) "above a pile of shit. See," he continued above a chorus of laughter, "we don't know as much as we think we do about horses."

I met Donny when he'd put on a cutting clinic at the barn where my wife and I stable our horses and pasture our cattle. In his younger days, Donny nearly landed a job as the Marlboro Man, but he had to settle for runner-up and make himself available in case some misfortune—lung cancer, for example—befell one of America's cherished icons. I once had an opportunity to peruse his collection of promotional materials, and it didn't take much imagination to picture a billboard featuring Donny galloping into a desert sunset with a cigarette dangling from his weathered lips and the Surgeon General's dire warning superimposed over his dust trail.

Still smoking and always willing to share stories from his days as one of the finest cutting horse competitors on the East Coast, Donny warmed up to his subject. "By all rights, I should have gotten involved in jumping, foxhunting…you know, horse sports common to this area."

"So why Quarter Horses, Donny, and why all this cowboy business?" I asked, trying in vain to mask my uncommon curiosity, and hoping that he'd shed his self-deprecating manner long enough to teach me something about Old Dominion cowboys.

"Well, probably because nobody else was doing it, that's why I wanted to."

Those of us who knew Donny's contrary nature smiled.

"Back when I got started," he continued, oblivious to our knowing looks, "right after the Korean War, you had to go all the way to Chicago to find a Quarter Horse. They were in a real minority around here. Since then, there's been a tremendous increase in interest in Quarter Horses. Only problem is, everyone has gotten too specialized. In the old days, you'd do a little of everything. I think all of this specialization has taken the glamour out of the horse business."

I could see from his expression that Donny was lost in thought, perhaps traveling back to his youth when he'd competed against the big boys in Texas, or maybe just reflecting on the niche that he and other horse-loving pioneers had carved out among the foxhunters and dressage riders of Virginia.

"I think I know why folks around here like Quarter Horses."

---

commands quickly. Like any athlete, a successful *cow horse* (that is, a horse with an ability to work cattle) thinks quickly and moves with dexterity.

INVENTING TRADITION

Donny was back with us now, pulling on his cigarette and squinting beneath his perfectly shaped Stetson. He paused for emphasis and was clearly choosing his words carefully. I tucked my notepad behind my saddle horn and inched Colfax forward to make sure I didn't miss a beat.

"For one thing," he said, drawing deeply on what I assumed was a Marlboro, "they're athletic. People like athleticism. And another thing is, they have a mind. They've got something you can work with. You can go out and ride these horses, put 'em away, ride 'em again, put 'em away...they just have that athleticism and are smart enough so you can get 'em to do what you want 'em to do."

I stole a glance at Colfax's head to see her ears pointed forward and her eyes, unblinking, fastened on the arena.

Alright, girl, I get the point...

"Four. Your number is four." Barrett's voice over the public address system interrupted Donny's paean to Quarter Horses. All attention turned to the arena, where Larry, James, and Ashley were approaching the herd. Larry rode in first for the initial cut, and I could see that he was moving too fast. The herd scattered like a covey of quail.

"Back me up, Ashley!" Larry hollered. A scant fifteen seconds had passed, and Larry was already enveloped by dust. "Hey cow hey cow hey cow hey cow yayaya...!" Ashley's telltale war whoop pierced the air. Within seconds, she too, was lost in the melee. Only James was still visible, galloping from one side of the arena to the other in a desperate attempt to peel back the trash.

"They'll never get 'em back now," said Jason to no one in particular. "Come on, James," he yelled, "let's see some of that cowboy stuff!"

I looked down at my notepad and scribbled furiously, secure in the knowledge that nobody would give me a second thought as long as this disaster was playing itself out.

"Ah, shit," said Jason. Suddenly aware that the mood around me had changed, I glanced up to see James face down in the dirt. His horse, slinging globs of foam every which way and farting up a storm, was bucking furiously only fifteen feet from James' inert body. Ignoring the cattle, Ashley and Larry came looming out of the dust like spirits from another world to check on their fallen team mate. The digital clock stopped at 53.876 seconds, and for several tense seconds, you could have heard a pin drop, save for the staccato *pop pop pop* issuing from the horse's hindquarters and the sickening slap of stirrup leather against its sweat-soaked hide.

"Shit." Another expletive, from whom I couldn't tell. More seconds passed. Then, almost imperceptibly, James moved one leg, then another. After what seemed like an eternity, he lifted his head to reveal a dirt-covered face and what appeared to be the beginnings of a smile.

"Hey, James, you OK?" Jason, his voice quivering ever so slightly, broke the silence.

"Yeah, I'm OK. Where's my *goddamn* horse?"

James was rising to his feet now—shaky and spitting dirt and manure from his mouth, but clearly in command of his senses, and apparently unhurt.

As if on cue, a burst of laughter erupted from the sidelines. Comments came fast and furious from cowboys who, moments earlier, had been rendered speechless by James' brush with catastrophe.

"You told me you were gonna get wild! You sure as Hell did!"

"Hey, James, I missed it! Do it again!"

"Cowboy up, James! Let's see you ride that bad boy!"

"I was just tryin' to give you folks a thrill," James yelled as he retrieved his crushed cowboy hat and brushed off what he could of the dirt. More laughter ensued. Meanwhile, Larry had delved into his own repertoire of cowboy skills and managed to grab hold of the renegade horse's reins as it tore around the arena. It took several minutes for the handsome bay gelding to slow to a trot and, eventually, to a sedate walk.

Soon, the horse's glistening hide was the only evidence of the raging fury that had brought the penning to a standstill and opened a window into the wilderness that lurks beyond the pale of consciousness. I marveled at this transition from the wild to the tame—this return, from wherever the horse had been, to civilized behavior. As I looked around at my fellow sportsmen and women, all smiles and pumped with adrenaline from James' impromptu trip to the Wild West of the imagination, I couldn't help but speculate that the horse wasn't the only one to enjoy an excursion into an untamed past.

Larry handed his team mate the reins, and James, with a mock bow that elicited yet more guffaws from his audience, mounted his horse and loped off with Ashley toward the herd to settle it in preparation for the next ride. He knew that his unplanned dismount had resulted in his team's disqualification for this particular ride. He also knew that he had several more opportunities in the open division to redeem himself and, with a little luck, win back some of the entry fee that he'd just squandered.

I exhaled, leaned forward, and caught Colfax's eye.

So help me, I think she winked.

James' accident was quickly forgotten, and the open competition resumed with no more than the usual close calls and animated banter from the sidelines. "Next up are Jason, Andy, and Tom, and on deck are Judy, Teresa, and Jenny, and then we'll have a cattle change," said Barrett over the public address system. I thought about volunteering to help with the cattle change. Like two-legged athletes on grass-covered playing fields, cattle need subs every now and then to conserve their strength and, on blistering days like this, avoid heat stroke. At regular intervals, herds are substituted for one another. For a full-blown penning, cowboys count on a minimum of three herds of thirty cattle each, for a grand total of ninety cattle, with perhaps a few extras on hand in case any of them, for whatever reason, become incapacitated. Substitute herds are kept in corrals that provide easy access to the arena, and penners are expected to pitch in when it's time to retire one herd and bring in another.

I surveyed my surroundings and spotted a middle-aged man who I didn't recognize mounted on a handsome Palomino and visiting animatedly with other cowboys. I decided to let others handle the cattle change and rode over to join in the discussion.

"I been ridin' pretty much all my life," he was saying as I rode within earshot, "but all I ever did was *sit* a horse. You know, trail riding and such. Hell, mostly I played golf five days a week. But last year I took a trip to Montana, did some real *ridin'*, and got hooked. I came home and found me a trainer who taught me the difference between *sittin'* and *ridin'* a horse."

INVENTING TRADITION

"I know what you mean," said a bearded, fifty-something man next to him. I recognized him as a man I'd seen earlier in the day, when it was cooler, sporting a vest emblazoned with a colorful logo from the 2004 Team Penning Championship in Amarillo, Texas. "I've been in the trucking business since the 1970s and I've ridden for years, mainly trail rides. But seven or eight years ago, I started penning, and then my wife got into it. And it occurred to me, when I was into trail riding, I never really *did* anything. But this," he said, gesturing toward the pandemonium that was taking shape in the arena, "this is really *doing* something. I like working the calves."

"Me too," said Dina, a young woman, surely south of twenty, sporting a pressed Western shirt and earrings. She'd just returned to the arena from watering her horse at a nearby trough. "Vince," she said, pointing in the direction of a young cowboy visiting with another group of penners, "convinced me to switch from English to Western. It's fun and more relaxed. No pretensions, you know? I still ride English, but out here, I can be as rowdy as I wanna be!" With that, she spurred her horse in Vince's direction, leaving us with an ever-so-faint aroma of shampoo that wafted from a luxuriant head of hair flowing beneath her Stetson.

"How about you, Stanley? How'd you get in this game?" My question was addressed to a newcomer, Stanley, a bookish man in his early sixties who taught astrophysics at a prestigious university in Northern Virginia.

Stanley laughed as he removed his thick glasses and rubbed a bandana across his sweaty, unshaven face. "Well, I used to ride hunters and jumpers. You know, those snobby Thoroughbreds. But my wife has been showing Quarter Horses for years, and last year I tagged along to a show in Amarillo. I found out there was a team penning going on, and I decided to check it out."

He was beaming now, this astrophysicist-turned-cowboy, astride a muscular little horse perfectly suited to his wiry frame. I strained to listen.

"And right then," he continued, doing his best to coax a Western drawl from a nasal and decidedly northeastern twang, "I said to myself, 'Now that's for me: a bunch of old guys ridin' horses, chasin' cows, and hollerin' yahoo!'"

Everybody laughed at that one, perfectly at ease with a greenhorn who wasn't afraid to trade in his professorial persona and English riding togs for boots, chaps, cowboy hats, and a feisty little Quarter Horse that he'd bought shortly after his conversion experience and eventually placed with a trainer.

"I've had nine months to mess up this horse," he said in the self-deprecating manner so common to Old Dominion cowboys. "The way I see it, I'm an untrainer! I hope my trainer can straighten him out."

"I know what you mean about action," said Mitch, the senior executive who had already regaled listeners with his story about bathing his horse and getting water squirted in his face for his trouble. "Me, I'm the kind of person who has to stay active. I can't sit still and read a book. Well, that's not quite true, I mean, I do read. But whenever I think about retiring, I wonder what I'd do..."

His voice trailed off as though he'd come to the limits of his imagination and wasn't sure how to proceed. I imagined that Mitch, who looked nowhere close to his sixty-plus years and claimed to still enjoy what was surely a stressful career, would be in the saddle, both on the job and in his chosen form of recreation, for some time to come.

"So, this lady walks into the auto parts store and tells the dude behind the counter that her husband needs a can of 710 for his pickup."

Andy had taken over the public address system. I was startled to hear a masculine voice booming across the arena and decided that Barrett must have taken an outhouse break. I noticed that Judy, Teresa, and Jenny, the first all-girl team of the day, were in the arena and waiting for two of the cowboys who had just completed their ride to settle an increasingly restive herd. I tuned into what Andy had to say.

"So the dude gets this puzzled look on his face and says to the lady, 'What do you mean, 710?' And she says, 'Look here, my husband wrote what he needs on this piece of paper,' and she hands it to him. And he reads it, turns it around, and says to the lady, 'I think he needs some OIL'."

Amid peals of laughter, Andy concluded, "710–that's OIL upside down. Get it, ladies?"

The three women in the arena, clearly amused, joined in the fun. Judy, her wavy hair bouncing as her horse pranced fitfully beneath her shapely buttocks, shouted toward the judge's booth, "Hey, Andy, you'd better be nice. Me and Jenny won first place up north last month, remember?"

"Well, even a blind hog finds a nut once in a while!"

Andy's rejoinder elicited more laughs from men and women alike. I looked toward the picnic table, groaning with barbecue and fried chicken now that lunch time was approaching, to see several women, clad in shorts and either sneakers or flip flops, smiling and nodding knowingly at the entertainment that Andy was having at their gender's expense.

"Alright, ladies, the herd is ready."

I saw Andy exit the judge's booth as Barrett resumed command of the arena. "Your number is...two. Two, two, and two." Teresa, who co-owned an independent luggage store with her husband in a town about an hour's drive south of Golconda Farm, dashed into the herd and emerged seconds later trailing a beefy number two Angus and bellowing at the top of her lungs, "Hey cow hey cow hey two hey two get on outa here cow yayayaya!" Or something to that effect. Her team mates were equally adept and, incredibly, even more vocal. With a full twenty-five seconds left on the clock, they were hard on the heels of the three number twos and making tracks to the pen. When they had the cattle perfectly grouped some  fifteen feet from the pen's entrance, they made their final charge, and the three bewildered beasts had no choice but to cooperate. They entered the pen simultaneously at a dead run and slammed into the far panel, nearly upending the entire contraption. Three slender arms shot into the air at the entrance, and three very sweaty horses dug in their hooves for vertebrae-rattling halts. The clock stopped at 58.632 seconds.

INVENTING TRADITION

A round of applause greeted what was one of the finest displays of horsemanship so far in the open division. Teresa offered her team mates very subtle high fives, or to be precise, low fives, their hands barely brushing one another at the level of their knees. With little fanfare, they pushed the number twos, panting and slobbering into the dust, out of the pen and escorted them, at a much more leisurely pace, in the direction of the herd. It appeared that all three women were going to assist with the cattle change.

"Nice job, ladies," said Barrett over the public address system. "That's three head in 58.632 seconds. Now we'll have a cattle change. First up after the cattle change are..."

I ignored the rest of Barrett's announcement. Because open riders invariably stuck with their own, I hadn't been able to book any rides in the open division, and I only had three in the mixed. Besides, lunch was beckoning, and I needed a moment to organize my thoughts. Hoping one day to master the skills that Judy, Teresa, and Jenny had just demonstrated, I spurred Colfax and loped off to my horse trailer for a much-needed swig of water and a few minutes alone with my tape recorder.

Chow Time

Once the open division rides were over and prize money handed out to the top three teams, we broke for lunch. Horses, languid in the midday heat, were tied either to the arena or to their owners' trailers, dozing and swishing their tails, seemingly oblivious to cumbersome tack and human presence. A few competitors, myself included, remained mounted, balancing Styrofoam plates and soft drinks as best we could and visiting about whatever came to mind. From my perch on Colfax, I gazed out on a sea of cowboy hats and spotted Lamont, the only Black at Golconda Farm and, upon reflection, the only one I'd seen at a penning. He and his significant other, clad similarly in ball cap and sneakers, were friendly enough, but they tended to keep to themselves and apparently didn't think twice about flaunting the association's requirement that competitors dress, appropriately enough, in Western boots, jeans, and cowboy hats. I waived to them, and even though they smiled and nodded in my direction, it seemed clear that they weren't interested in socializing. I decided to nudge Colfax in the direction of some people who'd tethered their mounts nearby and were leaning against the arena, eating and swapping war stories from their day jobs.

"I woke up in the middle of the night, thinking about penning and thinking about work," said Frank, a fifty-something cowboy whose silver beard and deep set eyes made it difficult to imagine him spending his weekdays as a technician. "And I started thinking, I just don't care anymore. I'm there for a paycheck. This is the first time in my life I've felt this way."

"Well, I still love teaching, even after all these years," said Gloria as she gnawed on a drumstick. "But the state bureaucracy is getting harder to deal with, and I can tell you, there are more bitchy employees than problem solvers. I know so many people who are counting the days until they can retire, and they should, because they're not a positive influence on students."

"I just feel fortunate that the dean at my university allows me so much autonomy," said Stanley, whose crinkled cowboy hat and three-day stubble couldn't quite mask his academic demeanor. "What I hated about working at NASA was the bureaucracy. Really, I have all the freedom these days I need."

"Yeah, I get sick of the bureaucracy in my company." Ted, another fifty-something cowboy employed as a middle manager at a multinational manufacturing company near the Coast, decided to weigh in with his own real-world complaints.

"You know," he said between swigs from a water bottle, "our new hires are required to attend training sessions. A friend of mine has four hundred acres, and I got this bright idea that we should take the newbies to his place, put them on tame horses, and get them to herd cattle back and forth across the river. I thought it would be a good way to build team work. But, hey, I'm the only cowboy. Nobody went for it."

Ted started to walk toward the picnic table, then turned back to face us. "You know," he said with conviction, "all I want is to have fun. I'm in this for the camaraderie. Sure, I want to get better with my horse, but as far as I'm concerned, those hyper-competitive guys, forming their cliques and all..." he paused and nodded his head toward a cluster of open riders, "they can go their own way if they want to. The way I figure it, a bad day of penning is better than a good day at the office."

Ted sauntered off for another helping of fried chicken, leaving the rest of us to ponder his parting thought.

"Yeah, there are lots of ways to cut it," said Johnson, yet another member in good standing of the A.A.R.P crowd who'd spent most of his career as a fire fighter and paramedic. "Years ago I was into clogging. Then I took up karate, and now, well, here I am." He pointed toward his horse, a scrappy little pony with a huge brand on its left flank that he'd picked up at an auction in Texas.

"I guess every ten years or so I need to reinvent my life." Beneath his droopy handlebar mustache, I detected a self-satisfied grin.

Mitch, with his snappy Yankee accent, was the next to chime in. "With all the stress we have, it's nice to come out and play 'cowboy.' I mean, come on, every boy grows up wanting to be a cowboy! See, I got my granddaughter shoveling manure at our place."

Unable, by his own admission, to remain still for very long, Mitch mimicked a laborer, hard at work with a shovel—a comic sight indeed, with his chaps flapping, spurs jingling, and natty cowboy hat pulled practically to the bridge of his nose. "And I says, 'Look, I had to go to college to do this. See, you have to make enough money so you can afford to have horse manure on your place!'"

We all laughed, a bit sheepishly, perhaps, at this candid glimpse of ourselves. I excused myself and spurred Colfax toward my trailer, where I hoped to sit quietly before the mixed and novice rides and record some notes. Given the conversation that I'd just taken part in, I wasn't surprised when I passed by some of the younger, more serious competitors and overheard them waxing philosophic about the perils of adulthood.

"My mother said I'd never grow up," said one, probably in his early forties, astride a jet-black gelding with rivulets of foam dripping from its breast collar.

"I'll never grow up," said the young, sinewy fellow next to him. I recognized him as Jake, a man in his early twenties who was dead set on making it to the big leagues. He traveled as far as Texas and Oklahoma to pen cattle and often returned home several thousand dollars richer, only to blow his winnings on horses and probably impressionable young women. Jake looked reasonably healthy considering the broken shoulder and shattered leg that he'd sustained only twelve weeks earlier when the competition turned rough. He'd actually removed his own cast when he got tired of waiting for the doctor to give him a clean bill of health.

"No profit in it," was the terse rejoinder from a cowboy I didn't recognize.

I rode a little further and spotted Dudley, one of the most accomplished penners in Central Virginia. Clad incongruously in shorts and sneakers, he was perched in a lawn chair on the platform beside the judge's booth, where he was taking a break from flag duty and offering advice to anyone who cared to listen. I asked him why he wasn't competing.

"Chronic kidney stones," he said without a hint of emotion. "I rode last week, took lots of pain killers." I imagined that he must be in dire straits today. Otherwise, he'd surely be in the thick of it.

"Hey, Mike, I hope your horse feels better."

I turned around to see an enormous pile of manure in my trail and Mickey, an aspiring open rider of sixteen or so who often wore his jeans tucked inside his boots like some John Wayne wannabe, snickering with his friends.

So call the press, buddy, my horse just took a crap.

"Sorry, girl," I said to Colfax as I spurred her out of earshot.

A dust devil rose specter-like out of the ground, and whatever else they had to say was lost to the wind. I noticed that several of the highly rated riders were already mounted and warming up in the arena. The knot that had been forming in my stomach suddenly tightened, and the butterflies just south of my esophagus started flapping their wings. It was almost time for the sociologist to take a back seat and let his alter ego take over. Time, that is, to cowboy up. For the rest of the afternoon and probably right through cocktail hour, I'd be spending more time observing cattle than people.

Without prompting, Colfax broke into a lope.

Lordy...

Cowboy Up!

After a few reflective moments in my stifling trailer, I answered Barrett's summons to the mixed division rides. My notepad, formerly a repository of ethnographic scribbling, quickly became a scorecard as I recorded the details of my rides. My first two rides in the mixed division were classic blow-outs.[9] In the first one, two trash cows squirted out of the herd and my team mate, Jessica, failed to intercept them before they crossed the barrier. The next one fell apart when Colfax and I rode too quickly into the herd and scattered the cattle like bird shot.

"I've never seen such a mess!" screamed my team mate, Jake, as he spurred his horse in a desperate attempt to control a situation that was clearly beyond controlling. An accomplished penner, Jake had agreed to ride with me, and I could see from his dour expression as we held the herd for the next team that he'd lived to regret it.

---

[9] A *blow-out* is pretty much what it sounds like—a complete failure, with no cattle penned.

My third and final ride in the mixed division was more successful, not enough to warrant a call back, but good enough to win back some self-respect and remind the more accomplished riders that they didn't own the arena. My team mates were two women I'd never met, and we managed to coax two cattle into the pen in just over seventy seconds. I helped settle the herd and returned to the sidelines, where the women's husbands were congratulating them and offering suggestions for next time.

No sooner had I brought Colfax to a standstill than I became aware of a commotion behind me. I swiveled in my saddle and saw one of the newcomers riding at a dead gallop through the parking area, apparently out of control. I was about to ride to his assistance when I realized that some other people had beat me to it. Two riders caught up with him and slowed his horse down enough so that one of them could grab its reins. The horse stopped, a very frightened man quickly dismounted, and the drama passed.

"Man, I can't believe this shit." Jake, pointing in the direction of the near disaster and chuckling with his young, hard-riding friends, was clearly enjoying the spectacle of a rookie who couldn't control his horse. Making a mental note to record what appeared to be a clear clash of interests between recreational riders and their competitive counterparts, I returned my attention to the arena and watched patiently as the mixed division rides drew to a close.

The final ride in the mixed division was delayed when only one rider on the previous team remembered to stay in the arena to settle the herd. I was about to volunteer my services when I heard someone call out, "Hey, Sammy, how about holding the herd for the last ride?"

An older man next to me, clad in worn shotgun chaps and scowling, shook his head with a defiance that I didn't understand. He refused to budge, and another man rode into the arena to help out.

"Come on, Sammy, it's a two-way street," called someone else. I noticed several others pointing in Sammy's direction and shaking their heads in disbelief.

"Sammy's such an asshole. He's in this for himself." It was Mitch, talking to nobody in particular, and apparently voicing a common sentiment about Sammy's go-it-alone attitude. Meanwhile, the herd was settled, and the final team entered the arena.

The mixed division concluded at 4:00. Barrett called for a cattle change, and I joined other novice riders in the arena to warm up. I'd noticed that the cows were already getting *sticky*, cowboy vernacular for tired cattle whose clustering instincts are all but impervious to horse and rider. That spelled trouble for novice division riders like myself who'd have to contend with cattle from Hell, not to mention exhausted horses, as the day wore on. I found out just how sticky they were on my first two rides as cattle careened around the arena like billiards.

I found redemption on my third ride with Stanley and Johnson. The penning gods must have been smiling. As soon as Colfax's nose crossed the barrier and the flagman signaled the beginning of the ride, I spotted two number eights that we'd been assigned to pen practically hugging each other on my left. I rode in quickly, separated them from the herd, and finished them—that is, Colfax and I drove them far enough toward the pen so that they'd more than likely stay on the far side of the arena and leave my team mates and me alone as we probed for the third number eight.[10]

---

[10] Any penner knows that it's easier to *finish* two cattle than one. A single cow is driven by instinct to return to its mates, whereas two cows are more or less content to be with one another. Many rides turn to blow-outs when a lone cow that's been separated and driven toward the pen decides to circle back and rejoin the herd.

Stanley, peering through his thick lenses, quickly spied the third one and rode gingerly into the herd. "I found him, white cow on the right! Watch the trash!" he screamed in a decidedly unprofessorial manner. Slowly and deliberately, Johnson and I peeled back the trash, and just before the thirty second warning buzzer, we had all three cows perfectly positioned for a successful charge to the pen. I took the sweeper position on the far right, Johnson took the wing position between me and the pen, and Stanley made a dash for the hole, a gap of ten feet or so between the pen and the left side of the arena that all too often becomes an escape hatch for cattle desperate to rejoin the herd.

Like a three-pronged pincer, we forced the number eights into an ever tighter configuration. When I was sure that Stanley had the hole properly blocked, I spurred Colfax toward the pen and gave her her head. She responded, and the cattle dashed into the pen with Johnson and me inches behind their flailing hooves. Our right arms flew into the air, and the clock stopped at 58.383 seconds.

"Nice job, guys. That's three head in 58.383 seconds. Next up are..."

I didn't hear the rest of Barrett's announcement. Practically oozing adrenaline, I quietly offered congratulations to my team mates, and Johnson and I returned the number eights to the herd and settled the cattle for the next team while Stanley rode to the sidelines, basking, no doubt, in praise, and perhaps picking up some suggestions on how we might have shaved off a few more seconds.

"The cattle are ready," said Barrett over the public address system once Johnson and I had them settled. "Your number is...two. Two, two, and two." With our cue to skedaddle, Johnson and I wheeled our horses and raced one another to the gate. I waited until the last second to tug on Colfax's reins and beat Johnson to the gate by half a horse length. Behind us, the next team was already in the thick of it, fully aware that ours was now the time to beat.

I met with modest success on my final two rides in the novice division. On my fourth ride, Ted, Johnson and I managed to pen one cow in 63.912 seconds, and on my last ride, Gloria, Ted and I drove two cows into the pen in just under seventy-five seconds. As penning ratings are cumulative and based on a combination of the number of cows penned and the time it takes to pen them, I knew that those rides would boost my standing vis a vis other competitors. But it was my third ride with Stanley and Johnson that not only helped my overall ratings for the season; it also catapulted our team into the call backs, where the top ten teams out of the twenty-seven that had entered the fray would vie for the prize money.

The dust was still settling from the last novice division ride when Barrett requested a cattle change and a few minutes to tabulate results from the first go. I knew that Stanley, Johnson and I had done well enough to make the call backs, but like everyone else, we had to wait for Barrett to announce the lineup. I rode to my trailer for a drink of water, hoping I'd have enough time to record some observations on my tape recorder.

"OK, folks, here's the lineup for call backs."

Conversations were cut short, and the loudspeakers became the center of attention. Even though I could hear Barrett clearly from my trailer, I quickly mounted Colfax and returned to the sidelines. It turned out that, with three head penned in 58.383 seconds, we'd finished third in the first go, which meant that we'd ride seventh in the call backs. I swung my right leg over my saddle horn, fiddled nervously with my rowel[11], and settled in for the first six rides, knowing that every blow-out would bring Stanley, Johnson and me closer to the winnings.

My best shot at a share of the jackpot was approaching. True to form, sticky cattle and tired horses confounded the first four teams. The fifth team managed to pen two head in a tad over seventy seconds, and the sixth team went down in flames (dust, that is) as trash cattle zoomed across the barrier like mall shoppers at a blue light special.

"That's a no-time," announced Barrett matter-of-factly as two disappointed cowboys loped off to settle the herd. The third, a seasoned penner but still, as near as I could tell, on the fringes of the open rider clique, hunkered down on the sidelines for some post-ride banter.

"Hey, man, easy come, easy go," he said as he rubbed his fingers together, reflecting the Old Dominion cowboy nonchalance about money and refusal to express disappointment. "But like I say, I wish I'd been born rich instead of pretty!"

"Next up are Stanley, Johnson, and Mike, with three head in 58.383 seconds in the first go."

The butterflies were now in full flight, and my insides were turning to mush. Colfax's rearing and prancing as we went through the gate weren't helpful. I took a deep breath and said to my team mates, "How about if I ride in first. She seems to do better at that."

"Suits me," said Stanley and Johnson, practically in tandem, as they assumed flanking positions.

"Guys, these cows are getting sticky," said Stanley as we approached the herd. "All we need are two head in a decent time, and we can probably win this thing. So if we get two in a hurry, let's take 'em home."

Johnson and I nodded. No sense getting greedy. The barrier was no more than ten feet in front of us. The herd was settled, and the flagman was poised to drop his flag. I glanced at the leather cow counter dangling below my saddle horn.[12] My record keeping wasn't perfect, but fortunately, I'd remembered to check off at least some of the numbers since the last cattle change.

"Forget six, three, four, and seven!" I yelled.

I detected nods on either side. You find advantages wherever you can.

The flag dropped, and Barrett's metallic voice told us all we needed to know.

"Your number is one. One, one, and one."

"On your left! Two ones, both black! I got your back!"

Stanley was hollering at the top of his lungs, but riding slowly, to the left and behind me, to avoid sending the cattle into their customary panic. I'd spotted them already. Ominously,

---

[11] The rowel is the business end of a spur and comes in all sizes and degrees of severity. Mine are pretty much middle of the road, neither too large nor too sharp. I like to say that I use them for persuasion, not cruelty, and that they remind my precocious horses that, at least theoretically, I'm the boss.

[12] A cow counter is a leather strip with ten slits in it, and each slit is fitted with a piece of metal that can be moved from one side to the other. It can be hooked unobtrusively to a saddle and is used to keep track of the cattle that the judge designates. Cowboys outfitted with these handy devices know which cattle have been used in a given herd, and when it's their turn to pen, we know at a glance which cattle will not be designated for their ride. I've seen homemade cow counters, but I purchased mine at the National Saddlery in Oklahoma City.

INVENTING TRADITION

Colfax reared once, then settled down and went straight for them. With some careful maneuvering, we got behind them and sent them flying toward the pen.

"Finish the sons-a-bitches, Johnson!" I screamed. "I see the third one!" Sure enough, there he was, big as life and twice as ugly, moving along the fence to my right. Colfax didn't flinch as we snuck up behind him. A little light spurring and sidestepping and we had him right where we wanted him.

"Watch the trash, Stanley, watch the trash!" I yelled as I dug in my spurs.

He did, and we were home free.

And that's when all Hell broke loose.

To this day, I'm not sure why Colfax acted the way she did. Maybe there was a horsefly looking for a snack on her rear end, or maybe she had a touch of rain rot that was starting to itch under her sweat-soaked saddle blanket. It's possible (though I am loath to admit it) that, in the heat of the moment, I was a bit too persuasive with my spurs. But in all likelihood, the penning gods simply decided that enough good fortune was...enough. All I remember is that, half-way to the pen, going at a dead gallop and trailing three panicked cows, Colfax stuck her nose in the dirt and started to buck.

Instinctively, I thrust my feet forward in the stirrups and threw my weight—what there is of it—backward. At the same time, I jerked violently on the reins, knowing full well that Colfax's bit was designed more for fast maneuvering than stopping. But to no avail. Something in that little horse brain of hers was telling her to put me in the dirt, and there wasn't much I could do about it.

Two other things about the incident remain fuzzy: how I stayed in the saddle, and how Stanley, Johnson and I managed to put those cows in the pen in 65 seconds flat. I do remember

Sean, a seasoned penner who offered clinics to beginners nearly every Friday night at a nearby arena, jumping off the fence to give me a hand. I also remember that he didn't need to, because something else in Colfax's little horse brain told her to knock it off a split second before we would have slammed into the fence. She lifted her head, and I wheeled her around just in time to see Sean skedaddle over the fence to safety and my team mates lift their arms in triumph.

"Nice job, guys," announced Barrett. "That's three head in 65 seconds."

My head cleared enough to help Johnson settle the herd. Returning without incident to the sidelines, I watched the next team pen three head in less than sixty seconds. The final team blew out. I couldn't be sure until Barrett announced the results, but it seemed certain that Stanley, Johnson and I had finished in second place. Not bad, since I'd just returned from a near-death experience and could think of nothing but a hot shower and a cold beer. I rode slowly to a nearby trough to let Colfax slake her thirst.

"OK, here are the results from the novice division."

I turned toward the judge's booth and listened carefully. Sure enough, Stanley, Johnson and I had finished in second place. I breathed a sigh of relief and tugged on Colfax's reins, anxious to collect my winnings and head for home to enjoy the aforementioned amenities. I approached the booth in time to see Stanley, the professor with whom I felt a special kinship, gracefully accepted his share of the loot from Barrett, presented in a simple white envelope. We'd won a grand total of $40.00 each, not quite enough to compensate for my entry fees and the gas it took to get over the mountain, but enough for a six pack and a night on the town with my wife.

Suddenly, Barrett disappeared into the booth. Then the public address system crackled to life.

"There's been a protest about the second place team. We have a request that they be disqualified because Sean jumped into the arena to stop that crazy horse."

I froze in my tracks, wondering how this unexpected turn of events would play out. Even though neither Colfax nor I had come in contact with him, Sean's courageous intervention was, potentially, a breach of the rules.

I overheard Barrett talking to someone at the window of the booth. "So who's protesting?" I heard her ask.

"I'm not sure," was the puzzled reply. "I guess it's anonymous."

Great. Leave it to Colfax and me to create an incident.

What I heard next over the public address system was slightly muffled, as though Barrett didn't mean to make a general announcement. But all of us heard it, and, as the late President Reagan might have said with his fabled fancy for Western bravado, it made my day.

"Far as I'm concerned," said Barrett indignantly to a larger audience than she perhaps intended, "anyone who can hang on to a bucking horse like that and still pen cattle deserves an award."

Apparently, that settled it. The few folks who were milling around the judge's booth were laughing, perhaps wondering, as I was, who had had the gall to register a protest. The controversy quickly gave way to jokes at my expense, which I accepted with the self-deprecation that we expect from one another. Sean was one of the first. "Hey Mike, you owe me one," he said, dismissing his leap in front of my deranged horse as all part of a day's work. "I missed it, Mike, do it again!", "Great job, thanks for the show," and "You're in the wrong sport, Mike—this ain't rodeo!" were the kind of comments I answered with a smile and a shrug of my shoulders, determined not to let on that my insides had turned to soup, wondering how we'd managed to get those cattle penned, and resigned to a nickname that would never fly back at the university.

Quittin' Time

Johnson showed up after a trip to the watering trough to accept his envelope, and we shook hands and said our goodbyes. Stanley already had his envelope. As soon as the controversy abated and he was sure it was his, he clutched it like a Nobel Prize. I tucked mine in my shirt pocket, right behind my fieldnotes. My pen was no doubt pulverized somewhere in the arena. After a round of congratulations and good wishes, we headed for our trailers.

Christy, a young woman I didn't know very well with children in tow, was walking a very sweaty horse to her trailer.

"So, how was your day?" I asked.

INVENTING TRADITION

"You know, this is the only sport I do where I hurt from smiling," was her reply. Judging from the grin on her face, I had no doubt that she'd wake up Sunday with a sore jaw.

"So, how about you, Tom?" I asked another acquaintance in his early forties who had recently retired from the Navy and was looking forward to a second, albeit related, career.

His answer rivaled Christy's in its simplicity. "It's a pretty day. I got to ride. I'm pleased with that." I was glad to know that his less than stellar performance that day in the arena hadn't been a deal killer.

I glanced behind me and saw Hank, an accomplished rider who was equally at ease with open riders and novices, riding in my direction. Judging from his generally upbeat nature, I knew what to expect, but I asked him anyway.

"Good day?" I asked as he rode by on the way to his trailer.

"Any time I'm riding, I'm having a good day," he said. And with that, he laughed and spurred his horse toward a trailer crammed with veterinary supplies that he used in his equine dentistry practice.

Jim, a novice rider who lived somewhere near Washington, DC, was sitting quietly on his horse and smiling. He had a long way to go in terms of skills, and I admired his effort.

"What'd you think, Jim?" I asked as I passed by.

"Where else can you have so much fun for so little money?" he replied, perhaps wondering why I would ask such a foolish question.

I couldn't help smiling. Here was a young man living a stone's throw from one of the world's great metropolises, with unlimited opportunities for entertainment at his doorstep, getting his kicks by driving three hours south to chase cattle from the backside of a horse.

My last encounter was with a man in his twenties who was new to penning. I couldn't remember his name, but I remembered his awkward forays into the herd. His distinguishing feature was the cord dangling from his hat to a point several inches below his chin, which gave him a slightly comical appearance—a stark contrast with more common and decidedly more macho headgear sported by seasoned cowboys and aspiring novices.

"So, how'd it go?" I asked. "Think you'll stick with it?"

"I don't care if I look like a goober," he said. *That's probably a good thing...* "I like this. I can see getting hooked."

The crowd was dissipating. When we reached my trailer, I dismounted and bent over to unfasten my chinks and spurs. Colfax took that as her cue to rub her sweaty nose (a bit too vigorously, considering my exhausted state) against my backside. Rigs were bouncing past us on their way to the gate. Waves and goodbyes were exchanged over the din of clanging metal. Sunlight glinted off bumpers and tailgates. The valley was bathed in an eerie, twilight glow. Long shadows fanned out across the grass.

An earthy aroma of manure and hay, cooked to a yeasty brew, greeted me as I opened my trailer and grabbed a bottle of water to sooth my parched insides. I removed Colfax's bridle, replaced it with a halter and lead rope, and secured her to the trailer. Even though the grass was no doubt tempting, she was too tired to protest. She groaned with relief as I slid the saddle off her drenched hide and loosened her lead rope so she could graze for a few minutes before loading.

I stowed my saddle and blanket in the trailer and emerged to find that Colfax and I were alone in the pasture. All that remained of the mighty rigs was a trail of dust along the entrance to Golconda Farm. The only activity was back in the arena, where Andy and his sons were herding the cattle from their holding pens into the pasture. I knew they'd soon find the water they so richly deserved after a day of putting up with Old Dominion cowboys.

"Showtime's over, sweetheart," I said to Colfax as I led her to the back of the trailer. "Let's go home."

I swear...

Never mind.

Chapter Seven — A Sociology of Cowboy Sports

"It was either this or a red sports car."

Old Dominion cowgirl
Ruckersville, VA

Culture, Cowboy Sports, and the Seamless Web

The previous chapter was fun to write. Compressing data gathered from my fieldnotes into a day-long narrative unleashed a torrent of memories and rekindled the visceral jolt that pulls Old Dominion cowboys to the arena. Jake, the seasoned penner referenced in Chapter Six who competes in the big leagues, expressed more than he knew in an offhand remark about the allure of team cattle penning. "It's not just an obsession," he said with a grin. "Hell, it's a disease!"

Sociologically, the narrative is meant to illustrate the porous boundary between sport and culture and illuminate the multi-faceted lens through which ethnographers perceive collective behavior. I approached my units of analysis in all their dimensions, aware of and deeply involved in what was happening in real time even as I probed for symbols, interaction rituals, historical antecedents, and cross-cultural comparisons—all reflections of the sociological imagination, and all key to understanding the formation of identity and expression of culture. From the beginning, I was drawn to a dichotomy that I tried to incorporate in the foregoing narrative and that I will revisit shortly: cowboys' much-touted independence and self-reliance ends at the arena, where cultural norms, rules, and regulations become vital to expressing cowboy ways. No matter how independent we perceive ourselves or, sociologically speaking, no matter how much agency we lay claim to within institutional frameworks and normative systems, we are all susceptible to the lure of groups whose activities enable us to transcend, if only fleetingly, the paramount reality that directs the course of our lives.[1] What is true in the broader culture certainly holds for Old Dominion cowboys. Social structures are simultaneously enabling and constraining insofar as they open up channels for identity formation and cultural expression even as they wrap us in webs of conformity (Hays 1994).

My status as an Old Dominion cowboy allowed me to indulge my preference for direct over mediated experience and, specifically, to revel in the emotional and historical mimesis that comes with the territory. Yet warning bells sounded as I stepped into the shifting sands of authenticity. Regardless of how energized I felt in my connection to America's mythic past and its resonance in sport, I had to remind myself that authenticity is not so much an inherent quality

---

[1] Borrowing from Cohen and Taylor's (1976) lexicon cited in Chapter One, "Old Dominion Cowboys," I define paramount reality very broadly as the reality of everyday life: a familiar, stable, and by and large friendly world whose established constructions envelope us on all sides and mold our consciousness. It is the tension between paramount reality and the human drive to establish an identity—that is, between reality work and identity work— that compels us to seek avenues of escape.

as it is a social construction, subject to the vicissitudes of time and evolution of attitudes (Berger and Luckmann 1967). My challenge thus became two-fold: as a cowboy, I needed to hone my skills and shape my persona to the contours of cowboy ways; and as a sociologist, I had to keep arm's length from the whole business—secure in my surroundings, yet mindful of the tension between complete membership status (Adler and Adler 1987) and objective research.

Yearning for authenticity has deep roots in American culture. Orvell (1989), cited previously in connection with turn-of-the-century Wild West shows, detected among Americans an increasing fixation on the real thing between 1880 and 1940, when advances in technology were opening a cornucopia of mediated experience for the price of a ticket, thus substituting the fabricated world for the natural one. As the curtain closed on the frontier experience and American-style entertainment came into its own, opportunities for direct, unmediated experience seemed more vital than ever. As we have seen, Elias and Dunning (1986) went so far as to link direct experience, and particularly the perils of athletic competition, with the maintenance of mental health. Perhaps Simmel (1990: 67) said it best when he suggested that "the power and the rhythm of emotions" lie at the core of human motivation.

As an observant participant—that is, as a cowboy first and an observer second—I brought a sensitivity to my units of analysis dating back to youthful experiences in my home state of Oklahoma as well as New Mexico and Texas. Even at a remove of some thirty years, my cowboying days remain seared in my consciousness and continue to serve as wellsprings of self-reflectivity. Simply put, I think that my experiences as a common ranch hand constitute a bridge between the range cattle industry, the West of the imagination, and the cowboy sports that celebrate and commemorate them.

The frontier narrative, its *dénouement* in the closing decades of the nineteenth century, and its revitalization by turn-of-the-century culture producers bent on salvaging a civilization in peril from the juggernaut of modernization, coalesced in America's foundation myth. Nurtured by mass entertainment and embedded in collective memory, the myth has survived, battered but far from beaten, in the West of the imagination. It survives as a continuum, ranging from film and Country and Western music to rodeo and everyday experiences on cattle ranches, where working cowboys ply their trade in much the same way, and according to much the same ethos, as their trail-blazing ancestors. Somewhere along this continuum lie cowboy sports and the Old Dominion cowboys who keep them alive. Our sports are thus part of a seamless web in which distinctions between work and play, sport and leisure, even experience and imagination, dissolve into a rich cultural stew that is peculiarly American and specifically Western. That's hard to capture in documents, and it's not altogether clear from the backside of a horse. But put those perspectives together and season them with a little up-close-and-personal experience in cow country, and I think you've got something worth pondering as we blaze a trail into the twenty-first century.

With this in the way of background, I offer an analysis of fifteen themes that I teased from my fieldnotes and incorporated into my narrative. Unless otherwise noted, ethnographic data referenced in my thematic analysis come from the preceding chapter. Of course, delineating themes and treating them separately is artificial insofar as cultural attributes feed on and reinforce one another. In the social world, they can no more be separated than the ingredients of a recipe once the concoction is bubbling away in the oven. Nevertheless, it is only through this kind of scrutiny that I can lay bare the attributes of cowboy sports. I treat themes systematically, beginning with the most obvious ones and moving on to higher levels of abstraction. Throughout this analysis, I address the dichotomies between the wild and the tame, dependence and

INVENTING TRADITION

independence, and especially authenticity and invented traditions: in short, the unresolved tensions that have characterized American culture since its inception and crystallized both in our collective memory of the frontier experience and in expressions of cowboy ways in sport.

Reference has been made to the cultural trinity—Theodore Roosevelt, Frederic Remington, and Owen Wister—and the role they played in promoting their versions of cowboy ways to an angst-ridden nation. Borrowing from Hobsbawm and Ranger's (1983) lexicon, I have suggested that the cowboy type, a collage of characteristics that has provided fodder for mass entertainment since the late nineteenth century and has long since taken up residence in our collective memory, constitutes an invented tradition insofar as it represents selective borrowing from an historic text rather than wholesale mimicry. This is not to suggest that turn-of-the-twentieth-century culture producers had anything to do with cowboy sports. In their day, rodeo was embryonic, and cowboy sports were not even on the horizon. Indeed, organized sports as we know them were just beginning to assume their present form between 1880 and 1920. The frontier was receding into history, modernity was coming into focus, and athletics were increasingly seen as a means of regeneration in a rapidly secularizing society (Mrozek 1983). Yet the cultural trinity and its ilk, together with an entertainment industry that was already profiting from endless retellings of America's foundation myth, was pivotal in making sure that modernization didn't jeopardize such virtues as independence, self-reliance, and stoicism. These quintessentially Western attributes were wrested from centuries of pushing back a wilderness, were fundamental to life in the great outdoors, and were imperiled by the closing of the frontier.

The task at hand, then, is to suggest which themes in cowboy sports represent authentic cowboy ways, which ones reflect selective filtering in the service of cultural engineering, and which ones can be attributed to a century of cultural change. As we have seen, establishing a baseline for authenticity is problematic insofar as it reflects the myriad prisms through which individuals shape their identities and construct meaning in their lives.[2] Yet in a cultural study rooted in historic discourse, the risk is unavoidable. After all, cowboys didn't simply arise from thin air. They were, and are, agricultural laborers whose trade originated on the cattle frontier, and their legacy is a constellation of skills and attributes subsumed under the rubric of cowboy ways. Somewhere at the intersection of history and sociology is a typology whose makeovers since the closing of the frontier in no way belies its genesis in the practical and decidedly authentic business of providing Eastern markets with Western beef. To clarify my analysis, I occasionally fall back on memories from my own cowboying days in the American Southwest. They may be thirty years behind me, but they remain crystal clear in my mind's eye, and they serve as a conduit between an authentic, albeit idealized, past and a postmodern present.

Like the cattle trails leading to Abilene, my thematic analysis of cowboy sports is thus woven from distinct, yet complementary, threads. Of course, returning to the analogy with cooking, culture is both organic and dynamic, and we need to be careful about drawing distinctions that obscure more than they reveal (Swidler 1986; Hays 1994). At the risk of making chaos out of sublime and symbiotic relationships, I thus enter my units of analysis like a cowboy easing himself into a herd, anxious to separate designated cows from the trash, yet mindful of just how sticky cattle can be.

Once themes are revealed and clarified, I will be in a position in Chapter Eight, "Postmodern Cowboys," to suggest connections between America's frontier narrative, the

---

[2] See Chapter Three, "Cowboys in History, Literature, and Showbiz," pp. 45-46, and the subsequent review of cowboy memoirs under *Honest-to-Goodness-Cowboys*.

traditions that it spawned, and the sports that keep them alive both in the arena and in the cultural imaginary. Then, like a cowboy who's spent a night gathering mavericks[3] before pushing his herd to its final destination, I will reassemble these themes, return to the questions that sparked this inquiry, and suggest ways that cowboy sports serve as vehicles of identity formation and cultural expression in our postmodern age. Finally, I will hazard some conclusions about macro social forces that keep cowboy sports alive and, perhaps even more important, develop a theoretical prism to help us situate Old Dominion cowboys in a sociological context and understand the salience of cowboy sports in the twenty-first century.

Themes

Cowboying

Perhaps the most obvious feature of cowboy sports is the athleticism required of horse and rider. Whatever our skill levels as reflected in our ratings, all of us aspire to become better competitors, and all of us spend plenty of time and treasure to do so. Once committed, there seems to be no turning back: there is always another saddle or bridle to try, always a new training video to watch, and often another horse trainer to contact whose techniques just might be the ticket to a competitive edge. But clearly, nothing trumps the quest for the ideal horse. Conversations about horses dominate the sideline banter in any cowboy sporting event that I have attended, and the arena buzz often centers on a horse that one of us has acquired, or entrusted to a trainer, since the last competition. Donny, the runner-up Marlboro Man who claimed that horse trainers aren't very far above "a pile of shit," had this in mind when he praised Quarter Horses for their athleticism and intelligence. In Chapter One, "Old Dominion Cowboys," I footnoted an instance when one of my fellow competitors, a woman in her fifties, was thrown from her horse and suffered a  broken arm. She was the inspiration in Chapter Six for Gloria. Moments before her accident, she gave me the lowdown on her new horse that was, in my estimation, far too large and perhaps too powerful for her diminutive frame. As I watched her husband load their two horses into their

---

[3] Mavericks are unbranded cattle whose ownership is in question. The term originated in the mid 1800s when a South Texas rancher by the name of Samuel A. Maverick gained a reputation for letting his cattle run wild. People around San Antonio became accustomed to the sight of Maverick's cattle roaming at will across the range. Eventually, all unbranded cattle were referred to as mavericks, and the moniker continues to describe anyone who refuses to go along with the crowd. An online source for the etymology of Western expressions is available at http://www.tsha.utexas.edu/handbook/online/index.html.

trailer and rush her to the hospital, I reflected on the lengths to which all of us go to become better cowboys.

Beneath the good humor and camaraderie is an expectation that participants take their sport seriously and do what they can to improve their cowboying skills. Horsemen such as Tray, the trainer who gave me some pointers after assessing my degree of seriousness, are clearly interested in selling their services, but they also share a commitment to promoting Western horsemanship and raising the caliber of competition. Skill-building thus constitutes what is no doubt the clearest, not to mention the most authentic, connection between Old Dominion cowboys and the mythic past that we commemorate. As we have seen, the cowboys depicted in literature and films spend more time shooting one another and rescuing towns from desperadoes than tending cattle. Not so with cowboy sport competitors. For us, cowboying is not an invented tradition. Beneath the rituals, rules, and procedures that define cowboy sports are genuine skills, acquired at the risk of injury and even death, which enable competitors to enjoy mimesis on two levels: entering the flow of our nation's foundation narrative and, at the same time, experiencing the emotional rush of penning, sorting, and cutting cattle.

A little less talk and a lot more action

Closely related to cowboying is the preference for action over introspection. Time and again, competitors mentioned their attraction (addiction?) to fast-paced action. Contexts and histories varied: a truck driver who had been a trail rider throughout his adult life was delighted to learn the difference between *sittin' a horse* and *ridin' a horse*; several people schooled in English riding techniques jettisoned their jodhpurs and sleek Thoroughbreds for cowboy hats and scrappy Quarter Horses because they relished the chance to *get rowdy*; one high-level corporate manager admitted a disinclination to sit still for any length of time; and a university professor was wooed into team penning when he found kindred spirits who enjoyed "ridin' horses, chasin' cows, and hollerin' 'yahoo'!" I was particularly intrigued with a man who'd spent his career as a firefighter and paramedic and took up team penning as an alternative to his previous recreational activities: clogging and karate. "I guess every ten years or so I need to reinvent my life," he said one day as he reflected on a lifetime of action-packed recreation.

What these and other competitors too numerous to mention shared is an attraction to what cowboy-turned-president Theodore Roosevelt would have called "the strenuous life." Much the same can be said for Frederic Remington. From the comfort of his studio on the St. Lawrence River, he sank ever deeper into nostalgia for cowboys and their action-oriented ways, and his art promoted Western adventurers to the point of hagiography. Meanwhile, Owen Wister and a legion of dime novelists spawned an entertainment genre with their depictions of cowboys who'd just as soon shoot first and ask questions later. Yet as we have seen in memoirs left by Andy Adams (1903), Teddy Blue Abbott (1939), and Charlie Siringo (1950), the prism through which turn-of-the-century culture producers interpreted the frontier experience left little room for the mindless drudgery that was the cowboy's lot.

In my reflective moments between rides and traveling to and from competitions, I have wrestled with an inner conflict: Even as I savor the action of penning, sorting, and cutting cattle, and although I am convinced that horses enjoy playing their part in the animate trinity, I am aware of the artificiality and perhaps even cruelty of working horses and cattle to the point of exhaustion. Simply put, in the real world, no cowboy worth his salt would deliberately wear out his horse and run weight off his cattle. I am reminded of Hugh, an old timer with whom I had the privilege to work at the Double U Bar Ranch in Colfax County, New Mexico, in the summer of 1974. His connection with the land defies the modern imagination. In all his seventy-plus years, he had never strayed further from home than brief visits to Arizona and Arkansas. He became visibly agitated whenever the young cowboys at the ranch got together on their days off for impromptu roping contests. "Horses have feelings, too..." he muttered as he limped off to the bunkhouse on a pair of bowed legs that touched the ground only when absolutely necessary. For Hugh and, I suspect, a generation of aging cowboys whose memories of the cattle frontier were barely beyond the purview of lived experience, business was business, and there was something suspicious about young men who overworked livestock just to prove a point.

In their evolution from proletarian necessity to structured competition, cowboy sports sacrificed authenticity for action. Of course, even in our technological age, there are circumstances on farms and ranches that call for deft maneuvering from the backside of a horse, particularly in terrain unsuited to mechanization. Yet pushing horses and cattle to the limits of their endurance, particularly in the heat of summer, has more to do with our cultural obsession with athletic competition than genuine cowboy ways. Developing skills that their pastoral ancestors reserved for specific purposes and dire emergencies, Old Dominion cowboys thus participate in an invented tradition, extracting skills from a collectively remembered past that lend themselves to sport while eschewing the context from which they came. Like so many activities that have evolved through the centuries, cowboy sports are simulacra, far removed from the socioeconomic context that spawned them.

The cowboy says it salty

Cowboy sports provide an ideal arena (pun intended) for considering communication as a dimension of culture. Historically, Americans have been biased toward the technological marvels that facilitate communication. Yet communication defined simply as sending and receiving information is only one way to conceive of this most ancient form of human interaction. An alternative to the so-called transmission model is the view that communication constitutes a ritual experience aimed less at extending messages across distance than in maintaining society across time. Carey (1989) noted that the simple act of reading a newspaper reveals communication on two levels: even as readers glean information about their world, they participate in a ritual that strengthens cultural ties and maintains meaning systems embedded in communicative symbols. To update Carey's illustration of communication as culture, think of the morning routine that plays itself out in offices worldwide as white collar professionals boot up their computers and log onto their email accounts. Beneath the obvious level of sharing information is a deeper expression of culture in action, with untold millions of people using technology as an extension of themselves, coding and decoding messages in the certainty that they belong to a vast network based on technological savvy and meaning systems familiar to all. Communication, then, runs far deeper than technology and economics. It lies at the heart of culture, shapes community, and informs the myriad of activities that make up our daily lives. No matter how social life is produced and reproduced, "it is through communication, through the intergraded relations of symbols and social structure, that societies, or at least those with which we are most familiar, are created, maintained, and transformed" (p. 119).

Cowboy sportsmen and women interact through language whose symbolic richness shines through a veneer of disarming minimalism. Reflecting a simplicity bordering on the banal, Marvin, the horse trainer and champion cutting horse competitor, admonished a gathering of wannabe cutters to remember what's required in a *finished* (that is, well-trained) horse: "There are three things you need in a cow horse: a horse that's broke, showmanship, and an ability to work cattle." I might as well admit that such bare-knuckles oratory washes over this cowboy-turned-sociologist like a cool mountain shower after a week in the halls of academe.

Communication in and around the arena might not always pass muster as the King's English. But it is certainly expressive, and it serves as an insider's code to cowboy communication as well as a portal into a mythic past. Penners quickly learn that a *cow horse* is not the result of genetic engineering gone haywire, but is instead a mount with, in Marvin's terse lexicon, "an ability to work cattle." *Cow work* might raise suspicions among labor activists, but cowboys recognize the moniker as shorthand for what we do. *Cow* is a perfectly good verb, *cowy* is a good thing for a horse to be, *cow sense* is a good thing for a horse to have, and *sticky* is a bad thing for cows to be when you're trying to coax them out of a herd. When it comes to good horsemanship, everyone knows that *making a horse* has less to do with amorous liaisons than with good training and clear signals between man and animal. Similarly, a horse *with a handle on him* doesn't make him easier to haul through an airport, but it does ensure some measure of compliance, particularly if you can remember to apply pressure with your *cow leg* and *cow rein*, both of which depend on the location of your sought-after cow. (And trust me: That changes really fast!) If a horse is *soft in his side*, then you'd better use your spurs gently and perhaps infrequently. But if he's *soft in his face and in his shoulders*, then that's good, because he'll react quickly to commands. Merely *sittin' a horse* is about as exciting as watching grass grow. And when someone from the sidelines hollers, "Let's see some of that cowboy stuff!", you can practically hear the synapses clicking on rowdy, wild, and Western riding, complete with colorful sound effects, and never mind the dust.

Not only is cowboy vocabulary expressive; it is profoundly descriptive, particularly when used in the service of metaphor. As we have seen (Abbott 1939; Adams 1903; Adams, 1971; Boatright 1949; Siringo 1950), cowboys have always reflected the immensity of their landscape and hardscrabble nature of their work by painting word pictures, using exaggeration to the point of absurdity to illustrate a point. My favorite expression fell from the lips of a farrier and weekend cutter who was handing over his business to a young man of exceedingly small stature: so small, in fact, the he was "no bigger 'n a cake of soap after a hard day's washin'." Equally vivid images were conjured up by cowboys who likened a good penning horse to an expensive lawn mower or a set of high-tech golf clubs. Not surprisingly in a sport derived from an agricultural enterprise, earthy allusions were about as common as ticks on a dog's back. Donny's suggestion that horse trainers are "about this far (the distance between his outstretched hands) above a pile of shit" comes to mind as a particularly memorable slice of scatological humor that couldn't be much more descriptive. Tray's reference to a girl who hesitated to speak her mind as someone "who wouldn't say shit if she had a mouthful of it" was an indelicate turn of phrase, to be sure, but was certainly expressive, and utterly to the point. Mickey's observation that Colfax had left an uncommonly large pile of manure behind her, annoying though it was, typifies the way that cowboys embrace bodily functions as part of our cultural milieu. Thus do vocabulary and the uses to which it is put contribute to the perpetuation of cowboy culture: earthy, prone to exaggeration, and tuned to the rhythms of the animate trinity.

A third and final aspect of cowboy communication is the self-deprecating humor that we expect of one another. In activities as wild and unpredictable as cowboy sports, opportunities abound for amusement at our own expense. James' fall from his horse and Colfax's attempt to unseat me during our charge to the pen were nothing less than chances to demonstrate acceptance of group norms. Once our comrades determined that we were unhurt, James and I were compelled to swallow our pride and play along with the ribbing that we knew was coming. Similarly, no matter how accomplished we are, we know better than to brag about our prowess. Marvin's admission that he was "just a stupid horse trainer," Donny's  admission that we can never understand everything about horses, Andy's jokes about female contestants (over the public address system, no less!) and the women's willingness to join in the fun just before turning in a stellar performance, and Stanley's claim that he'd had "nine months to mess up his horse" were typical examples of cowboy modesty laced with humor.

Unlike athletes who spike balls after touchdowns and pounce on one another after goals or home runs, cowboys signal the end of a successful ride with low fives and subtle nods of appreciation to their team mates, hardly the kind of exuberance that makes for a good photo op. And how about unsuccessful rides and blow-outs? Not surprisingly, cowboys rarely let their disappointment show. When Jake hollered at the top of his lungs "I've never seen such a mess!" just before our team blew out in the mixed division, he was expressing more than a vision of impending failure; he was also signaling his nonchalance and even amusement about losing his entry fee. Everyone knows that even the best riders can be undone by contrary cattle.

Thus do vocabulary, metaphor, and self deprecating humor coalesce into yet another trinity: a communicative trinity linking authentic cowboy ways with the sports that mimic them. Abbott (1939), Adams (1903), and Siringo (1950) certainly provided glimpses of communication as an expression of culture in their memoirs. It was left to their descendants on ranches and in arenas and, as we have seen, policy makers at the highest levels of governance to keep cowboy ways alive through communication. In short, there is nothing invented about the cowboy's salty lingo. And trust me: It still comes in right handy when you're caught between a rock and a hard place on a horse that's gone plumb loco.

The hoss bidness

When it comes to finances, cowboy sports are a slippery slope. Horses can be plenty expensive, but over the long run, the initial outlay for a horse pales in comparison to the ongoing burden of equine maintenance and purchasing tack, feed, and supplies. What's more, there is no shortage of opportunities to add to one's *remuda*.[4] It should thus come as no surprise to find that the horse business (or, to use the proper inflection, the *hoss bidness*) is a constant topic of conversation. Analogies are routinely drawn between horses and equipment. Although even the most taciturn cowboys exhibit some degree of affection toward their mounts, horses that don't perform up to expectations can look forward to an early retirement. It is not unusual for a cowboy sportsman to recognize somebody's horse more readily than its rider. In cutting horse competition, announcers make reference to horses' names and, for all intents and purposes, ignore their riders. I have certainly subscribed to the group norm: in just two years as a cowboy sportsman, I have already bought two horses, and I don't exactly run for cover when a seller shows up. On the other hand, neither of my horses, Haskell and Colfax, carries the ultimate badge of distinction: a brand, either on the shoulder or flank, indicating provenance from a ranch—most likely from the far side of the Mississippi, and more than likely from Texas.[5]

Much the same can be said about vehicles, trailers, tack, equipment, and especially saddles. Some saddles are bought off the rack in a tack store; others are custom-made to fit particular human and equine backsides.[6] I was intrigued to learn about *fitting clinics* where people learn how to buy a saddle based not on their own physiques, but rather on contours and musculature unique to their horses. Other accouterments include bridles, bits, pads, blankets, and regalia worn by either horse or rider that have functional value as well as symbolic significance known only to the *cognoscenti*.[7] I have also detected an undercurrent of communal expectations reflected in Western paraphernalia. Indeed, one of my most consistent findings is the reluctance of competitors, and particularly men, to remove their hats. An exception is made when prayers are offered before the competition gets underway. I can only ascribe this custom to the cowboy hat's status as an icon of the West. Barcheaded, cowboys aren't quite naked, but they certainly appear incomplete and perhaps even a bit ridiculous. All I know is that, whenever I remove my hat to catch a breeze or just wipe the sweat off my brow, I feel uncomfortable and vulnerable in a way that is hard to describe. So generally speaking, I keep my hat on, even when I think a little unfiltered sunshine and a cool breeze would suit me just fine.

Under the rubric of the *hoss bidness*, we thus find a curious mix of hard-nosed practicality and invented traditions made possible by the miracle of mass production and its twin, mass consumption. Whether driving a herd up the Western Trail or cutting cattle in a covered arena under the blare of loudspeakers, horses and tack must certainly be up to the task. Yet the

---

[4] A *remuda* is a herd of horses from which a cowboy selects his mount. The word comes from the Spanish verb *remudar*, to exchange.

[5] Haskell and Colfax are registered with the American Quarter Horse Association (A.Q.H.A.) in Amarillo, Texas. Haskell was born in Moneta, Virginia, and Colfax was born in White Bluff, Tennessee.

[6] At a practice penning that Colfax and I attended, the guest of honor was a famous saddle maker. With typical good-natured ribbing, the announcer let it be known that an older man who was flirting with the ladies was one of America's most renowned saddlers.

[7] I have owned two saddles from the Billy Cook Saddlery in Sulphur, Oklahoma, and my chinks were custom made at the National Saddlery in Oklahoma City. Aside from their durability and comfort, these pieces of equipment serve as good luck talismans from my home state.

availability of equipment and an endless array of options give modern day sportsmen an opportunity for acculturation that would bewilder our pre industrial forebears. Cowboy sport competitors are, after all, consumers. Honed like the rest of the industrialized world to the lure of the marketplace, we support our cowboying proclivities with our wallets, ever watchful for that special horse or piece of equipment that just might make us better cowboys, or at least make us look better. In the meantime, there's nothing we enjoy more than baking in the hot sun astride our mounts, discussing the *hoss bidness* in all its manufactured glory, and surrounded by the tools of our trade that facilitate cowboying skills even as they bind us to our collectively remembered past.

Cowboy up!

In 1994, Jersey Films and New Line Cinema released *8 Seconds* to wide acclaim. The film chronicles the life and tragic death of Lane Frost, a rodeo cowboy from Oklahoma who bucked his way to the pinnacle of success as the Pro Rodeo Cowboys Association (P.R.C.A.) Bull Riding World Champion in 1987. In one memorable scene, Frost (played by Luke Perry) suffered a severe kick to the groin from a bull that had just thrown him to the arena floor. His best friend and three-time World Champion Tuff Hedeman (played by Stephen Baldwin) followed his injured buddy from the arena and stayed by his side in the infirmary. As the young man was clutching his genitals and writhing in pain, Hedeman, utterly nonplused, looked him square in the eye.

"I got two words to say to you," said Hedeman.

"What's that?" croaked Frost through gritted teeth.

"*Cowboy up!*"

He did, and he went on to earn bragging rights as the best bull rider in the world before tasting dirt one last time at the Frontier Days Rodeo in Cheyenne, Wyoming.

Hedeman's advice has come back to me time and again as I have watched, and experienced, the mishaps that are the price of admission to cowboy sports. James' near-death experience, Gloria's broken arm, Jake's broken bones and subsequent decision to remove his own cast before it was medically prudent to do so, the injury to my right hand that I sustained when Haskell inexplicably pitched a fit and dumped me on the ground as I was gathering cattle in the pasture where my wife and I stable our horses and maintain our cattle,[8] and other incidents too numerous to mention are universally dismissed as part of the bargain. Nonchalance toward misfortune speaks to one of the most pervasive norms in the arena: Ride through the pain, don't complain, and if at all possible, laugh about it once the dust settles. In other words, *cowboy up!*[9]

The meaning of this terse admonition applies not only to injuries, but also to illness and even death. Dudley, the seasoned penner whose kidney stones were finally getting the best of him, remained stoic in what must have been severe discomfort, and he clearly had no interest in being pitied for his plight. Even an untimely death failed to elicit much emotion. Although Andy's announcement that Glenda had perished in a fall from her horse was greeted with

---

[8] See Chapter One, "Old Dominion Cowboys," p. 12 fn 5.

[9] *Cowboy up!* and its gender-specific equivalent, *Cowgirl up!*, seem to be an increasingly popular means of self-expression. In recent years, I have noticed quite a few decals and bumper stickers, exclusively on pick-up trucks, proclaiming these messages. As near as I can tell, the attitude being extolled lies somewhere between stoicism and *joie de vivre*.

INVENTING TRADITION

prayers, we accepted the fallen cowgirl's fate with equanimity, tinged with memories of our own close calls.

The determination to *cowboy up!* in the face of adversity brings to mind one of Andy Adams' (1903: 276) recollections from life on the trail. Reflecting on the end that awaits us all, one of his comrades with the Circle Dot herd, Rod Wheat, gave voice to an attitude toward death that has lost none of its resonance: "As for myself, I'm not going to fret. You can't avoid it when it comes, and every now and then you miss it by a hair." There's nothing new, and certainly nothing invented, about cowboy stoicism and its bedfellow, fatalism. Not even the cultural trinity could touch those. You might say they just let them slip into modernity like a trash cow dashing across the barrier, from their century to ours, and never looked back.

Easy come, easy go

Old Dominion cowboys are not immune from financial pressures. Sooner or later, most of us own up to some degree of concern about the costs of penning, sorting, and cutting. Yet the prevailing attitude is that money should never be a barrier to participation. At our modest level of competition, winning a piece of the jackpot might compensate for a few blow-outs, and it might even put the winner in the black after entry fees and transportation and all the other costs of a day of penning. But in the long run, winnings cannot hope to defray the ongoing costs of purchasing and maintaining livestock and all that goes with it. Still, people show up at competitions with wads of cash that they seem perfectly willing to spend. A reliable source of cowboy humor is the ease with which we part with our hard-earned money. Even cowboys such as Jake, who have the time and inclination to compete at higher levels of competition, treat their wins and losses with a carefree attitude that seems out of place in our money-driven culture. "Easy come, easy go" is a common refrain from cowboys returning to the sidelines after a blow-out.

Once again, my mind travels back to my days as an itinerant cowboy. It was the summer of 1975, and my horse and I were helping a feisty, seventy-something South Texas cowboy named Bub and his horse, Smokey, herd an unwilling Santa Gertrudis bull into a corral at *Quien Sabe* Ranch near Leesville, Texas. The bull, pawing and snorting and bellowing like the Minotaur of Greek legend, was getting the picture, but a touch more persuasion was in order. With the business end of his bullwhip cracking around the bull's ears and Smokey rearing back on his hind legs, Bub, sporting a grin as wide as the Rio Grande and as authentic as South Texas salsa, shouted through the billowing dust, "Goddamn, Okie, we ain't got money, but we sho' got fun!"[10]

Cowboy democracy

Complementing cowboys' spendthrift attitude is an aversion to distinctions based on anything but ability. Cowboy hats, jeans, and Western boots are not only the requisite attire at formal competitions; they are also a way to mitigate socioeconomic differences between

---

[10] Since the days of the Great Depression, native Oklahomans such as myself have been known colloquially as *Okies*. As a Texan, Bub was practically honor-bound to nickname me *Okie* in deference to the Red River rivalry between Texas and Oklahoma. In nearly two months of cowboying at *Quien Sabe* Ranch, I doubt that my comrade, mentor, and friend ever called me by any other name.

competitors. Gazing at a sea of cowboy hats and sweaty horses, I have no way to distinguish between highly paid professionals and blue collar employees. Dan's insistence that everyone be treated as equal ("We can't treat a rich man one way and a poor man another way.") comes as no surprise in a nation whose commitment to equality is one of its most notable birthrights. As Tocqueville (1945 vol. 1: 46) noted more than a century and a half ago,

> "Many important observations suggest themselves upon the social condition of the Anglo-Americans; but there is one that takes precedence of all the rest. The social condition of the Americans is eminently democratic; this was its character at the foundation of the colonies, and it is still more strongly marked at the present day."

Cowboy democracy, and particularly its insistence that cowboying skills trump pretty much everything else, was challenged when an anonymous protest was filed against my hair-raising ride in the novice division call backs. At first, I was pleased to know that my ability to hang onto a bucking horse and still pen cows had not gone unnoticed. Yet upon reflection, I realized that there was a principle at stake. Although a protest was probably warranted, it was beyond the pale of consideration and perhaps even contemptible under the circumstances. I suspect that the protester's goals were twofold: to nudge my team out of the way and collect a piece of the jackpot (modest though it was!); and to lower my and my team mates' scores in the association rankings and thereby boost his or her own ranking. Either way, the protester was attaching more value to the jackpot and rankings than the skills I mustered to finish in the money.

I have since wondered who crossed the line and attempted to have my team disqualified. He or she clearly violated group norms, but not the rules, by trying to invoke sanctions against a hapless cowboy who found himself in a fix. Recourse to technicalities might be a sign of the times, but it was clearly out of place on that hot summer day when Colfax pitched a fit. Simply put, it failed the test of cowboy democracy.

It's mighty white out there...

With rare exceptions, Hollywood's version of the cowboy has been a white male: tall, dark, handsome, and most certainly the progeny of Anglo-Saxon stock. Picking up where dime novels, theatrical productions, and Wild West shows left off, modern mass media perpetuated the type. From the singing cowboys of the 1920s to gunslingers and desperadoes roaming the vistas of popular culture, Western heroes cast up by the entertainment industry have conformed to an image personified by John Wayne, Gary Cooper, Robert Duvall, and other icons of our media-saturated culture. Much the same can be said for advertising, where we encounter the Marlboro Man and his ilk posed against an awe-inspiring landscape.

Such impressions fade when we recognize the cattle frontier as rich blend of cultures and ethnicities.[11] White males made room for Mexicans seeking opportunities north of the Rio Grande and former slaves with a yen to start their lives anew in the unsettled West (Durham and Jones 1965; Porter 1971; Savage 1976). Native American cowboys, their blood filtered through generations of racial mixing on the frontier, contributed to the collage, as did others whose

---

[11] See Chapter Three, "The Cowboy in History, Literature, and Showbiz," p. 44.

provenance will never be known and whose passing was marked by shallow graves and makeshift crosses fashioned out of whatever materials the prairie could provide.

The cowboy type can be attributed to cultural biases embedded in the era that spawned him. Settlers of Western European stock looked askance at Mexicans and their alien ways, and Indians were just another obstacle to the fulfillment of America's manifest destiny. Special contempt was reserved for people of African descent who were a scant generation or two removed from slavery. Coming from elite backgrounds in the stratified East, it is hardly surprising that the cultural trinity both reflected and reproduced the social Darwinism that shaped their worldviews. Theirs was a Eurocentric world, and the cowboy type was constructed in their image. Nurtured by an entertainment industry that was likewise a product of its time, the type hardened into a stereotype, clearly at odds with the historical record, that has never quite lost its grip in either our collective memory of the cowboy or the cultural imaginary where it resides.

Nor has the stereotype lost its grip on cowboy sports. In all my experience as an Old Dominion cowboy, I have yet to meet anyone of Latin American or Native American descent. I have seen only two or three black competitors, and to the best of my recollection, I have ridden on a team with only one. Moreover, the few black cowboys who I have encountered have segregated themselves in the way they dress: ball caps, collarless t-shirts, and sneakers instead of cowboy hats, button-down shirts, and Western boots. In my efforts to be inclusive, I have tried to engage my black comrades in sideline banter, but to no avail. Granted, generalizing from such a minuscule sample might not stand up to scientific scrutiny, and my choice of ethnography as a methodology precludes the kind of data gathering that would reveal variables that aren't apparent on horseback. Yet the dearth of black cowboys, particularly in a Southern state with a significant black population, may be evidence enough to conclude that cowboy sports are homogeneous enclaves, not through overt discrimination, but rather as a result of systemic and deliberate stereotyping across generations.

Unlike the cattle frontier that produced them, cowboy sports are overwhelmingly white. Racial homogeneity in the arena is thus a reflection of invented traditions, and its persistence reminds us that America's foundation myth doesn't quite capture the whole story. When Mitch declared emphatically that "every boy grows up wanting to be a cowboy," he left out a key descriptor: *white*. Children of color are welcome to the cowboy, but chances are they're looking for other heroes, and other myths to live by, as they construct their identities and express their cultural affiliations.

Cowboys and cowgirls

Cowboys might have come from many races and ethnicities, but they were represented by only one gender. One has to cast a large net to find a more male-centered world than America's range cattle industry. Ancient Sparta comes to mind, or perhaps seafaring cultures that discouraged women from boarding ships for fear of bad luck. Andy Adams (1903), the cowboy chronicler from Texas, gave us a glimpse into cow country's masculine milieu when he described his comrades' clumsiness in discussing matters of the heart. Our other memoirist, Teddy Blue Abbott (1939: 13), was on to something when he hinted at the fear that underlay cowboys' distrust of the opposite sex: "In fact there was only two things the old-time cowpuncher was afraid of, a decent woman and being set afoot." After two years of cowboying on the Dakota range, Roosevelt spent the rest of his life extolling the manly virtues that he found among his hard-riding comrades. Remington, who never exactly rode to the beat of a hardy life himself, spent his later years mourning the passing of men "with the bark on," while Wister left us with an enduring image of masculine gallantry at the edge of civilization. As we have seen, Dale (1937), an historian from Oklahoma and an accomplished herdsman in his own right, characterized cow country as the *father* of the new civilization that emerged on the great prairies after the Civil War: primal, pastoral, and wary of women and their civilizing ways. And in my own experience on Western ranches, I can't say that I ever had the privilege of rounding up strays or branding calves with a woman at my side, even eight decades after civilization put an end to the open range. In short, the world that fired the Victorian imagination was not only white; it was overwhelmingly masculine, testosterone-charged and resistant to female persuasion. Even as they subsumed diverse races and ethnicities into a culture of Anglo-Saxon hegemony, culture producers reflected and reproduced the sharp gender distinctions that shaped their world.

Among the social changes wrought by modernity, none looms larger than the relationship between the sexes. This is certainly apparent in cowboy sports, where men and women compete on an absolutely equal footing. Equality is apparent not only in the arena, but also on the sidelines, where people sit on their horses and engage in conversation with no apparent regard for gender. Although women sometimes shed their hats during the midday heat, attire isn't much use as a signifier of male and female. If it weren't for the occasional bare head or ponytail bouncing beneath the broad brim of a Stetson, a casual observer, at least from a distance, would be hard-pressed to distinguish between cowboys and cowgirls.

But sociologists are not casual observers. As is true of so many social relationships that have been transformed by modernity, distinctions between the sexes have not simply disappeared; rather, they have become more nuanced and less readily apparent. Differences certainly manifest themselves in cowboy humor at women's expense. Andy's joke about the woman buying oil for her husband's pick-up, and the way he trivialized the accomplishments of an all-girl penning team that was preparing to compete ("Even a blind hog finds a nut once in a while!"), are indications that gender bias is alive and well among Old Dominion cowboys. Gender roles have also arrived pretty much intact at the modern arena. Women, usually clad as though they were at the beach rather than a cowboy sporting venue, take charge of picnic tables and small children, and they sometimes assume supporting roles for their husbands and boyfriends by signing them up for rides and handling their bankrolls. Clearly, both men and women continue to acknowledge gender inequalities. Laughing about them softens the edges, but it certainly doesn't eliminate them.

Thus have cowboys and cowgirls accommodated themselves to the nuances of modernity: equal as competitors, but still tethered to communicative patterns and roles that favor men and devalue women. Even so, women have reserved at least two dimensions of cowboy sports for themselves. In their capacity as announcers and score keepers, they exert a powerful influence on events unfolding in the arena. They are also undisputed champions when it comes to hollering at cattle. Any lingering frustration over their subservience to men is surely dispelled in

INVENTING TRADITION

the heat of penning,[12] when women's war cries and decibel levels know no bounds. In those emotionally-charged moments, female acquiescence to male privilege is lost in the dust. Displays of such unladylike behavior would have scandalized the cultural trinity, and they have no place in the patriarchal culture that cowboy aficionados of another era reflected and reproduced. When it comes to gender differences, male privilege thus takes a back seat to the social upheavals that upended Victorian culture and narrowed the chasm between men and women, and certainly between cowboys and cowgirls.

What kind of outfit is this anyway?

In *Run for the Wall: Remembering Vietnam on a Motorcycle Pilgrimage* (2001), coauthors Raymond Michalowski (a sociologist) and Jill Dubisch (an anthropologist) chronicled their experiences on an annual cross-country bike trip from California to the Vietnam Memorial in Washington, DC, undertaken to commemorate soldiers who were killed and wounded in the Vietnam War.[13] One can only imagine the early pilgrimages, when former warriors and war protesters came together in a ritual healing that spanned the continent. Theirs was a classic folk association, cobbled together by volunteers with a shared vision. According to Michalowski and Dubisch,

> "Folk organizations are grass-roots voluntary associations that develop spontaneously and nonhierarchically, and that tend to use semiformal institutional frameworks to organize their activities and ensure their continuation. Folk organizations differ from formal voluntary associations such as the March of Dimes or the League of Women Voters by being more spontaneous and do-it-yourself in character, and by the desire of their members to avoid creating formal structures of authority and responsibility" (p. 220).

The Run for the Wall (or, to use the acronym, RFTW) thus began in much the same cultural context, and was fueled by the same ideology of free association, that drove pilgrims to American shores and spawned countless political and religious organizations. This tendency was firmly rooted in American soil by the time Tocqueville (1945) crossed the Atlantic in 1835. "In no country in the world," wrote the peripatetic Frenchman,

---

[12] Team cattle penning and sorting require competitors to make full use of their vocal cords. Cutting competitions, on the other hand, are quiet, reminiscent of a golf tournament or tennis match.

[13] See Chapter One, "Old Dominion Cowboys," p. 5.

"has the principle of association been more successfully used or applied to a greater multitude of objects than in America. Besides the permanent associations which are established by law under the names of townships, cities, and counties, a vast number of others are formed and maintained by the agency of private individuals" (vol. 1 p. 191).

Once established, folk organizations can either wither or flourish. Decline brings its own set of problems, but so does growth. In the case of the RFTW, the pilgrimage's increasing popularity exposed a tension between bikers' ideology of personal freedom and the need for structure. Arguably, freedom is an abstraction and means different things to different people. Structure, by contrast, is anything but abstract. It is embedded in routine practices, and it determines fundamental questions: Who does what? Who contacts whom? Who gets what? The answers to these questions are key indicators of an organization's structure insofar as they reveal both its day-to-day character and, more than likely, the source of its problems.

When Michalowski and Dubisch mounted their bikes for the RFTW in 1996, the spontaneity that characterized early pilgrimages was giving way, however grudgingly, to organizational imperatives. Informal gatherings were becoming forums for choosing leaders, mapping routes, and debating policies. Suspicions that the RFTW had been highjacked by a small clique of insiders led to emotional outbursts and even defections from the cause. Fragmentation threatened the group's solidarity, and new ways of coexistence were needed to mitigate the clash between individualism and community that is inevitable as folk organizations grow into formal associations. As Michalowski and Dubisch (2001: 222) concluded, "What binds these fragile structures into effective organizations is a sense of purpose and community shared among the members that is powerful enough to override the tensions that result from ambiguities surrounding matters of leadership and reward."

Like the RFTW, the Blue Ridge Team Penning Association began as a folk organization whose founders wanted to build a community of cowboys to enhance their sports in Central Virginia. Original members enjoyed talking about the old days when the organization was family-oriented and children were the focus of attention. When I joined the association in the summer of 2004, I learned that membership was declining as disgruntled people opted for other cowboy venues or sought other forms of recreation altogether. Since then, the ebb and flow of membership has accelerated. Some have drifted off to less competitive groups, while others have sought higher levels of competition. Perhaps the most glaring change is the absence of children, a development that doesn't bode well for long-term stability.

Mary's comment to the newcomer ("There's a lot of politicalness in this.") thus expressed a widely-held conviction that the fun and camaraderie from the organization's family-centered days have been sacrificed to competitive zeal. Disagreements over leadership and rankings, exacerbated by a growing rift between open riders and aspiring cowboys, were threatening either to transform the association into something else or undo it altogether. To borrow from Wuthnow's (1994) assessment of the small-group movement that has been quietly reshaping America's sense of community, the Blue Ridge Team Penning Association is an intentional community. Members of tribes and families are free to gripe about one another, but at the end of the day, they know they have to live with one another. Not so with intentional groups. Recognizing that they can always move on, dissatisfied cowboys can simply load their horses and skedaddle. "They have to decide whether they really want to be involved, listen to their

INVENTING TRADITION

feelings for cues, and worry about whether they are getting enough to make the time worthwhile" (p. 15).

But there's more to the rifts in Old Dominion cowboy culture than attitudes toward varying levels of competition. As we have seen, all sport is imbued with a sense of the sacred. Even as they hone their skills and build their bodies, athletes participate in rituals that reveal connections with each other even as they tap into spiritual dimensions. Thus do the quest for community and spirituality coalesce in sport, where postmodern angst finds a haven from the breakdown of community and social fragmentation.

Disaffection with the association thus posed more of a threat than lost entry fees and organizational headaches. In a Weberian sense, the Blue Ridge Team Penning Association was suffering from nothing less than a "disenchantment of the world" (Gerth and Mills 1946: 51) insofar as the magic and mimicry embedded in cowboy sports were threatened by organizational change and the tensions that it creates. Nothing could have been further from the minds of culture producers like Roosevelt, Remington, and Wister, for whom frontier themes were ends in themselves, perfectly suited to binding Americans to their collective past, and perhaps even immune to the rationalization and bureaucratization that are the price of modernity. One thing is certain: solidarity cannot long survive in an organization whose members differ on questions of purpose and community. Jake's contempt for the young cowboy on the runaway horse ("Man, I can't believe this shit!") pretty much said it all. It certainly left me wondering: What kind of outfit is this anyway?

The animate trinity

We come now to themes that are not so apparent—themes that call not just for observing or riding into a herd, but for elaborating on theory. I occasionally draw from sociological theory

that has something to say about cowboy sports, but for the most part, I draw inferences from my observations. I begin with a theme that pervades this entire investigation and underlies practically everything I've written so far. I tried to get at it in Chapter Six, "Showtime," when Colfax and I had the morning all to ourselves. Throughout the narrative, I kept coming back to it whenever I used italics to indicate an imagined dialog between my horse and me, and whenever something in her gestures or demeanor made me question what was going on in that little horse brain of hers. Broadening my field of perception, I looked for it, and more often than not found it, in the myriad ways that cowboys treated and talked about their horses and speculated about bovine ways. It's not a theme that's readily discussed among people who prefer action over introspection. Besides, it's a bit too abstract when you're focused on the decidedly practical task of penning, sorting, and cutting cattle. But the real problem lies in the fact that this theme, like the others that occupy the closing pages of this work, operates beneath the surface. I refer, of course, to the animate trinity of human, horse, and cow. In a Durkheimian sense, it is a social fact, visible in its outward manifestations, and comprehensible in terms of the extraordinary bond between man and animal that is a vestige of our ancient past.

In the first part of my narrative, I referenced Ike's mantra—simple, yet loaded with meaning, with regard to Colfax's penning proclivities and innate cow sense: "She *enjoys* it. She's got Doc Bar in her, she *can't help* it." Marvin's insistence on acquiring control of a horse's mind as a prerequisite to establishing trust, together with his assessment of horse and rider as *partners*, provided glimpses into a relationship that doesn't lend itself easily to words. "Ride your horse with respect," said Marvin. "Always *ask* a horse to do somethin'. If you don't get a reaction, then tell him, but always *ask* first." Donny, our other self-deprecating horse trainer, was expressing much the same sentiments in his paean to the Quarter Horse's athleticism and intelligence. In terms of horse care, Greg said more than he knew when he voiced his aversion to keeping his mount cooped up in a stable. "I wouldn't any more keep a horse in a stable than I'd keep someone in prison," he said as cowboy hats bobbed around him. Ted's suggestion that his company's new hires be put on horseback and herd cattle as a team-building exercise struck me as a stroke of genius. What better way to instill team work in the denizens of corporate America than to introduce them to the most fundamental team of all: the animate trinity?

Whenever attention turned to a particular horse's peculiarities, it seemed that the tables were being turned. Suddenly, we were discussing the ways that horses treat *us*. Mitch's account of bathing his horse and being squirted with water was a reminder that, like all relationships, the tie between people and horses works both ways. For their part, cattle were the subject of grudging admiration. Even as they frustrated us with their Houdini-like maneuvers, they earned our respect for putting up an honest fight. "That little bastard can slip through anything," said Gloria after her successful run was nearly thwarted by a number four Longhorn with a mind of its own. Slow cattle that were too easy to manipulate were subject to derision, as though they were somehow unworthy of our trouble. Turning to the horse-as-equipment analogy, cowboys who compared horses to machines were certainly strutting their *machismo*, trying their best to feign a no-nonsense attitude toward their sport. But on a deeper level, I believe that they were simply using a modern metaphor to describe a symbiosis that predates the machine age and even cowboys. It is surely older than civilization.

If the bond between man and animal is indeed lodged in ancient memory, then it is certainly beyond the purview of invented traditions, and cowboying is simply one act in a very old drama. We certainly learn more about it in cowboy memoirs than we do from the cultural trinity. Jim Flood, the foreman of Andy Adams' outfit who guided the Circle Dot herd from Texas to Montana in 1882, expressed something akin to reverence for the animate trinity when he said that "no better word can be spoken of a man than that he is careful of his horses" (Adams 1903: 29). Siringo (1950: 113) relied on frontier metaphor to describe his remorse at abandoning his horse: "Leaving Whisky-peet behind was almost as severe on me as having sixteen jawteeth pulled." Roosevelt's fixation on the strenuous life, Remington's infusion of Christian imagery into his depictions of a vanishing world, and Wister's dubious portrayals of cowboys who seemed to have little time for cattle, speak to a preoccupation with human values and their salience at the onset of modernity rather than the man-animal connection. The traditions that they played a part in inventing and promoting were aimed at saving a culture from disintegration, and animals were just part of the package. Leave it to cowboys, past and present, to remind us of a more basic tradition.

INVENTING TRADITION

The wild and the tame

In her anthropological study of rodeo, Lawrence (1982) identified the dichotomy between the wild and the tame as a persistent theme in the range cattle industry and the sports that it fostered. Caught between a love for unspoiled nature and an impulse to manipulate it in the service of civilization, cowboys in both milieus have participated in a ritual taming of animals and their environment. As we saw in Chapter Two, "The Frontier in American Character Development," Nash (1967) traced the civilizing impulse to America's beginnings, when settlers sought to carve a new Eden out of a hostile wilderness. As the wilderness showed just how stubborn it could be, its would-be conquerors came to see it as demonic, an evil presence standing in the way of paradise. Eventually, wild regions succumbed to the axe. Attitudes softened, and writers and social critics rushed to defend what was disappearing. Defoe's (1986) Robinson Crusoe found moral rejuvenation in the clash between man and nature, while Rousseau (1968) found nothing but corruption as our species emerged from a state of nature and started down the path of civilization. By the late eighteenth century, the call of the wild and the allure of civilization were reconciled, at least temporarily, in a pastoral ideal reflected in Jefferson's vision of an agrarian republic (Marx 1967). Since then, from the manifest destiny that sent settlers scurrying across the continent to the Weberian "iron cage"[14] that regulates life in the new millennium, wilderness has suffered from the march of civilization, and Americans have wrestled with the same dichotomy that Lawrence (1982) found on the trail as well as in rodeo: a yearning for wildness even as we find ever more ingenious ways to subdue it.

Like rodeo, cowboy sports reflect the dynamic tension between the wild and the tame. Bound by regulations and confined to arenas, cowboy sports have clearly lost the spontaneity of their workaday origins. Mimicry, authentic though it seems in the heat of penning, sorting, and cutting cattle, is a far cry from duplication—until, that is, things get wild and Western. James' fall from his horse and my own flirtation with disaster when Colfax tried to separate me from my saddle were greeted with undisguised rapture. As long as James and I were uninjured, all of us enjoyed a taste of danger and unpredictability that are tempered in standardized competition. I detected a hint of this in Andy's admonition following his prayer to "ride hard, and take lots of chances!" Although contestants had various ways of describing the difference between *sittin'* and *ridin'* a horse, the preference for action over introspection, tinged with an impulse to flirt with wildness, was unambiguous. Greg's comment, "I wouldn't any more keep a horse in a stable than I'd keep someone in prison," struck me as more than a recommendation on horse care. In the context of cowboy sports, Greg was expressing nothing short of a philosophy of life, certainly relevant to horses, but also applicable to people caught in the matrix of paramount reality (Cohen and Taylor 1976), struggling to formulate identities against the homogenizing flow of everyday life.

Drawing on Goffman's (1959) dramaturgical perspective positing people as actors and everyone else as members of the audience, Old Dominion cowboys thus acquire "tactical repertoires" (Calhoun 2002: 29) enabling us to manage identities that must constantly navigate between the wild and the tame, and our creativity and individuality give us leeway to carve out unique niches and ensure at least a modicum of human agency in the context of structured sports in such a way as not to threaten communal values. "In the end," wrote Goffman, "our conception

---

[14] Kalberg (2002: 123) translated this most Weberian of phrases as the "steel-hard casing."

of our role becomes second nature and an integral part of our personality. We come into the world as individuals, achieve character, and become persons" (p. 52).

With dozens of cowboying events under my belt, I find that we don't need to depend on unscripted displays of horsemanship to experience wildness. I tried to capture a sense of it when I described the run up to a day of penning. Colfax's playfulness with the other horses, Canadian geese brushing us with the wind off their wings, and the shadows cast by mountains in the early morning stillness, all point to a place in our souls that needs filling. Throughout the day, wildness beckoned from dust devils cast up by the wind and searing heat that left all of us, humans, horses, and cattle, sweat-soaked and panting. In this context, scatological humor is more than an expression of cowboy camaraderie. Deployed in the presence of ubiquitous feces, such humor reminds us that bodily functions are the ultimate levelers insofar as they transcend the veneer of civilization. It reduces us to the level of biology and thus  strengthens the bond among members of the animate trinity. I returned to the porous boundary between wildness and tameness when the competition drew to a close and my comrades expressed their satisfaction with the day's events. Surely Simmel (1990: 67) had something like this in mind when he suggested that "the power and the rhythm of emotions" lie at the center of human experience. Attuned to natural rhythms and mindful of the hazards, Old Dominion cowboys are thus delicately poised between the wild and the tame.

Perhaps the ultimate irony is that the wildness we seek is only possible under the sway of regulations and within the parameters of an arena, where we ride trained horses and chase domesticated cattle as the time displayed on a digital clock flashes by in thousandths of a second. Civilization, it seems, is the great enabler, opening us to primal emotions even as it entwines us in webs of rationality and predictability. Like the animate trinity, the dichotomy between the wild and the tame certainly predates modernity and the culture producers who sought to mitigate its pernicious effects through invented traditions. In one form or another, this dichotomy also draws us to the dawn of civilization, when our ancestors recognized the chasm that was opening up between themselves and the natural environment.

A community of mavericks[15]

In Chapter Two, "The Frontier in American Character Development," I situated frontier metaphors in a modern context by alluding to the resilience of cowboy themes in politics. From Roosevelt's rough-riding days and Kennedy's choice of frontier imagery to describe postwar challenges to Kissinger's gunslinger diplomacy during the Nixon Administration, pundits have detected an independent streak in American foreign policy that leads straight back to the cowboy. Perhaps the clearest example is the (George W.) Bush Administration's much-ballyhooed cowboy diplomacy. No sooner had the Twin Towers collapsed in a heap of rubble on September 11, 2001, than President Bush reached for his six shooter (metaphorically, thank

---

[15] For the etymology of maverick, see p. 143 fn 3 above.

goodness) and summoned the greatest military power in the world to bring in Osama bin Laden dead or alive. Virtually ignoring more prudent counsel from the United Nations, Bush unleashed the dogs of war in the Middle East and proceeded to taunt North Korea and Iran for their refusal to holster their nuclear arsenals. Although this go-it-alone approach to world affairs is a recipe for disaster in the twenty-first century, it continues to resonate in a nation weaned on the principle of equality and the independent spirit that it fosters. As usual, we rely on Tocqueville (1945: vol. 2 287) for historical and sociological context:

> "The principle of equality, which makes men independent of each other, gives them a habit and a taste for following in their private actions no other guide than their own will. This complete independence, which they constantly enjoy in regard to their equals and in the intercourse of private life, tends to make them look upon all authority with a jealous eye and speedily suggests to them the notion and the love of political freedom."

Blending personal experience with their nation's foundation stories, Roosevelt, Remington, and Wister certainly did their part to promote the cowboy as the personification of independence and self-reliance. As new communication technologies came on line in the early 1900s, America's entertainment industry reflected and reproduced their version of the cowboy. Its success can be measured by global acceptance of the stereotype: a lone horseman, quick on the draw and bound by a strict code of morality, rescuing a hapless town from desperadoes and then, in his moment of glory, riding into the sunset to the cheers of a grateful citizenry. Generations removed from lived experience, we share a collective memory of this lonely individual who can never quite reconcile himself to the society he is honor-bound to save. For Bellah et al (1996), this mythic individualism is uniquely American insofar as it suits a people who yearn for independence even as they seek community. The cowboy certainly has special talents and a keen sense of justice that are needed by civilized folk. Yet these same characteristics make him so unique that he can never fully embrace his fellow man. His destiny is to defend society without ever joining it. Shane immortalized himself by riding off into the sunset, and the Lone Ranger roamed from town to town with his Indian comrade, Tonto, as his sole human companion. But the cowboy is neither isolated nor antisocial. "Rather, his significance lies in his unique individual virtue and special skill and it is because of those qualities that society needs and welcomes him...It is as if the myth says you can be a truly good person, worthy of admiration and love, only if you resist fully joining the group" (pp. 144-45).

I frankly don't know if any Old Dominion cowboys fancy themselves as Shane or the Lone Ranger or Tonto, for that matter. What I do know is that the sense of community in cowboy sports is far more prevalent than rugged individualism. Tray's impromptu lesson in horsemanship ("Well, I could see you're trying. As long as someone's working at it, I'm glad to help."), Ted's suggestion that newcomers to his company be put on horseback to develop team spirit, and the group's censure when Sammy refused to help hold the herd, all point to the communal nature of cowboys sports. Ted voiced a common sentiment when he declared that he was "in this for the camaraderie." At the risk of pointing out the obvious, team cattle penning and sorting are *team* sports, and cutting horse competitors rely on herders and turn-back men to keep the cattle in check as they go about their business. And let's not forget our four-legged comrades. The animate trinity itself is, after all, a team. As Marvin so eloquently put it, a rider and his horse are partners, deserving of mutual respect. In their formal and informal dimensions, cowboy sports thus belie the myth of rugged individualism. Just as tame arenas and structured competition make it possible for cowboys to walk on the wild side, so, too, does the sense of community enable mavericks like us to shape our identities and express our attraction to cowboy ways.

Taking a longer view, cowboy sports enthusiasts could no more compete alone in an arena than an honest-to-goodness cowboy could have driven a herd from Texas to Montana by himself. Adams (1903), Abbott (1939), and Siringo (1950) certainly captured the communal nature of cowboying in their memoirs. Citing group endeavor as a prerequisite to conquering the frontier, Boatright (in Hofstadter and Lipset 1968; in Speck 1973) dismissed cowboy independence as one of the West's most misguided myths. Team work (or should I say the lack thereof?) comes to mind as I recall an incident at the Double U Bar Ranch in Colfax County, New Mexico, in the summer of 1974. Everyone at the ranch capable of mounting a horse was on hand to drive a thousand head of cattle from a five thousand acre pasture through a gate (far too small, as it turned out) that opened into the mountains and the summer grazing lands beyond. With some clear instructions from the ranch foreman and a bit of cooperation among us cowboys, we might have succeeded. Instead, what was supposed to be an orderly cattle drive degenerated into pandemonium. We knew trouble was brewing when we rode too fast and prevented the calves from keeping up with their mothers. Instinctively, the mothers peeled back to find their babies. At that point, the jig was up. Cattle came charging down the narrow mountain pass in a torrent that couldn't be stopped. In desperation, some cowboys broke out their six shooters and bullwhips, but that probably just made a bad situation worse. I vividly recall one cowboy firing his gun into the air just a few feet away and hollering at me through the dust and smoke to dig in my spurs. It's probably just as well that I wasn't wearing any. Eventually, we all maneuvered our horses to whatever shelter we could find from the marauding bovines and let the stampede spend itself. I left the Double U Bar Ranch shortly thereafter to cowboy at the family place back in Haskell County, Oklahoma. To this day, I'm not sure if those rugged individuals ever did get those cattle to the high country.

In our choice of leisure activities, we Old Dominion cowboys brand ourselves as mavericks who'd rather pen, sort, and cut cattle than participate in activities more suited to our time and place. Those of us who compete at higher levels, and the few who have the land and livestock to host events, are in it to some extent for the money. But for the most part, we simply buy into the mimicry of it all, relishing what amounts to an invented tradition of rugged individualism even though we know better. We are thus a community of mavericks, united by a common desire to construct identities in the Western mold and belong to a subculture that values independence even as it facilitates social bonding. As accurate an assessment of Old Dominion cowboys as I have found comes from Wuthnow's (1994) study of the small-group movement that attempts to mitigate the fragmentation of our postmodern age.

> "Small groups draw individuals out of themselves, pull them out of their isolated personal lives, and put them in the presence of others where they can share their needs and concerns, make friends, and become linked to wider social networks. Small groups provide a way of transcending our most self-centered interests; they temper our individualism and culturally induced desire to be totally independent of one another. The attachments that develop among the members of small groups demonstrate clearly that we are not a society of rugged individualists who wish to go it entirely alone but, rather, that we are a communal people who, even amidst

INVENTING TRADITION

the dislocating tendencies of our society, are capable of banding together in bonds of mutual support" (p. 12).

Ritual: the ties that bind

Perhaps the best way to situate cowboy sports as ritual is to borrow from Stoeltje's (1993) analysis of rodeo.[16] Her model for the study of ritual genres begins with recognition that power is more than a manifestation of domination and subordination. Power is also evident in its "capacity to create, transform, or otherwise make things happen" (p. 140). Specifically, her model posited three sources of power: *form*, a term that embraces all aspects of ritualized performance; *discourse*, which includes communication, oral and written, that contributes to the performance; and *production*, the organization of resources needed to stage the event. Like rodeo, the basic forms of cowboy sports were forged on the cattle frontier in the late nineteenth century, and the discourse paralleled and fostered the evolution of the cowboy type. As organized sports wove themselves into the fabric of American life between the closing of the frontier and the outbreak of World War I (Mrozek 1983), the discourse emanating from frontier themes flowed through the prism of culture producers bent on mitigating the disruptive effects of modernity. Molded to contours of their liking, the discourse captivated a burgeoning entertainment industry and, by extension, the collective memory of a nation entranced by cowboy imagery. The discourse also informed the myriad of logistical challenges that constitute the production of rodeo and its kissing cousins, cowboy sports. Thus was ritual hewn from the bedrock of custom. Power manifested in yet another trinity—form, discourse, and production—transformed the workaday skills of the herdsman into ritualized sports linking an historical era with a space in the high country of the imagination: America's "fifty-first state of mind" (West 1995: 131).

It is a short step from recognizing sports as communal activities suffused with ritual to drawing parallels between sports and religion (Birrell 1981; Edwards 1973; Frey and Eitzen 1991; Weiss 1969). I suspect that my fellow penners, sorters, and cutters would resist the notion that our cowboying proclivities have anything to do with religious practices. Nevertheless, the signs are all there. Immersing ourselves in unmediated nature, if not exactly religious, is surely an avenue to spirituality. Overt examples of religiosity range from prayers and playing the national anthem at the beginning of a competition to gathering around picnic tables for shared meals. Andy's announcement of Glenda's death in a horseback riding accident, and the muted, yet poignant response that it elicited from her fellow cowboys is a particularly striking example of togetherness in religious form. Given her rough-riding ways, there could have been no more fitting tribute. Finally, the rules and regulations that govern cowboy sports fit squarely within the rubric of what Elias (1978: 44) called "the civilizing process," evident in Europe since the High Middle Ages, in which "social events, like natural phenomena, form part of an ordered process." What began as custom among men on horseback trying to scratch a living out of the prairie has thus become ritual tinged with a sense of the sacred, perfectly suited to Old Dominion cowboys looking for the ties that bind.

---

[16] See Chapter Five, "From Custom to Ritual: Identity Formation and Cultural Expression through Rodeo and Cowboy Sports," p. 106.

The West of the imagination

I concluded Chapter One, "Old Dominion Cowboys," with an anecdote from an awards banquet that the Blue Ridge Team Penning Association held to commemorate the 2004 season. I returned to it in the heading to this chapter, and I use it now to introduce the final theme that I have wrested from my fieldnotes. As the reader will recall, I asked the man across the table from me how he got into team penning. Without waiting for his reply, his wife, Gloria, interjected, "It was either this or a red sports car."

I remember feeling momentarily stunned. Predictably, the rest of the conversation drifted off into safe territory—something about the man's hunting trips out West and a career that had long since lost its luster. It was about as exciting as the iced tea and roast beef that graced our dining table. Here we were, denizens of the Information Age, breaking bread together in a nondescript diner some two hours south of the nation's capital, contending for Western belt buckles and jackets emblazoned with logos to signify our success at *cowboying*, bound by an attraction to the animate trinity and the cultural richness that it radiates…

And it was either this or a red sports car?

In hindsight, as I explored methodologies that would be most effective in developing a sociology of cowboy sports, I think that was the moment when I scratched formal interviews with participants off my list. I have had many opportunities to reflect on Gloria's cryptic, yet revealing response to my question. None was more poignant than the incident five months later when Gloria's horse bucked her off.[17] She writhed in pain for what seemed like an eternity before she managed to spit the dirt and manure out of her mouth and tell the rest of us, anxiously surrounding her with placid horses in tow, that she had not simply had the wind knocked out of her. A trip to a nearby hospital revealed a broken bone just below her shoulder. When I phoned her the following evening to see how she was doing, she exhibited the stoicism and nonchalance that I have since come to expect from Old Dominion cowboys. I mean, what are a few steel pins and a boat load of pain killers to a fifty-something-school-teacher-turned-cowgirl?

And it was either this or a red sports car?

The little grey cells have been working overtime ever since. I decided early on to throw a wide loop around my units of analysis, and I think that was a wise decision. It led to forays into history, entertainment, collective memory, and sports, all distinct fields of inquiry, yet all connected within the rubric of cultural sociology. On weekends I trailered my research assistants around the state to penning, sorting, and cutting events and scratched my observations on dusty notepads. During the week, I cleaned up and tackled the literature. And now, as I return to my research questions and prepare to draw some conclusions, I find that the final theme in my repertoire might be the most salient of all. I refer to it here and elsewhere as "the West of the imagination."

This theme takes up more space in my field notes than any other, bar none. It showed itself when cowboys hollered to someone the arena, "Let's see some of that cowboy stuff!" and when people reacted to accidents that might have turned catastrophic with undisguised delight. "Great job, thanks for the show," was probably my favorite comment following my wild ride in the novice call backs. Penning prowess is one thing; hanging onto a rampaging horse is something else entirely, and I think it summons feelings that don't get to come out very often in our scripted, mediated lives. I also think this is what Elias and Dunning (1986) were getting at in their essay on the quest for excitement in leisure. In their estimation, sports don't simply provide

---

[17] See Chapter One, "Old Dominion Cowboys," p. 12 fn 5.

INVENTING TRADITION

relief from tension. Fact is, sports, and particularly those steeped in the Western stew, open up an imaginative space where we experience tensions that help us to keep a grip on sanity.

As Cohen and Taylor (1976) suggested in their exploration of identity formation in our homogenizing culture, there are many ways to manage immersion in "paramount reality," which I find as good a way as any to describe the numbing routines of daily existence. Drawing on Goffman's (1959) dramaturgical perspective of identity formation and Simmel's (1990) insight into the tensions between the individual and society, they posited escape routes that are available to people who have had... enough. One avenue of escape is through "activity enclaves" where, in the context of leisure activities or hobbies, one "suspends self-consciousness because the activity in itself provides an adequate opportunity for self-expression" (Cohen and Taylor 1976: 97). Not that activity enclaves are immune from contamination. Witness the rift between open riders and novices in the Blue Ridge Team Penning Association that threatened to unravel the entire outfit. Nevertheless, cowboy sports are certainly one means of escape, not as a way of avoiding life's hassles altogether, but rather, as an imaginative space laden with opportunities for identity formation and cultural expression, and with the promise of rejuvenation. As the curtain closed on the frontier narrative, culture producers, together with the entertainment industry, looked to this kind of stimulation as a palliative for people roiled by social and economic forces they could neither understand nor control. Look through the clutter of postmodernity, and I think you'll see that they were onto something.

A craving to visit the high country of the imagination came through loud and clear when people talked wistfully about their conversion experiences out West and when they bragged about a new horse, often carrying a brand on its flank or shoulder indicating provenance from some ranch in Texas. A yearning for things Western, suffused with frustrations about work or home life, was unmistakable when people described their feelings about cowboy sports. None said it more succinctly than Ted during our lunch break: "A bad day of penning is better than a good day at the office." Using language more suited to working cattle than unraveling the secrets of science in the halls of academe, Stanley took top billing for eloquence to describe his attraction to penning cattle: "Now that's for me—a bunch of old guys ridin' horses, chasin' cows, and hollerin' yahoo!" Then there was the newcomer who didn't care if he looked "like a goober." He'd latched onto something satisfying, and he intended to stick with it. But it was Mitch, swaggering around in his worn chaps and stylish cowboy hat that would look downright silly in boardrooms where he no doubt clocked much of his time, who cut straight to the chase with his frank assessment of just what we were up to: "With all the stress we have, it's nice to come out and play 'cowboy.' I mean, come on, every boy grows up wanting to be a cowboy!"

Not an astronaut or a lumberjack, and certainly not a red sports car driver. A cowboy.

Chapter Eight — Postmodern Cowboys

> "In sport there is redemptive simplicity. You always know
> what's at stake, and you always know where you stand.
> This is a world with clear boundaries. They are marked.
> There are defined ends and obvious means."
>
> Thomas De Zengotita
> Mediated: How the Media
> Shapes Your World and
> the Way You Live in It (2005)

> "There are three things you need in a cow horse:
> a horse that's broke, showmanship,
> and an ability to work cattle."
>
> Horse trainer
Stanley, VA

Inventing Tradition and the Elusive Postmodern

In the early stages of writing the dissertation that became this book, one of my mentors at the university challenged my insistence on situating cowboy sports in the context of postmodernity. How, he asked, did I define postmodern, and why was it relevant to a cultural study? He cut to the quick when he said that the word seemed more ornamental than substantive, as though juxtaposing cowboys and postmodernity might simply be a good marketing ploy. True, they are unlikely bedfellows. And frankly, there is something alluring about an exploration that promises to reconcile opposites. I remember being taken aback by his skepticism, and I'm sure that whatever rationale I offered at the time was pretty lame. I was encouraged to use the concept of invented tradition as the fulcrum of my study and to leave postmodern theorizing for later. Or maybe never, now that I think about it.

Two things occurred to me about those formative discussions. First, the admonition to frame cowboy sports in the context of invented tradition was right on track. The more I learned about the emergence of sports in American culture around the turn of the twentieth century, the more I appreciated the symbiosis between the cultural trinity's mission to alleviate the pressures of modernity and the entertainment industry's money-making imperative. These cultural juggernauts came together in the cauldron of postfrontier culture to promote a fascination with cowboy ways that has never lost its appeal. Of course, it would be unrealistic to credit Roosevelt, Remington, and Wister with singlehandedly shaping the cowboy myth and promoting it to a receptive public. Yet they were certainly the most prominent members of their generation to wrestle with frontier anxiety, and they wielded more influence than their peers. Using the bully pulpits they had at their disposal, they served as prisms between the real West and an imagined West—between official history and the images, authentic and mediated, that created the Western genre of entertainment and situated themselves in our collective memory. Yet theirs was not a process of manipulation. As Hobsbawm (1983) recognized, manipulation becomes something else entirely when it serves preexisting needs. Culture producers recognized a need, and they used their unique talents to fill it. The entertainment industry seized on this union of history and invented traditions, and cowboy ways have been a pillar of mediated experience ever since.

Neither the cultural trinity nor the entertainment industry had to look very far in their search for symbols. Unlike so many representations of the past that lie outside our symbolic universe (Confino 1997), the frontier does not languish in symbolic isolation. If anything, it suffers from an embarrassment of riches, suffusing contemporary culture with symbols rooted in the frontier experience and molded to the contours of popular culture. Borrowing from Swidler's (1986) lexicon, the Old West bequeathed to subsequent generations a cultural tool kit brimming with opportunities to fashion identity and express cultural affiliation. Memory in this case does not have to speak for itself. Nor does it have to rely on historians to keep it alive. It survives through a host of symbolic intermediaries, from music, film and fashion to metaphors that encapsulate America's unique approach to diplomacy.[1] Memory is thus nothing less than an expression of culture and a bridge between representation and reality that reveals itself in cultural practices (Confino 1997). And we would be hard-pressed to find cultural practices in which the blend of authentic and invented traditions are more clearly manifested than in cowboy sports.

The second thing that occurred to me leads to a consideration of the postmodern condition. Given the thrust of this investigation, it should come as no surprise that I accept postmodernity as an apt descriptor of our time. Media theorist and historian Denis McQuail (2000: 114) gave us a deceptively simple definition of postmodern culture as "volatile, illogical, kaleidoscopic, and hedonistic." Although his focus was on media, I think that his characterization applies to a wide range of practices and structures in contemporary culture, including what we do in our leisure time.

It is not without trepidation that I conclude this investigation in such unstable territory. Like the quicksand of the South Canadian River that bedeviled Andy Adams (1903) and his Circle Dot herd, postmodernism is treacherous ground. And, like Western imagery, it suffers from an embarrassment of riches ranging from aesthetics and architecture to epistemology, literature, and mass communication. Anderson (1998) traced its shadowy beginnings to the Hispanic inter-world of the 1930s, when avant-garde writers began to challenge the literary canons of their day. According to Mills (1959: 165-66), our species somehow made it through Antiquity and the Dark Ages to arrive at The Modern Age, only to see it crumble in the advance

---

[1] See Chapter Two, "The Frontier in American Character Development," for an overview of frontier rhetoric in political discourse.

of a postmodern period that he called, rather apocalyptically, "The Fourth Epoch." Berman (1982) used the imagery of a world in which "all that is solid melts into air" to describe the contradictions and ambiguities of these fluid times. For Lyotard (1984), social fragmentation meant the eclipse of grand narratives, "the great historico-philosophical schemes of progress and perfectibility that the modern age threw up" (Kumar 1995: 133). One of the most celebrated expressions flowed from the pen of Baudrillard (1988), who claimed that postmodernity's rupture with history is so complete that reality has been subsumed by *simulacra*, or images and representations of the past that have no sense of the past that they represent. "What society seeks through production, and overproduction, is the restoration of the real which escapes it" (p. 180). Harvey (1990: 38) looked to the turbulence of late 1960s as the tipping point between modernist culture and its successor, postmodernism, a "full-blown though still incoherent movement" that rails against rationalism and bureaucracy. Fukuyama (1992) boldly declared that history ground to a halt with the collapse of Communism and left us with a world (the developed part, anyway) united by trade and devoid of ideology. As it turns out, he was a bit premature. Kumar (1995) traced the development of three varieties of post-industrial theory—the idea of the information society and theories of post-Fordism and post-modernity—to give us a sweeping perspective of our times.

    Turning to social theorists with a bent toward media, we encounter a sea of provocative commentary on the postmodern condition. Advertising-executive-turned-polemicist Jerry Mander (1978), arguing that television has created a culture of passive and commercialized consumers who have relinquished control over their lives to corporate interests, went so far as to recommend the elimination of the electronic altar altogether. In a similar vein, Postman (1985) claimed that television has produced a culture obsessed with trivialities and entertainment to such an extent that we are quite literally amusing ourselves to death. Recognizing shades of an Orwellian Ministry of Information in the current climate of corporate-controlled media, Bagdikian (2000) has made it his business since the 1980s to apprise us of mergers and acquisitions that place control over the levers of communication in fewer and fewer hands. McChesney's (1999) primary concern was with a public sphere that has sputtered into irrelevance in a nation committed to the principles of free market capitalism and wary of governmental controls. Gitlin (2002) claimed that democracy itself is in peril as media-saturated consumers tune out the real world and surrender themselves to electronic stimulation and the disposable emotions that it engenders. For a truly sobering assessment of the postmodern condition, we turn to De Zengotita's (2005) polemic against media's capacity to reshape our lives. His monster vision is of a world, already in the making, in which "humanly created options that endow ordinary people with entitlements no mortal in history, no matter how exalted, could ever have assumed before" (p. 266) have obliterated time and space and placed mankind on a par with the divine. Ascending from media to mythology, De Zengotita suggested that Neietzsche's Overman has replaced the God of creation with gods of his own making, feverishly devising ever more alluring means of satisfying every conceivable desire.

    Even as postmodernists and media theorists have sought to make sense of a world that seems to be tipping ever further on its axis, sociologists and their ilk have been turning their attention to the decline of community. Riesman (1953) gave us the "lonely crowd" to express the emergence of a character type that depends less on internalized adult authority than on peer pressure. Unlike miners, lumberjacks, ranch hands, and similar sturdy stock from earlier generations who eschewed conformity to externalized norms and relied on their elders for direction, "other-directed" individuals spend their lives seeking the approval of others.

INVENTING TRADITION

"Approval itself," wrote Riesman, "irrespective of content, becomes almost the only unequivocal good in this situation: one makes good when one is approved of" (p. 66). In their study of modern consciousness, Berger et al (1974: 182) used the metaphor of homelessness to describe the anonymity of contemporary life:

> "This anonymity carries with it a constant threat of anomie. The individual is threatened not only by meaninglessness in the world of his work, but also by the loss of meaning in wide sectors of his relations with other people. The very complexity and pervasiveness of the technologized economy makes more and more social relations opaque to the individual. The institutional fabric as a whole tends toward incomprehensibility."

Using the demise of bowling leagues as a metaphor for decreasing participation in civic life, Putnam (1995) provided empirical evidence to confirm suspicions that Americans are joining fewer voluntary associations. Following a rich tradition stretching back to Tocqueville, Putnam emphasized the importance of civic participation in maintaining personal well-being and developing social capital. Bellah et al (1996) relied on extensive interviews to reveal a cult of individualism that was threatening communal values. Wuthnow (1994) injected a dose of optimism into the debate with his suggestion, backed by empirical evidence, that a small-group movement was reinvigorating the body politic. His detection of a pulse in America's public culture failed to stem hand wringing among academics. Angst in the academy made its way to the kitchen table when the mainstream media discovered McPherson et al's (2006) article in the *American Sociological Review*, "Social Isolation in America: Changes in Core Discussion Networks over Two Decades." Replicating a 1985 study based on General Social Survey (GSS) data of social networks, the researchers found that Americans are far more socially isolated than they were two decades ago. The social environment of core confidants that people count on for emotional support "has become smaller, more densely interconnected, and more centered on the close ties of spouse / partner" (p. 372). Moreover, the types of bridging ties that connect people to community and neighborhood have withered as confidant networks have closed in on smaller core groups. Clearly, the social ties that captured Tocqueville's (1945) attention have either frayed beyond recognition or undergone restructuring whose outlines are far from delineated.

Thus have legions of social theorists worked overtime to understand the *zeitgeist* of our age. I began this project with a suspicion (or, sociologically speaking, an hypothesis) that postmodern theory might have something to say about Old Dominion cowboys, and vice versa, and I haven't backed off. In several years of alternating between working literature and cattle, I am more convinced than ever that a case can be made for situating cowboy sports within a postmodern paradigm and the social changes that go with it. Perhaps the most effective way to approach this marriage of hard-riding sport and lofty theory is to return to my suggestion at the end of Chapter One, "Old Dominion Cowboys," that my fellow competitors and I are simultaneously at odds with, yet symptomatic of, the postmodern age. In other words, cowboy sports are embedded in postmodernity, even as they lure participants to activities rooted in the nomadic and decidedly pre-modern culture of America's great prairies. Much of what I have to say in conclusion has been expressed, if not explicitly, then at least implicitly, somewhere along the way. But, just in case we've missed a few mavericks, now's the time for a final round-up.[2]

Identity Formation and Cultural Expression through Cowboy Sports

Early on,[3] I mentioned two social theorists whose work is particularly germane to this study: Georg Simmel, who wrote extensively on tensions between the individual and society; and Erving Goffman, for his dramaturgical perspective and focus on the role of symbols in human interaction. Like Cohen and Taylor (1976) in their exploration of escape attempts, my debt to these sociologists is more implicit than explicit. Rather than cite them *ad nauseam*, I allow their influence to nourish my interpretations of Old Dominion cowboys and their contrary ways. But now may be the time to close ranks with Simmel and Goffman to suggest that cowboy sport participants are in a constant process of identity formation and cultural expression that transcends postmodernity. With arenas as our stage and collective memory of the frontier as our cultural tool kit (Swidler 1986), we compensate for the rootlessness of postmodern culture by identifying with others who share a nostalgia for cowboy ways and an urge to mimic them. Bauman (2004: 24), who was likewise indebted to Simmel and Goffman, put it this way in his book-length interview with Italian journalist Benedetto Vecchi: "Once identity loses the *social* anchors that made it look 'natural', predetermined and non-negotiable, 'identification' becomes ever more important for the individuals desperately seeking a 'we' to which they may bid for access."

Identity formation and cultural expression pervaded my units of analysis on individual as well as group levels. Individually, it was evident in a former golf fanatic's conversion to cattle penning after a vacation in Montana; in invidious distinctions that many people drew between *sittin'* and *ridin'* a horse; in Ted's comment that he "was the only cowboy" in his company; in Johnson's frank admission, "I guess every ten years or so I need to reinvent my life"; and in Mitch's assumption that "every boy grows up wanting to be a cowboy!" On a group level, identity formation and cultural expression revealed themselves most clearly as open riders and novices squared off in subtle and not so subtle ways to determine the purpose of the Blue Ridge Team Penning Association. In these and other instances, it was clear that identity formation and cultural expression were dualistic processes: cowboys were negotiating for a sense of community—a "we," in Bauman's terse description—even as we expressed our individualism. Whether we're working on our cowboying skills, participating in sport ritual, or paying a visit to the West of the imagination, we thus rely, personally and collectively, on our stock of cultural symbols to confirm our identity as cowboys, maintain our sense of community, and shield ourselves from the glare of postmodernity.

---

[2] Unless otherwise noted, anecdotes and examples cited in these concluding pages are drawn from Chapter Six, "Showtime."

[3] See Chapter One, "Old Dominion Cowboys," p. 11.

INVENTING TRADITION

Livin' on the Edge

Even as they challenged me to explore the notion of invented tradition and rethink the applicability of postmodern theory to my units of analysis, my mentors at the university suggested that I look into the similarities and differences between cowboy sports and so-called extreme sports. Well, I suppose that ethnographers need to be prepared for most anything. I could have joined a motorcycle gang or invested in a high-tech skateboard, or maybe taken a header off a cliff with a rubber band strapped to my ankles. Perhaps, in keeping with my own research interests, I should have climbed on the back of a two-thousand-pound bull to see if there was a correlation between its gyrations and my longevity. In fairness, my mentors were a reasonable bunch, and they settled for some dabbling in sport sociology. Which I did, mainly in the form of a literature review to contextualize rodeo and cowboy sports.[4]

My exploration in this area led me to Michalowski and Dubisch's (2001) account of their experiences on a cross country motorcycle trip from California to the Vietnam Memorial in Washington, DC, to commemorate the dead and wounded from the war in Southeast Asia. I credit their work for helping me to situate myself as an observant participant in my sporting activities. Granted, riding a motorcycle on an interstate highway doesn't entail the risk associated with truly extreme sports. Nobody was in danger of being gobbled up by a shark or frostbitten to death on some godforsaken mountain, and rampaging bulls were the least of their concerns. Nevertheless, hurtling across the continent on a motorcycle for hours on end, subject to the vicissitudes of nature and tied to the fate of people whose biking skills are a matter of conjecture, certainly has its perils. What their book did for me was to stimulate some thinking about just how *culturally specific* such activities are. Not that there aren't points of contact. Reflecting on bikers' place in popular culture, the authors had much to say about escaping the constraints of everyday life that would be familiar to Old Dominion cowboys and the frontier imagery that animates them. "Such images," wrote the academics-turned-bikers,

> "resonate with an idea that has played an important historical role in American ideology and popular culture—the concept of the frontier, a space that is open, empty, waiting to be explored and conquered. While such a frontier has long disappeared (and indeed the frontier as an empty space never really existed in America in any case, as these 'empty spaces' were already populated by native peoples), it can be recaptured through modes of travel that create the illusion of exploring new space by moving down the road" (p. 122).

Cowboys and bikers: unlikely as kindred spirits, but similar in their reliance on frontier imagery to construct their identities and supply symbols of group interaction. As I ponder these and other opportunities to experience excitement in leisure, it occurs to me that a few of my own sporting interests, aside from cowboying, definitely venture into extreme territory. Specifically, I can't help but wonder about three of them that might not be as death-defying as bungee jumping and bull riding, but that clearly lie at the outer edges of safety: sailing, scuba diving, and sky diving. Like cowboying and cross country biking, all three of these sports offer an escape from paramount reality through an imaginative frontier, and all three require an eagerness to

---

[4] See Chapter Five, "From Custom to Ritual: Identity Formation and Cultural Expression through Rodeo and Cowboy Sports," *The Sociology of Sport*.

embrace life, if only for a short time, on the edge, and to risk injury and death for the sake of adventure. As a sailor, I have bloodied my knees on supposedly controlled jibes in the capricious winds of Lake Michigan; as a scuba diver, I have followed sharks through coral canyons in the Caribbean and stared down cormorants in the waters of Lake Malawi in southern Africa; and as a sky diver, I have watched the Earth draw near in a sixty-second free fall from twelve thousand feet. Although a comparative analysis lies beyond the scope of this investigation, it certainly seems plausible to imagine correlations between extreme sports in terms of the ways that we fashion identities and express cultural affiliations, not just in our interaction through symbols, but also in our decision to do things that can get us killed.

Similarities between cowboy sports and extreme sports notwithstanding, cowboy sports remain on a range of their own. As America's favorite sandbox (Deverell 1994), and as a tool kit (Swidler 1986) brimming with cultural artifacts, the cattle frontier is culturally specific, and the lessons that it has to teach lie at the core of American history and our collective memory of it. The mimicry that we experience as Old Dominion cowboys does not end when the adrenaline subsides and our pulses return to normal. It extends to our sideline banter, the metaphors we use, the way we joke with one another, the stories we tell about our day jobs, and the feelings that peek through macho veneers when we talk about horses and, yes, even those contrary cattle. It shows up in the clothes we wear and the vehicles we drive. Based on my observations of parents and children, I strongly suspect that mimicry of cowboy ways is reflected in our child-raising predilections. The point is that cowboy sports are not just about athletics, and not just about excitement in leisure. As expressions of a distinct culture, they serve as links with the frontier that shaped us, and they provide communal resources to foster individual needs. Never mind that official history does not always square with the way things are remembered. Hewn from history, modified, and served up as an antidote to the destabilizing effects of modernity, the cowboy type has yet to be dethroned from its privileged position in America's mythological hall of fame. Other sports no doubt have their own myths. But that's another story.

As I write these words on a quiet Sunday morning in August, an aching muscle in my lower back reminds me that our postmodern, media-saturated world isn't quite done with cowboys. Colfax and I were after a cow at a penning last night, just before midnight. She cut fast and caught me off balance. I stayed on and we got the cow penned, and now I'm paying the price. The B.R.T.P.A. president wasn't there. Seems he busted some ribs when his mare pitched a fit and landed on top of him. A couple of guys were wearing back braces—precautionary, I'm sure, but no doubt signs that something was hurting. A man with his arm in a sling and steel pins in his shoulder showed up just to watch. Someone else is undergoing hand surgery next week. A horse broke loose back by the trailers and took off at a dead gallop with no bridle. Damn near ran over my wife. Several of us scrambled to stop it before something really bad happened.

And so it goes—small prices to pay for a stake in America's epic.

The Lure of Cowboy Ways

My third research question has to do with macro forces, historical and social, that contribute to the resilience and popularity of cowboy sports. Answers to this question can be found throughout this inquiry and probably don't bear repeating, except to reiterate that my units of analysis reveal the porous boundary between history and sociology. Spencer (Burke 1992) claimed famously that historians, stuck in the minutiae of time, place, and circumstance, are valuable only insofar as they carry the bricks that sociologists use to construct buildings. Such invidious distinctions between historical empiricism and sociological theory might provide fodder for academic debates, but they don't seem very useful in explaining social phenomena, and they don't do much to bridge disciplinary divides. The kinship between history and sociology was perhaps most forcefully expressed by Giddens (Abrams 1982: xviii) when he asserted that, "with the recovery of temporality as integral to social theory history and sociology become methodologically indistinguishable." Distinctions between the disciplines blur completely when we look to the past for clues to current behavior. Impatient with arcane debates that have done little to advance our understanding of society, Abrams (1982: x) had this to say about the symbiosis between history and sociology:

> "In my understanding of history and sociology there can be no relationship *between* them because, in terms of their fundamental preoccupations, history and sociology are and always have been the same thing. Both seek to understand the puzzle of human agency and both seek to do so in terms of the process of social structuring."

Seen as mutually supporting rather than antagonistic, history and sociology thus deliver to us a past that is more than the womb of the present; it is in fact the *only* raw material we have to fashion our present. From my experience as an observant participant, it seems clear that the historical and sociological forces behind cowboy sports collide in collective memory. It is here that the aggregation of individual memories, embedded in and filtered through specific social contexts, bumps up against phenomena that are accessible through rites and symbols (Halbwachs 1992; Olick 1999). Like Durkheim's collective conscience, collective memory is more than the sum of its parts, both in its intrinsic properties and its patterned persistence over time. It is a social fact, and it militates against our tendency to distinguish too sharply between the individual and society. Simply put, individuals and society construct one another. The process is abetted by collective memory's access to technologies of memory such as language, narrative, and dialogue, as well as museums, archives, and even professional historiography, all of which lie beyond the individual's grasp. Seen in this light, cowboy sports are nothing less than a technology of memory, perfectly suited to maintaining cowboy culture and perpetuating it across generations.

Did the cowboy type, forged on the cattle frontier, filtered through turn-of-the-twentieth-century angst and the traditions it spawned, and celebrated throughout a century of mass entertainment, produce Old Dominion cowboys? Sure. But it's just as true that Old Dominion cowboys are constantly making and remaking the cowboy type—that is, ourselves.

At least our horses know who we are.

Cowboy Sports and Postmodernity

And so we wind up where we began, pondering the resilience of premodern themes in a postmodern culture. Of all the contradictions that we've touched on—the wild versus the tame, agency versus structure, freedom versus community—this one might be the most intriguing of all.

To recapitulate: We now have a reasonably clear understanding of the socio historical processes that created the cowboy type, and we appreciate the role of cultural leaders who, between the closing of the frontier and the outbreak of World War I, chose the cowboy to represent their nation's most cherished values: independence, freedom, and rugged individualism. Following in the tradition of dime novels, theatrical productions, and Wild West shows that celebrated the West when it was still wild, a burgeoning entertainment industry dressed those values in cowboy garb and served them up as a palliative for the stresses of modernity. Over time, historical accuracy became less important than the symbols and imagery used to portray the frontier. Fact and fiction blurred in the collective memory of a nation seeking networks of familiarity (Bauman 2004) to counter a rising sense of instability and rootlessness. Meanwhile, organized sports infiltrated popular culture and enabled us to experience, both vicariously and personally, the life-sustaining thrill of athletic competition (Elias and Dunning 1986). Finally, within the rubric of sport sociology, we can see how rodeo and cowboy sports evolved from custom to ritual through the *form* of cowboying, the *discourse* of cowboy ways, and the *production* of events that commemorate the cattle frontier (Stoeltje 1993).

Now it's time to turn the question around and ask what cowboy sports have to teach us about these postmodern times. Simply put, what can Old Dominion cowboys and their brand of mimesis tell us about the broader culture? Are there lessons to be gleaned from a subculture that, as I claimed in Chapter One, "Old Dominion Cowboys," is curiously at odds with, yet symptomatic of, our postmodern age?[5]

Frankly, the first part of this assertion, that Old Dominion cowboys feed their peculiar habits outside the swirl of postmodernity, is an appeal to common sense. In several years as an Old Dominion cowboy, I have never ceased to be amazed simply by the *existence* of this robust subculture. Even as I strap on my spurs and saddle up to pen, sort, or cut cattle, I summon whatever objectivity I can muster and take in my surroundings. Aside from vehicles and cell phones (nowadays strapped to saddles in stylish pouches), evidence of our technology-saturated world is hard to come by. The air is laden with the pungent aroma of manure and fresh-cut grass. Except for the hum of traffic on some distant highway, sounds are reduced to the rhythms of nature: birds chirping; horses snorting, urinating, and defecating. Once in awhile there's thunder from an approaching storm. Canadian geese signal their presence as they fly overhead, oblivious to our existence. If I arrive early enough for a daytime competition, I am struck by people's muted voices, as though they (we) are reluctant to break the spell. At those moments, even the pounding of hooves beneath some lone rider warming up in the arena seems unnaturally muffled. On occasion, the only sound is...silence. Dust is everywhere. Insects are enough to drive you crazy. Somehow spitting seems okay, and the outhouse is no match for a visit to the rear of my trailer. And I have yet to be greeted by anything other than a smile from cowboys and cowgirls who are surely relishing the moment, just as I am.

In my mind's eye, I conjure up memories of similar moments, long ago, when the same sensations were a prelude to a hard day's work. Visions of cowboying in Haskell County, Oklahoma, Colfax County, New Mexico, and Gonzales County, Texas, invade my consciousness and connect me to a place deep down in my soul where I feel whole and secure. It's a place that's not accessible to my comrades, but I know from observation and experience that they have their own places to visit, their own memories to treasure, and their own longings to fulfill. In my thematic analysis and elsewhere, I refer to this collective watering hole as "the West of the imagination."

---

[5] See Chapter One, "Old Dominion Cowboys," p. 14.

INVENTING TRADITION

Media historian and theorist Denis McQuail (2000: 114) gave us a sort of shorthand when he characterized postmodernity as "volatile, illogical, kaleidoscopic, and hedonistic." If that's true—and I believe it is—then cowboy sports are surely an antidote. Historically and sociologically, they lie outside the paradigmatic flow of postmodernity. They contribute to what Goffman (Calhoun 2002: 29) might call "tactical repertoires" that enable us to manage our identities and defend ourselves from excessive scrutiny and criticism. For Cohen and Taylor (1976: 97), they are "activity enclaves" where participants can suspend self-consciousness because their sports provide more than enough opportunity for self-expression. Though subject to change, Old Dominion cowboy culture provides a set of norms and expectations within the highly structured parameters of sport. At the end of the day, there's nothing in commonly accepted definitions of postmodernity to recommend it. As Marvin, the horse trainer from Tennessee said to his group of listeners with a simplicity that borders on banality, "There are three things you need in a cow horse: a horse that's broke, showmanship, and an ability to work cattle."

Now, how kaleidoscopic is that?

This is not to say that Old Dominion cowboys are somehow immune to the need for community. Quite the contrary: like any activity enclave, cowboy sports are the arena of choice (pun intended) for people who choose to identify with the animate trinity and all that it represents. They serve as a haven for people rendered homeless in these mobile times. In their exploration of late twentieth century anxiety, Berger et al (1974: 184) provided as clear an explanation as I have seen for people to cluster in like-minded communities:

"A world in which everything is in constant motion is a world in which certainties of any kind are hard to come by. Social mobility has its correlate in cognitive and normative mobility. What is truth in one context of the individual's social life may be error in another. What was considered right at one stage of the individual's social career becomes wrong in the next. Once more, the anomic threat of these constellations is very powerful indeed."

If, as Berger et al (1974) and other scholars (Bellah et al 1996; McPherson et al 2006; Putnam 1995; Riesman 1953; Wuthnow 1994) have suggested, the loss of community is a defining feature of our age, then what are we supposed to do about it? The choices offered up by technology appear to be a double-edged sword. Even as they open up new worlds to explore (that is, for those who can afford to venture out), they remind us that our identities are of our own making. Peering through the formative haze of postmodernity, Slater (1970) recognized the *anomie* that is inevitable when people lose their sense of stability and enduring connections with others. Bauman (2004) saw that predictions of a rootless society had come to pass. "One becomes aware that 'belonging' and 'identity' are not cut in rock, that they are not secured by a lifelong guarantee, that they are eminently negotiable and revocable;

and that one's own decisions, the steps one takes, the way one acts—and the determination to stick by all that—are crucial factors of both" (p. 11). McPherson et al (2006) put the empirical stamp of legitimacy on all this in their study of social isolation in America. "Many more people talk to no one about matters they consider important to them in 2004 than was the case two decades ago" (pp. 353-54).

Great. Not only is postmodernity a jumbled and ever-shifting mosaic. Turns out we don't even have anyone to talk to anymore.

It doesn't help when you can't find groups with some history behind them, with rituals and symbols that retain their meaning over time rather than change with the prevailing winds.

Imaginative space has been colonized by media.

Sports arenas coddle us in air-conditioned comfort, pushing us ever further from the thrill of lived experience.

Advances in transportation and communication have ripped the heart out of communities, or at least transformed them into something else, maybe accessible only with a mouse click.

Social mobility leaves us homeless, literally and figuratively.

When you get right down to it, it's hard to know where to go, and even what to be.

Unless, maybe, you're a cowboy.

Postscript

There's an expression from cow country that's been circulating among Old Dominion cowboys: "There's never been a horse that couldn't be rode, and there's never been a cowboy that couldn't be throwed."

Hopefully, in this investigation of cowboy sports in a postmodern age, I have managed in some small measure to hang onto the horse that I chose to saddle up. Not that it's been a flawless ride. There are no doubt reams of literature that I missed, and I'm sure that there are clues in my ethnographic data that I failed to pick up on. Surely scholars will find gaps in my effort to link so many bodies of literature. Most of all, I am fully prepared for scholars to take issue with my attempt to situate cowboy sports in the context of postmodernity. Maybe it's just plain hubris to think that my units of analysis belong in the same, rarified air as theory more given to aesthetics and literary criticism than hard-riding cowboys.

So maybe I'm just another cowboy that got himself throwed. But I doubt it. I think that my position as an observant participant, committed to my sports long before I decided to write about them, represents an effective methodology. As near as I can tell, condensing two years of field work into one day is a novel technique in presenting units of analysis. This approach avoids the tedium of chronicling, in laborious detail, activities that are ritualized and, let's face it, repetitive—until all Hell breaks loose, which it usually does. What might be problematic for the historian turns out to be efficient for the sociologist, and I don't think that the thematic analysis suffers as a result. If anything, a condensed narrative brings a sharper focus to observations that might lose their salience over time.

Then there's the research. Frankly, I was a bit surprised to wind up on so many trails. Cowboys are supposed to be a simple lot, and yet there I was, rooting around in history, film criticism, myth making, collective memory, and sports, all within the rubric of cultural sociology, and all situated precariously in the shifting sands of postmodernity. But the deeper I probed, the more convinced I became that my forays were necessary to answer my research questions. Without wide-ranging research, I might have missed the distinction between history and collective memory that became a fulcrum of this study. Maybe I would have overlooked the role that Roosevelt, Remington, Wister and their ilk played in sculpting frontier values to the contours of an angst-ridden nation. More than likely, I would have been reluctant to wrap my arms around the elusive concept of authenticity to establish a baseline for mimicry of cowboy ways.

Perhaps the wide loop I threw around the literature, and the kind of cultural analysis that got me chasing so many mavericks, will suggest ways for researchers to breach the walls that separate them and tackle social phenomena from a multidisciplinary perspective. Turns out that history and sociology aren't such strange bedfellows after all. Both seek to understand collective behavior across time and culture, and neither can stand alone in explaining who and what we are and why we do what we do. Ideally, this exploration of cowboy sports from the backside of a horse will inspire others to begin where they are, and to use their own unique interests and activities as windows to explore the social world and the riches it has to offer.

Like the man said, "that's a thrill. You'll get hooked. There's nothing like it!"

Index

A

Abbott, E.C. "Teddy Blue", 42, 52, 53, 54, 56, 61, 62, 75, 77, 92, 113, 144, 146, 147, 152, 161
Adams, Andy, 42, 43, 46, 47, 48, 49, 50, 51, 52, 53, 54, 57, 61, 75, 77, 144, 146, 147, 150, 152, 157, 161, 166
Adventures of Huckleberry Finn, The (Twain), 21
agency, as freedom within structure, 94, 98, 99, 100, 101, 102, 140, 155, 158, 172
Alamo, 36, 42
American Dream, 7, 32, 37, 66, 74, 99
American exceptionalism, 9, 17, 18, 22, 103
animate trinity (human, horse, cow), 2, 13, 47, 55, 61, 87, 90, 111, 115, 145, 147, 156, 157, 159, 160, 163, 174
anomie, 32, 86, 168, 174
anxiety and angst
    as modern condition, 35, 38, 156, 174
    as postfrontier, 6, 26, 63, 76, 77, 111, 142, 166, 172, 176
associations, as voluntary, 18, 120, 130, 151, 154, 155, 156, 168
athletes and athleticism, 1, 4, 7, 10, 95, 97, 98, 102, 108, 109, 110, 141, 143, 147
    bovine, 127
    equine, 51, 55, 115, 126, 143, 157
    special status of, 14, 93, 97, 142, 156, 171, 173
authenticity, 87, 142
    as modern craving for, 12, 58, 61, 65, 76, 78, 141
    in frontier representations, 39, 46, 53, 54, 60, 61, 74, 77, 83, 140, 142, 144, 145, 147, 150, 158, 166, 176

B

bandeirante, 26, 37
barrel racing, 10, 112
bison. *See* buffalo
Blue Ridge Team Penning Association (B.R.T.P.A.), 15, 114, 116, 120, 155, 156, 163, 164, 169
Boone, Daniel, 34, 37, 38, 78, 90
bronc riding, 10, 105, 112
buffalo, 48, 57, 70
Buffalo Bill. *See* Cody, William Frederick
Buffalo Bill's Wild West Show, 60, 62
bull riding, 10, 112, 170
Bumppo, Natty, 20, 37, 38
Bunyan, Paul, 57, 78, 90
Bush, George W., 29, 30, 159, 160

C

Calamity Jane, 62
calf roping, 10, 112
Caroline (author's horse), 11, 114, 115
Carson, Kit, 38
cattle. *See* animate trinity
cattle frontier, nineteenth century, 3, 8, 14, 27, 40, 41, 43, 44, 45, 46, 47, 48, 49, 50, 52, 53, 54, 56, 62, 63, 64, 74, 84, 90, 100, 102, 104, 105, 106, 111, 141, 142, 145, 151, 152, 157, 158, 162, 171, 172, 173
census of 1890, 7, 23, 27, 63
Chicago School sociology, 4
chivalry, among cowboys, 52, 73, 74
Circle Dot herd, 47, 48, 50, 51, 150, 157, 166
Cody, William Frederick "Buffalo Bill", 57, 58, 59, 60, 61, 62, 76
Colfax (author's horse), 3, 4, 11, 114, 115, 116, 117, 118, 120, 121, 123, 124, 126, 127, 130, 131, 132, 133, 134, 135, 136, 137, 138, 139, 145, 146, 147, 148, 151, 156, 157, 158, 159, 161, 171, 173
collective conscience and consciousness, 27, 57, 73, 81, 86, 172
collective memory, 10, 11, 69, 70, 78, 84, 85, 86, 87, 88, 89, 91, 106, 111, 141, 142, 152, 160, 162, 163, 166, 169, 171, 172, 173, 176
    collected memory, in contrast to, 88
    generational effects on, 88
    history, in contrast to, 85, 89, 166
    lieux de mémoire (sites of memory), 86, 87, 90
    social memory studies, 84, 88
    technology, effects of, 85
communicative trinity. *See* humor, metaphor, vocabulary
Cooper, James Fenimore, 20, 77, 78
cowboy diplomacy, 29, 30, 159
cowboy sports (penning, sorting, cutting), 1, 3, 4, 6, 9, 10, 11, 12, 13, 55, 70, 89, 90, 99, 100, 102, 105, 109, 111, 141, 142, 143, 147, 149, 150, 152, 153, 156, 158, 160, 161, 163, 164, 165, 166, 168, 170, 171, 172, 173, 174, 176
    comparisons to rodeo, 10, 101, 103, 111, 112, 158
    etymology and origins of, 8, 102, 109, 142
    evolution from custom to ritual, 111, 145, 162, 173
    mimesis, emotional and historical, 46, 87, 90, 141, 144, 156
cowboy ways, 3, 10, 29, 30, 39, 42, 46, 66, 71, 72, 76, 79, 84, 90, 91, 111, 140, 141, 142, 145, 147, 161, 166, 169, 171, 173, 176

cowboy, as type, 10, 35, 37, 38, 41, 67, 74, 75, 78, 79, 81, 83, 84, 90, 106, 142, 151, 152, 162, 171, 172
cowboys. See Chapter Three, The Cowboy in History, Literature, and Showbiz. See also animate trinity; cattle frontier, nineteenth century; cowboy sports; cowboy ways; cowboy, as type; frontier; horsemanship; mimesis, in cowboy sports; Old Dominion cowboys; rodeo; West of the imagination; Western genre of entertainment
Cowboys Turtle Association, 106
Crèvecoeur, J. Hector St. John de, 16, 17, 18, 19, 24, 33, 38
Crockett, Davy, 35, 37, 57
cultural entrepreneurs, 7, 10, 39, 89, 90
cultural imaginary, 91, 143, 152
cultural trinity (Roosevelt, Remington, Wister), 70, 74, 76, 106, 142, 150, 152, 154, 157, 166
Custer, George Armstrong, 36, 58
custom. See Chapter Five, From Custom to Ritual. See also cowboy sports, evolution from custom to ritual
cutting, 1, 2, 10, 12, 13, 90, 91, 100, 109, 110, 111, 112, 116, 124, 125, 144, 145, 146, 148, 150, 156, 158, 160, 163

D

Defoe, Daniel, 19, 20, 158
Democracy in America (Tocqueville), 18
dime novels, 7, 10, 38, 57, 58, 64, 65, 67, 68, 74, 77, 78, 103, 144, 151, 173
discourse, as source of power, 106, 111, 162, 173
Double U Bar Ranch (New Mexico), 3, 145, 161
Durkheim, Emile, 14, 84, 97, 172

E

Eden, concept of America as, 7, 18, 32, 33, 34, 35, 63, 89, 158
ethnography, 3, 4, 5, 6, 10, 152
   access to field, 4, 104
   analytic autoethnography, 6
   objectivity, 14, 141, 173
   observant participation, 4, 13, 14, 141, 170, 172, 176
   participant observation, 4, 6
   self-reflexivity, 5, 6
   subjectivity, 14
   units of analysis, 4, 11, 92, 140, 141, 142, 163, 169, 170, 171, 176

F

Farafield Farms (Oklahoma), 3
fatalism, among cowboys, 150
Fink, Mike, 57

form, as source of power, 106, 111, 162, 173
frontier. See Chapter Two, The Frontier in American Character Development. See also anxiety and angst, as postfrontier; census of 1890; cowboy, as type; cultural imaginary; *Significance of the Frontier in American History;* Turner, Frederick Jackson; West of the imagination; West, as America's fifty-first state of mind

G

gauchos, 26, 37, 41, 45
Goffman, Erving, 4, 5, 11, 14, 94, 97, 158, 164, 169, 174
Golconda Farm (pseud.), 114, 116, 120, 129, 130, 139
Great Train Robbery, The, 76, 77
Gunsmoke, 12, 81

H

Halbwachs, Maurice, 10, 85, 87, 172
Haskell (Judy Hightower's horse), 3, 4, 11, 12, 114, 115, 148, 149, 161, 173
Hickok, Bill, 62
Hobsbawm, Eric, 7, 8, 69, 85, 86, 89, 142, 166
Home of Champions Rodeo, 107
horsemanship, 3, 11, 13, 104, 118, 130, 144, 146, 159, 160
horses. See also animate trinity; athletes and athleticism, equine; Caroline; Colfax; Haskell; horsemanship
   Mustang, as breed, 40, 41, 43, 90
   Quarter Horse, as breed, 41, 42, 110, 125, 126, 128, 143, 144, 157
   represented in myth of White Mustang, 41
   symbolism of, 41, 45, 55
humor, in cowboy communication, 10, 29, 48, 49, 50, 83, 106, 111, 144, 146, 147, 150, 153, 159

I

independence, in American character, 11, 18, 19, 53, 63, 80, 83, 102, 140, 142, 160, 161, 173
Indian Territory, 43, 44
individualism, in American character, 11, 12, 18, 23, 24, 26, 27, 36, 42, 67, 79, 80, 91, 107, 155, 160, 161, 168, 169, 173
International Committee for the Sociology of Sport, 96
invented traditions, 7, 8, 11, 69, 86, 100, 106, 142, 144, 145, 148, 152, 154, 157, 159, 161, 165, 166, 170

J

Jefferson, Thomas, 16, 18, 22, 30, 33, 34, 158

Index

Judson, Edward Zane Carroll, 57, 58

K

Kansas, 41, 43, 44, 54, 73, 78, 103

L

Lazy B Growing Up on a Cattle Ranch in the American Southwest, The (O'Connor, Day), 28, 29
Leatherstocking Tales (Cooper), 20, 77
Letters from an American Farmer (Crèvecoeur), 16
Life and Strange and Surprising Adventures of Robinson Crusoe, The (Defoe), 19, 158
llaneros, 41, 45
Log of a Cowboy: A Narrative of the Old Trail Days, The (Adams), 46
Lone Ranger, 35, 160

M

Marlboro Man, as American icon, 125, 143, 151
media, 20, 58, 79, 83, 84, 85, 105, 166, 167, 168, 171, 175
    mass, 10, 29, 37, 68, 69, 81, 85, 87, 104, 151
    mediated experience, 62, 80, 83, 86, 140, 141, 166
metaphor
    in cowboy communication, 49, 50, 51, 146, 147, 157, 171
    in frontier imagery in politics and culture, 9, 10, 26, 27, 28, 30, 31, 37, 68, 73, 81, 91, 159, 166
mimesis, in cowboy sports, 12, 13, 14, 46, 87, 113, 140, 144, 173
modernity, 7, 11, 13, 21, 22, 27, 41, 47, 59, 64, 65, 66, 71, 74, 76, 77, 78, 80, 85, 86, 90, 97, 104, 106, 142, 150, 153, 156, 157, 159, 162, 166, 171, 173
Montana, 43, 46, 48, 51, 52, 54, 61, 62, 72, 104, 107, 127, 157, 161, 169
myth, America's foundational. *See* American Dream; American exceptionalism; collective memory; cultural imaginary; cultural trinity; Eden, concept of America as; invented traditions; metaphor, in frontier imagery in politics and culture; nostalgia; West of the imagination; West, as America's fifty-first state of mind; Western genre of entertainment

N

National Cowboy and Western Heritage Museum (Oklahoma City, OK), 62, 108
National Cutting Horse Association (N.C.H.A.), 110
National Team Penning Championships (N.T.P.C.), 110

Nebraska, 50, 52, 56, 57, 60, 102, 103, 104
New Heloise, The (Rousseau), 20
New Mexico, 3, 28, 42, 44, 49, 141, 145, 161, 173
norms, group, 69, 140, 147, 149, 151, 167, 174
nostalgia, 8, 10, 14, 32, 61, 67, 68, 69, 77, 81, 84, 86, 87, 90, 144, 169
    reflective, 86
    restorative, 86

O

O'Connor, Sandra Day, 28
Oklahoma, 3, 14, 22, 42, 45, 47, 54, 56, 62, 63, 83, 104, 108, 112, 124, 132, 135, 141, 148, 149, 150, 153, 161, 173
Old Dominion cowboys. *See* Chapter One, Old Dominion Cowboys; Chapter Seven, A Sociology of Cowboy Sports, Thematic Analysis
    and postmodernity, 168, 173
    as mimetic cowboys, 14, 173
    author as observant participant, 13, 14
    definition of, 3
    participation in the animate trinity, 13, 90
Old Glory Blowout, 60, 102

P

penning, 1, 2, 10, 12, 13, 15, 90, 91, 100, 109, 110, 111, 112, 114, 116, 117, 118, 119, 120, 124, 127, 128, 130, 131, 133, 134, 136, 138, 140, 144, 145, 146, 148, 150, 153, 154, 156, 157, 158, 159, 160, 163, 164, 169, 171
popular culture, 7, 35, 57, 59, 77, 78, 82, 85, 90, 151, 166, 170, 173
postmodernity, 11, 46, 87, 91, 100, 164, 165, 166, 167, 168, 169, 173, 174, 175, 176
Pro Rodeo Hall of Fame and Museum of the American Cowboy (Colorado Springs, CO), 108
production, as source of power, 106, 111, 162, 173
Professional Rodeo Cowboys Association (P.R.C.A.), 104, 106, 108
proletarian, as cowboy, 10, 51, 69, 76, 109, 145
Protestant Ethic and the Spirit of Capitalism, The (Weber), 99

Q

Quien Sabe Ranch (Texas), 3, 150

R

Ranch Life and the Hunting-Trail (Roosevelt), 71
Reagan, Ronald, 28, 32, 67, 137
Red Right Hand, or First Scalp for Custer, The, 58
religion
    as reflected in sport, 14, 71, 97, 98, 162

in cowboy communication, 50, 78
Remington, Frederic, 8, 10, 69, 71, 72, 73, 74, 75, 76, 77, 89, 90, 103, 106, 142, 144, 152, 156, 157, 160, 166, 176
ritual. *See* Chapter Five, From Custom to Ritual. *See also* cowboy sports, evolution from custom to ritual
rodeo, 30, 67, 102, 103, 104, 105, 107, 108, 112, 115, 137, 141, 149, 170, 173
    comparisons to cowboy sports, 10, 100, 101, 111, 112, 113, 142, 158
    etymology and origins of, 3, 8, 102, 103
    professional associations, 104, 106, 108, 149
    scholarly interpretations, 10, 76, 91, 99, 103, 104, 105, 106, 107, 108, 158, 162
Rogers, Roy, 35, 79
Romanticism, 22, 34, 64
Roosevelt, Theodore, 8, 10, 27, 28, 29, 30, 69, 70, 71, 72, 73, 74, 76, 78, 89, 90, 103, 106, 142, 144, 152, 156, 157, 159, 160, 166, 176
Rousseau, Jean-Jacques, 20, 22, 67, 158
routinization, as condition of modern life, 98

S

sacred, as element of sport, 2, 14, 96, 156, 162
Scouts of the Prairie, The, 58, 59
self-reliance, in American character, 28, 67, 140, 142, 160
Significance of the Frontier in American History, The (Turner), 9, 23
Simmel, Georg, 11, 93, 141, 159, 164, 169
Siringo, Charlie, 53, 54, 55, 61, 75, 77, 144, 146, 147, 157, 161
small-group movement, 155, 161, 168
social Darwinism, 64, 66, 71, 74, 78, 106, 152
sorting, 1, 2, 10, 12, 13, 90, 91, 100, 105, 109, 111, 112, 116, 144, 145, 150, 154, 156, 158, 160, 163
sports. *See* Chapter Five, From Custom to Ritual, Identity Formation and Cultural Expression through Rodeo and Cowboy Sports, The Sociology of Sport; Chapter Seven, A Sociology of Cowboy Sports. *See also* animate trinity; athletes and athleticism; barrel racing; bronc riding; bull riding; calf roping; cowboy sports; cutting; horsemanship; International Committee for the Sociology of Sport; penning; rodeo; sorting; steer wrestling; team steer roping
Startling and Soul-Stirring Attack upon the Deadwood Mail Coach, The, 60
steer wrestling, 10, 112
stoicism, among cowboys, 70, 142, 149, 150, 163
symbolic interaction, 4, 93, 94, 140, 146, 148, 166, 169, 170, 171

T

team steer roping, 10
Texas, 3, 29, 40, 42, 43, 44, 45, 46, 47, 48, 51, 52, 54, 55, 56, 58, 64, 78, 102, 104, 109, 110, 120, 124, 125, 128, 131, 132, 141, 143, 148, 150, 152, 157, 161, 164, 173
Texas Cowboy, or Fifteen Years on the Hurricane Deck of a Spanish Pony, A (Siringo), 53
theater, as locus of frontier themes, 10, 58, 59
thematic analysis, 11, 80, 81, 141, 142, 173, 176, *See* Chapter Seven, A Sociology of Cowboy Sports, Thematic Analysis
Tocqueville, Alexis de, 18, 19, 24, 38, 151, 154, 160, 168
Tonto (Lone Ranger's sidekick), 160
Transcendentalism, 22, 34
Turner, Frederick Jackson, 9, 22, 23, 24, 25, 26, 27, 28, 32, 33, 34, 38, 62, 63, 67, 68, 70, 72, 75, 77
Twain, Mark, 21, 77

U

United States Team Penning Association (U.S.T.P.A.), 109, 110

V

vaquero, 38, 42
Virginia, 3, 12, 14, 30, 40, 42, 104, 111, 112, 113, 114, 117, 125, 128, 132, 148, 155
Virginian, The (Wister), 42, 74, 75
vocabulary, in cowboy communication, 49, 146, 147

W

Wayne, John, 83, 132, 151
We Pointed Them North: Reminiscences of a Cow Puncher (Abbott), 52
Weber, Max, 93, 97, 99
West of the imagination, 39, 62, 106, 127, 141, 163, 169, 173
West, as America's fifty-first state of mind, 10, 162
Western genre of entertainment, 35, 61, 71, 76, 77, 79, 80, 81, 82, 83, 84, 166
Wild West shows, 7, 10, 68, 103, 106, 141, 151, 173
Winning of the West (Roosevelt), 70, 78
Wister, Owen, 8, 10, 42, 69, 74, 75, 76, 78, 89, 90, 103, 106, 142, 144, 152, 156, 157, 160, 166, 176
World's Columbian Exposition (Chicago, IL), 22, 62
Wyoming, 43, 74, 75, 76, 102, 104, 149

References

Abbott, E. C. ("Teddy Blue"), and Helena Huntington Smith (1939). *We Pointed Them North: Reminiscences of a Cow Puncher*. New York: Farrar and Rinehart, Inc.

Adams, Ramon F. (1971). *The Cowman Says It Salty*. Tucson: The University of Arizona Press.

Adams, Andy. (1903). *The Log of a Cowboy: A Narrative of the Old Trail Days*. Illustrated by E. Boyd Smith. Boston and New York: Houghton, Mifflin and Company.

Adler, Patricia A. and Peter Adler. (1987). *Membership Roles in Field Research*. Newbury Park, CA: Sage Publications.

Anderson, Leon. (2006). "Analytic Autoethnography." *Journal of Contemporary Ethnography* 35 (4): 373-95.

Anderson, Perry. (1998). *The Origins of Postmodernity*. London and New York: Verso.

Assmann, Jan and John Czaplicka. (Spring – Summer 1995). "Collective Memory and Cultural Identity." *New German Critique*, 65, Cultural History / Cultural Studies: 125-33.

Bagdikian, Ben. (2000). *The Media Monopoly*, 6th ed. Boston: Beacon Press.

Baudrillard, Jean. (1988). *Selected Writings*. Edited, with an Introduction, by Mark Poster. Stanford, CA: Stanford University Press.

Bauman, Zygmunt. (2004). *Identity: Conversations with Benedetto Vecchi*. Cambridge, U.K.: Polity Press.

Bellah, Robert N., et al. (1996). *Habits of the Heart: Individualism and Commitment in American Life*. Berkeley, Los Angeles, London: University of California Press.

Bendix, Reinhard. (1977). *Max Weber: An Intellectual Portrait*. With an Introduction to the new edition by Guenther Roth. Berkeley, Los Angeles, London: University of California Press.

Berger, Peter L., Brigitte Berger, and Hansfried Kellner. (1974). *The Homeless Mind: Modernization and Consciousness*. New York: Vintage Books.

Berger, Peter L. and Thomas Luckmann. (1967). *The Social Construction of Reality: A Treatise in the Sociology of Knowledge*. Garden City, NY: Anchor Books.

Berman, Marshall. (1982). *All That Is Solid Melts into Air: The Experience of Modernity*. New York: Penguin Books.

Berne, Eric. (1964). *Games People Play: The Psychology of Human Relationships*. New York: Grove Press, Inc.

Billington, Ray Allen. (1966). *America's Frontier Heritage*. New York, Chicago, and San Francisco: Holt, Rinehart and Winston.

Birrell, Susan. (December 1981). "Sport as Ritual: Interpretations from Durkheim to Goffman." *Social Forces*, 60 (2, Special Issue): 354-76.

Becker, Howard. (1963). *Outsiders*. New York: Free Press.

Bly, John. (1990). *Iron John: A Book about Men*. New York: Vintage Books.

Boatright, Mody C. (1942). "Frontier Humor: Despairing or Buoyant?" In Speck, Ernest B. (1973). *Mody Boatright, Folklorist: A Collection of Essays*, 39-60. Austin: University of Texas Press.

_____. (1949). "The Art of Tall Lying." In Speck, Ernest B. (1973). *Mody Boatright, Folklorist: A Collection of Essays*, 68-79. Austin: University of Texas Press.

_____. (Summer 1951). "The American Myth Rides the Range: Owen Wister's Man on Horseback." *Southwest Review*, XXXVI (3): 157-63.

_____. (1964). "Theodore Roosevelt, Social Darwinism, and the Cowboy." In Speck, Ernest B. (1973). *Mody Boatright, Folklorist: A Collection of Essays*. Austin: University of Texas Press.

_____. (Summer 1964). "The American Rodeo." *American Quarterly*, 16 (2), Part 1: 195-202.

Boorstin, Daniel J. (1974). *The Americans: The Democratic Experience*. New York: Vintage Books.

Boym, Svetlana. (2001). *The Future of Nostalgia*. New York: Basic Books.

Burke, Peter. (1992). *History and Social Theory*. Cambridge, U.K.: Polity Press.

Caillois, Roger. (1961). *Man, Play, and Games*. Translated from the French by Meyer Barash. New York: The Free Press of Glencoe, Inc.

Calhoun, Craig et al, eds. (2002). *Contemporary Sociological Theory*. Malden, MA ; Oxford, UK; Melbourne; and Berlin: Blackwell Publishing Ltd.

Carey, James. (1989). *Communication as Culture: Essays on Media and Society*. Boston: Unwin Hyman.

References

Cawelti, John G. (1971). *The Six-Gun Mystique*. Bowling Green, OH: Bowling Green University Popular Press.

Clark, Candace. (2002). "Taming the 'Brute Being': Sociology Reckons with Emotionality." Pp. 155-82 in *Postmodern Existential Sociology*, edited by Joseph A. Kotarba and John M. Johnson. Walnut Creek, CA: AltaMira Press.

Clementi, Hebe. (1981). "National Identity and the Frontier." *American Studies International*, 18 (3-4): 36-44.

Clifford, James and George E. Marcus, eds. (1986). *Writing Culture: The Poetics and Politics of Ethnography*. Berkeley: University of California Press.

Coffin, Tristram P. (October 1953). "The Cowboy and Mythology." *Western Folklore*, 12 (4): 290-93.

Cohen, Stanley and Laurie Taylor. (1976). *Escape Attempts: The Theory and Practice of Resistance to Everyday Life*. London: Allen Lane Press.

Collins, Jim. (Winter 1991). "Theorizing Cultural Memory: Totalizing Recall?" *American Literary History*, 3 (4): 829-40.

Confino, Alon. (December 1997). "Collective Memory and Cultural History: Problems of Method." *The American Historical Review*, 102 (5): 1386-1403.

Cooper, James Fenimore. (1964). *The Pioneers*. New York: New American Library.

Crèvecoeur, J. Hector St. John de. (1997). *Letters from an American Farmer*. Edited with an Introduction and Notes by Susan Manning. Oxford and New York: Oxford University Press.

Cronon, William. (April 1987). "Revisiting the Vanishing Frontier: The Legacy of Frederick Jackson Turner." *Western Historical Quarterly*, 18 (2): 157-76.

Dale, Edward E. (June 1937). "The Cow Country in Transition." *The Mississippi Valley Historical Review*, 24 (1): 3-20.

_____. (1965). *Cow Country*. Norman: University of Oklahoma Press.

Davis, D. (Summer 1954). "Ten-Gallon Hero." *American Quarterly*, 6 (2): 111-25.

Defoe, Daniel. (1986). *Robinson Crusoe*. Cutchogue, NY: Buccaneer Books, Inc.

Denzin, Norman K. (1997). *Interpretive Ethnography: Ethnographic Practices for the 21st Century*. London, Thousand Oaks, New Delhi: Sage Publications.

Deverell, William. (Summer 1994). "Fighting Words: The Significance of the American West in the History of the United States." *Western Historical Quarterly*, 25 (2): 185-206.

Dudden, Arthur P. (Oct. – Dec. 1961). "Nostalgia and the American." *Journal of the History of Ideas*, 22 (4): 515-30.

Durham, Philip and Everett L. Jones. (1965). *The Negro Cowboys*. New York: Dodd, Mead and Company.

Durkheim, Emile. (1995). *The Elementary Forms of Religious Life*. Translated and with an introduction by Karen E. Fields. New York: The Free Press.

Edwards, Harry. (1973). *Sociology of Sport*. Homewood, IL: The Dorsey Press.

Elias, Norbert. (1978). *The Civilizing Process: The History of Manners*. New York: Urizen Books.

Elias, Norbert and Eric Dunning. (1986). *Quest for Excitement: Sport and Leisure in the Civilizing Process*. New York: Basil Blackwell.

Elkin, Frederick. (October 1950). "The Psychological Appeal of the Hollywood Western." *Journal of Educational Sociology*, 24 (2): 72-86.

Errington, Frederick. (November 1990). "The Rock Creek Rodeo: Excess and Constraint in Men's Lives." *American Ethnologist*, 17 (4): 628-45.

Ewen, Stuart. (1976). *Captains of Consciousness: Advertising and he Social Roots of the Consumer Culture*. New York: McGraw-Hill Book Company.

Faragher, John Mack. (February 1993). "The Frontier Trail: Rethinking Turner and Reimagining the American West." *American Historical Review*, 98 (1): 106-17.

_____, ed. (1994). *Rereading Frederick Jackson Turner: "The Significance of the Frontier in American History" and Other Essays*. New York: Henry Holt and Company.

Fine, Gary Alan. (1995). *A Second Chicago School: The Development of a Postwar American Sociology*. Chicago: University of Chicago Press.

Fishwick, Marshall W. (April 1952). "The Cowboy: America's Contribution to the World's Mythology." *Western Folklore*, XI (2): 77-92.

Fontana, Andrea. (2002). "Short Stories from the Salt." Pp. 201-18 in *Postmodern Existential Sociology*, edited by Joseph A. Kotarba and John M. Johnson. Walnut Creek, CA: AltaMira Press.

References

Forbes, Jack D. (Spring 1968). "Frontiers in American History and the Role of the Frontier Historian." *Ethnohistory*, 15 (2): 203-35.

Frantz, Joe B. and Julian Ernest Choate, Jr. (1955). *The American Cowboy: The Myth and the Reality*. Norman: University of Oklahoma Press.

Frey, James M. and D. Stanley Eitzen. (1991). "Sport and Society." *Annual Review of Sociology*, 17: 503-22.

Fukuyama, Francis. (1992). *The End of History and the Last Man*. New York: Avon Books.

Geertz, Clifford. (1973). "Deep Play: Notes on the Balinese Cockfight." In *The Interpretation of Cultures*. New York: Basic Books.

George, Henry. (1942). *Progress and Poverty: An Inquiry into the Cause of Industrial Depressions and of Increase of Want with Increase of Wealth*. New York: Walter J. Black.

Gerth, H. and C. Wright Mills. (1946). *From Max Weber: Essays in Sociology*. New York: Oxford University Press.

Gitlin, Todd. (2002). *Media Unlimited: How the Torrent of Images and Sounds Overwhelms Our Lives*. New York: Henry Holt and Company.

Goetzmann, William H. and William N. Goetzmann. (1986). *The West of the Imagination*. New York and London: W. W. Norton and Company.

Goffman, Erving. (1959). *The Presentation of Self in Everyday Life*. New York: Doubleday.

_____. (1974). *Frame Analysis*. Cambridge, MA: Harvard University Press.

_____. (2002). "The Presentation of Self in Everyday Life." Pp. 51-65 in *Contemporary Sociological Theory*, edited by C. Calhoun et. al. Malden, MA; Oxford, UK; Melbourne; Berlin: Blackwell Publishing Ltd.

Gordon, David. (December 1981). "The Reality of Myths." *Reviews in American History*, 9 (4): 446-50.

Green, Rayna. (April – June 1984). Book review: "Rodeo: An Anthropologist Looks at the Wild and the Tame." *The Journal of American Folklore*, 97 (384): 230-33.

Groos, Karl. (1898). *The Play of Animals*. New York: D. Appleton and Company.

Halbwachs, Maurice. (1992). *On Collective Memory*. Edited, translated, and with an introduction by Lewis A. Coser. Chicago and London: The University of Chicago Press.

Hall, G. Stanley. (1907). *Youth: Its Education, Regimen, and Hygiene.* New York: D. Appleton and Company.

Harvey, David. (1990). *The Condition of Postmodernity.* Cambridge, MA and Oxford, UK: Blackwell Publishers, Ltd.

Hawthorne, Nathaniel. (2003). *The Scarlet Letter.* Introduction by Nina Baym. Notes by Thomas E. Connolly. New York: Penguin Books.

Hays, Sharon. (March 1994). "Structure and Agency and the Sticky Problem of Culture." *Sociological Theory*, 12 (1): 57-72.

Hobsbawm, Eric. (May 1972). "The Social Function of the Past: Some Questions." *Past and Present*, 55: 3-17.

Hobsbawm, Eric and Terence Ranger, eds. (1983). *The Invention of Tradition.* Cambridge: Cambridge University Press.

Hofstadter, Richard and Seymour Martin Lipset, eds. (1968). *Turner and the Sociology of the Frontier.* New York and London: Basic Books, Inc., Publishers.

Hofstadter, Richard. (1977). *The Age of Reform.* New York: Alfred A. Knopf.

Horkheimer, Max and Theodor Adorno. (2002). *Dialectic of Enlightenment.* Stanford, CA: Stanford University Press.

http://www.harmonicacountry.com/index.html. *Giant Harmonica Fakebook.*

http://www.nationalcowboymuseum.org/g_rode.html. National Cowboy and Western Heritage Museum.

http://www.nchacutting.com. National Cutting Horse Association (N.C.H.A.)

http://www.ntpc.us. National Team Penning Championships. (N.T.P.C.)

http://www.prorodeo.org. Professional Rodeo Cowboys Association (P.R.C.A.)

http://www.tsha.utexas.edu/handbook/online/index.html.

http://www.ustpa.com. United States Team Penning Association (U.S.T.P.A.).

Huizinga, Johan. (1968). *Homo Ludens.* Buenos Aires and Barcelona: Emecé Editores.

Jacobs, Wilbur R. (1994). *On Turner's Trail: 100 Years of Writing Western History.* Lawrence: University Press of Kansas.

References

Jenkins, Philip. (1997). *A History of the United States*. New York: St. Martin's Press.

Kalberg, Stephen. (2002). Max *Weber: The Protestant Ethic and the Spirit of Capitalism*. Los Angeles: Roxbury Publishing Company.

Kasson, Joy S. (2000). *Buffalo Bill's Wild West: Celebrity, Memory, and Popular History*. New York: Hill and Wang.

Kelly, J. M. (1992). *A Short History of Western Legal Theory*. Oxford: Clarendon Press.

Klein, Kerwin Lee. (Winter 2000). "On the Emergence of Memory in Historical Discourse." *Representations*, 69, Special Issue: Grounds for Remembering: 127-50.

Kotarba, Joseph A. and John M. Johnson, eds. (2002). *Postmodern Existential Sociology*. Walnut Creek, CA: AltaMira Press.

Kuenz, Jane. (Spring 2001). "The Cowboy Businessman and 'The Course of Empire': Owen Wister's 'The Virginian'." *Cultural Critique*, 48: 98-128.

Kumar, Krishan. (1995). *From Post-Industrial to Post-Modern Society: New Theories of the Contemporary World*. Oxford: Basil Blackwell.

Lawrence, Elizabeth Atwood. (1982). *Rodeo: An Anthropologist Looks at the Wild and the Tame*. Knoxville: The University of Tennessee Press.

_____. (1985). *Hoofbeats and Society: Studies of Human-Horse Interactions*. Bloomington: Indiana University Press.

Lehman, Harvey C. and Paul A. Witty. (1976). *The Psychology of Play Activities*. New York: Arno Press.

Leverenz, David. (Winter 1991). "The Last Real Man in America: From Natty Bumppo to Batman." *American Literary History*, 3 (4): 753-81.

Lipsitz, George. (1990). *Time Passages: Collective Memory and American Popular Culture*. Minneapolis: University of Minnesota Press.

Livingston, Phil. (1991). *Team Penning*. Colorado Springs: Western Horseman, Inc.

Lofland, John and Lyn H. Lofland. (1995). *Analyzing Social Settings: A Guide to Qualitative Observation and Analysis*, 3rd edition. Belmont, CA: Wadsworth Publishing Company.

Loy, John W. Jr. and Gerald S. Kenyon, eds. (1969). *Sport, Culture, and Society: A Reader on the Sociology of Sport*. London: The MacMillan Company.

Luschen, Gunther. (1980). "Sociology of Sport: Development, Present State, and Prospects." *Annual Review of Sociology*, 6: 315-47.

McDougall, William. (1926). *An Introduction to Social Psychology*. Boston: John W. Luce & Co.

Lyotard, Jean-François. (1984). *The Postmodern Condition: A Report on Knowledge*. Translated from the French by Geoff Bennington and Brian Massumi. Foreword by Fredric Jameson. Manchester, U.K.: Manchester University Press.

Mander, Jerry. (1978). *Four Arguments for the Elimination of Television*. New York: William Morrow.

Manning, Peter. (1973). "Existential Sociology." *The Sociological Quarterly*, 14: 200-25.

Matthews, Fred H. (1977). *Quest for an American Sociology: Robert E. Park and the Chicago School*. Montreal: McGill-Queen's University Press.

Marx, Leo. (1967). *The Machine in the Garden: Technology and the Pastoral Ideal in America*. London, Oxford, New York: Oxford University Press.

McChesney, Robert. (1999). *Rich Media, Poor Democracy: Communication Politics in Dubious Times*. Urbana: University of Illinois Press.

McNutt, James C. (January 1986). Book Review: "Rodeo: An Anthropologist Looks at the Wild and the Tame." *Western Folklore*, 45 (1): 69-71.

McPherson, Miller, Lynn Smith-Lovin, and Matthew E. Brashears. (June 2006). "Social Isolation in America: Changes in Core Discussion Networks over Two Decades." *American Sociological Review*, 71 (3): 353-75.

McQuail, Denis. (2000). *McQuail's Mass Communication Theory*, 4th edition. London, Thousand Oaks, and New Delhi: SAGE Publications.

Mead, George Herbert. (1934). *Mind, Self, and Society from the Standpoint of a Social Behaviorist*. Edited, with Introduction, by Charles W. Morris. Chicago and London: The University of Chicago Press.

Michalowski, Raymond and Jill Dubisch. (2001). *Run for the Wall: Remembering Vietnam on a Motorcycle Pilgrimage*. Rutgers, NJ: Rutgers University Press.

Mills, C. Wright. (1959). *The Sociological Imagination*. New York: Oxford University Press, Inc.

Mrozek, Donald J. (1983). *Sport and American Mentality, 1880-1910*. Knoxville: The University of Tennessee Press.

References

Munden, Kenneth J. (1958). "A Contribution to the Psychological Understanding of the Origin of the Cowboy and his Myth." *American Imago: A Psychoanalytic Journal for the Arts and Sciences*, 15: 103-48.

Murdoch, David Hamilton. (2001). *The American West: The Invention of a Myth*. Reno and Las Vegas: University of Nevada Press.

Nash, Roderick. (1967). *Wilderness and the American Mind*. New Haven and London: Yale University Press.

Nemerov, Alex. (Winter – Spring 1991). "Frederic Remington: Within and without the Past." *American Art*, 5 (½): 36-59.

Nisbet, Robert. (1976). *Sociology as an Art Form*. New York: Oxford University Press.

Noble, David. (1965). *Historians against History: The Frontier Thesis and the National Covenant in American Historical Writing since 1830*. Minneapolis: University of Minnesota Press.

Nora, Pierre. (Spring 1989). "Between Memory and History: *Les Lieux de Memoire*." *Representations*, 26, Special Issue: Memory and Counter-Memory: 7-24.

Nussbaum, Martin. (October 1960 – May 1961). "Sociological Symbolism of the 'Adult Western'." *Social Forces*, 39 (1): 25-28.

O'Connor, Sandra Day and H. Alan Day. (2002). *Lazy B: Growing Up on a Cattle Ranch in the American Southwest*. New York: Random House.

Olick, Jeffrey and Joyce Robbins. (1998). "Social Memory Studies: From 'Collective Memory' to the Historical Sociology of Mnemonic Practices." *Annual Review of Sociology*, 24: 105-40.

Olick, Jeffrey. (November 1999). "Collective Memory: The Two Cultures." *Sociological Theory*, 17 (3): 333-48.

Ong, Walter J. (1988). *Orality and Literacy: The Technologizing of the World*. London and New York: Methuen.

Orvell, Miles. (1989). *The Real Thing: Imitation and Authenticity in American Culture, 1880-1940*. Chapel Hill and London: The University of North Carolina Press.

Porter, Kenneth Wiggins. (1971). *The Negro on the American Frontier*. New York: Arno Press.

Postman, Neil. (1985). *Amusing Ourselves to Death*. New York: Viking.

Putnam, Robert. (1995). "Bowling Alone: America's Declining Social Capital." *Journal of Democracy,* 6 (1): 65-78.

Riemer, Jeffrey W. (1977). "Varieties of Opportunistic Research." *Urban Life* 5 (4): 467-77.

Riesman, David et al. (1953). *The Lonely Crowd: A Study of the Changing American Character.* Garden City, NY: Doubleday and Company, Inc.

Robertson, James Oliver. (1980). *American Myth, American Reality.* New York: Hill and Wang.

Roosevelt, Theodore. (1888). *Ranch Life and the Hunting-Trail. Illustrated by Frederic Remington.* New York: The Century Company.

Rousseau, Jean-Jacques. (1968). *Julie, or the New Heloise. Letters of Two Lovers, Inhabitants of a Small Town at the Foot of the Alps.* Translated and abridged by Judith H. McDowell. University Park and London: The Pennsylvania State University Press.

Russell, Charles M. (1927). *Trails Plowed Under.* Garden City, NY: Doubleday, Doran and Company, Inc.

Russell, Sharman Apt. (2001). *Kill the Cowboy: A Battle of Mythology in the New West.* Lincoln: University of Nebraska Press.

Samuels, Peggy and Harold, eds. (1979). *The Collected Writings of Frederic Remington.* Garden City, NY: Doubleday.

Sanford, Charles L. (1961). *The Quest for Paradise: Europe and the American Moral Imagination.* Urbana: University of Illinois Press.

Savage, William Sherman. (1976). *Blacks in the West.* Westport, CT: Greenwood Press.

Schein, Harry. (Summer 1955). The Olympian Cowboy. *The American Scholar*, 24 (3): 309-20.

Schuman, Howard and Jacqueline Scott. (June 1989). "Generations and Collective Memories." *American Sociological Review*, 54 (3): 359-81.

Schwartz, Peter Hammond. (December 1988). "Equestrian Imagery in European and American Thought: Toward and Understanding of Symbols as Political Texts." *The Western Political Quarterly*, 41 (4): 653-73.

Shively, J. (December 1992). "Cowboys and Indians: Perceptions of Western Films among American Indians and Anglos." *American Sociological Review*, 57: 725-34.

Simmel, Georg. (1990). *The Philosophy of Money.* Second enlarged edition. David Frisby, ed. Tom Bottomore and David Frisby, trans. London and New York: Routledge.

Siringo, Charles A. (1950). *A Texas Cowboy, or Fifteen Years on the Hurricane Deck of A Spanish Pony.* Bibliographical Study and Introduction by J. Frank Dobie. Drawings by Tom Lea. New York: William Sloane Associates.

Slater, Philip E. (1970). *The Pursuit of Loneliness: American Culture at the Breaking Point*. Boston: Beacon Press.

Slatta, Richard W. (Spring 1994). "In Their Own Words: Cowboy Memoirs." *Cowboys and Indians*, 2 (1): 45-50.

_____. (1997). *Comparing Cowboys and Frontiers*. Norman and London: University of Oklahoma Press.

_____. (Spring 1994). "Roots of Rodeo." *Cowboys & Indians*, 2 (1): 18-22.

_____. (Spring 1995). "America's Breed: The Quarter Horse." *Cowboys and Indians*, 3 (1): 20-27.

Slotkin, Richard. (Winter 1981). "Nostalgia and Progress: Theodore Roosevelt's Myth of the Frontier." *American Quarterly*, 33 (5): 608-37.

_____. (1992). *Gunfighter Nation: The Myth of the Frontier in Twentieth-Century America*. New York: Atheneum.

Smith, Henry Nash. (1950). *Virgin Land: The American West as Symbol and Myth*. Cambridge, MA: Harvard University Press.

Stoeltje, Beverly J. (October 1987). "Making the Frontier Myth: Folklore Process in a Modern Nation." *Western Folklore*, 46 (4): 235-53.

_____. (July 1989). "Rodeo: From Custom to Ritual." *Western Folklore*, 48 (3): 244-55.

_____. (April – October 1993). "Power and the Ritual Genres: American Rodeo." *Western Folklore*, 52 (2/4), Theorizing Folklore: Toward New Perspectives on the Politics of Culture: 135-56.

Sumner, William Graham. (1940). *Folkways: A Study of the Sociological Importance of Usages, Manners, Customs, Mores, and Morals*. Boston: Ginn and Company.

Swidler, Ann. (April 1986). "Culture in Action: Symbols and Strategies." *American Sociological Review*, 51 (2): 273-86.

Thelen, David. (March 1989). "Memory and American History." *The Journal of American History*, 75 (4): 1117-29.

Tocqueville, Alexis de. (1945). *Democracy in America*. Introduction, editorial notes, and bibliographies by Phillips Bradley. New York: Alfred A. Knopf.

Turner, Frederick. J. (1977). *The Frontier in American History*. Franklin Center, PA: The Franklin Library.

Twain, Mark. (1948). *The Adventures of Huckleberry Finn*. Introductions by Brander Matthews and Dixon Wecter. New York and London: Harper & Brothers Publishers.

Veblen, Thorstein. (1994). *The Theory of the Leisure Class*. New York: Penguin Books.

Vromen, Suzanne. (1993). "The Ambiguity of Nostalgia." In *Going Home*. Edited by Jack Kugelmass. Evanston, IL: Northwestern University Press.

Walker, Don D. (Winter 1960). "Reading on the Range: The Literary Habits of the American Cowboy." *Arizona and the West* II, 307-18.

Warren, Louis S. (2005). *Buffalo Bill's America: William Cody and the Wild West Show*. New York: Alfred A. Knopf.

Webb, Walter Prescott. (1964). *The Great Frontier*. Introduction by Arnold Toynbee. Austin: University of Texas Press.

Weber, Eugen. (1976). *Peasants into Frenchmen: The Modernization of Rural France, 1870-1914*. Stanford: Stanford University Press.

Weiss, Paul. (1969). *Sport: A Philosophic Inquiry*. Carbondale and Edwardsville, IL: Southern Illinois University Press.

West, Elliott. (1997). *The Way to the West: Essays on the Central Plains*. Albuquerque: University of New Mexico Press.

Westermeier, Clifford P. (1987). *Man, Beast, Dust: The Story of Rodeo*. Foreword by Bill Crawford. Afterword by Kristine Fredricksson. Lincoln and London: University of Nebraska Press.

White, Lynn Jr. (April 1965). "The Legacy of the Middle Ages in the American Wild West." *Speculum*, 40 (2): 191-202.

White, G. Edward. (1968). *The Eastern Establishment and the Western Experience: The West of Frederic Remington, Theodore Roosevelt, and Owen Wister*. New Haven and London: Yale University Press.

Wister, Owen. (2002). *The Virginian: A Horseman of the Plains*. Afterword by Max Evans. New York: New American Library.

Wolff, Kurt H. (1950). *The Sociology of Georg Simmel*. New York: The Free Press.

References

Wright, Will. (1977). *Six Guns and Society: A Structural Study of the Western*. Berkeley, Los Angeles, London: University of California Press.

_____. (Autumn 1982). "The Empire Bites the Dust." *Social Text*, 6: 120-25.

Wrobel, David M. (1993). *The End of American Exceptionalism: Frontier Anxiety from the Old West to the New Deal*. Lawrence, KS: University Press of Kansas.

Wuthnow, Robert. (1994). *Sharing the Journey: Support Groups and America's New Quest for Community*. New York: The Free Press.

Young, Mary. (April 1970). "The West and American Cultural Identity: Old Themes and New Variations." *Western Historical Quarterly*, 1 (2): 137-60.

Zengotita, Thomas de. (2005). *Mediated: How the Media Shapes Your World and the Way You Live in It*. New York: Bloomsbury.

Printed in the United States
110802LV00002B/2/P